Ethnologia Europaea

Journal of European Ethnology

Volume 42:2
2012

Guest editors: Karen Körber
and Ina Merkel

MUSEUM TUSCULANUM PRESS · UNIVERSITY OF COPENHAGEN

Printed in Sweden by Exaktaprinting AB, Malmö 2013
Cover and layout Pernille Sys Hansen
Cover illustration © iStockphoto/Cienpies Design
ISBN 978 87 635 4044 5
ISSN 0425 4597

This journal is published with the support of the Nordic board for periodicals in the humanities and social sciences.

Museum Tusculanum Press
University of Copenhagen
Birketinget 6
DK-2300 Copenhagen
Denmark
www.mtp.dk

CONTENTS

IMAGINED FAMILIES IN MOBILE WORLDS
An Introduction

Karen Körber and Ina Merkel

Families "on the move", "Euro-orphans", and "transnational mothers" – more than ever before, talk about the family is permeated with the opportunities and challenges currently presented by an increasing, border-crossing mobility.[1] A glance at European press and media coverage shows that the family has recently become an object of public attention, and one that seems to indicate primarily a state of crisis. For several years now, newspaper articles and TV documentaries have been reporting on women who take on housework and caring tasks in Western European dual-earner households, precariously employed as nannies and maids while their children are left behind in the depleted villages of Poland, Ukraine, and Moldavia as the "silent" victims of westward labour migration. This seems to continue, in a kind of distorting mirror, the trend diagnosed by US sociologist Richard Sennett as early as the 1990s. Sennett saw a new capitalism generating the values of a flexible society, whose most important dictum – "keep moving, don't commit yourself, and don't sacrifice" (1998: 25) – placed massive pressure on the institution of the family. These representations of feminized labour migration from East to West, South to North, reveal a new dimension of social inequality in global capitalism, but they also document a transformation in the gender order, at the symbolic heart of which stand contested images and discourses about "the" family.

The hypothesis of a crisis of the family has been refuted in past years primarily by numerous migration researchers, investigating the family within the domain that has been chiefly blamed for its decline (Lima 2001; Bryceson & Vuorela 2002; Sørensen & Guarnizo 2007). The global increase in migratory movements and altered or newly emerging patterns of migration and mobility have resulted in radical change to the perspectives of migration studies itself. Such research no longer revolves around the notion of linear, one-off, and completed migration processes from a society of origin to a receiving society; instead, the focus is on the complex, often largely stable and long-lived, "transnational" relationships between people, networks, and organizations across the borders of the nation state (Basch, Glick Schiller & Szanton Blanc 1994; Pries 2001; Vertovec 2009). In this context, the rise of the "transnational family" enhances the importance of a form of life that at first sight seems to embody a paradox: despite geographical distance and the experience of dispersal, the very social group whose core elements include spatial proximity and direct community is capable of sustaining the family virtually as its principal point of orientation and reference. As such, it is proving both resistant and creative in the face of the new demands of globalized societies.

This special issue critically addresses not only the prophecies of the end of the family, but also the apparent paradox inherent to the new models of familiarity under conditions of increased mobility. While working from very different angles, all the contributions join in querying a concept of family that makes the autochthonous family, located within national boundaries, the yardstick for all others. The Euro-American definition of family as a nuclear family characterized by settledness and geographically proximal relationships is here regarded as an articulation of "methodological nationalism" (Beck 2003) that obscures the cross-border practices constitutive for many different mobile and transnational family forms both past and present. Tracing the challenges, the creative potential, the cultural practices, and equally the constraints, of multi-locality for the meaning of family, our approach begins from a question that was raised in an earlier special issue of *Ethnologia Europaea*, "Double Homes, Double Lives?" (Bendix & Löfgren 2007): How do identity and feelings of belonging change under the conditions of dual location? Like that special issue, the present collection also pursues European ethnology's concern to address mobility and migration processes through both biographically oriented, ethnographic studies and the analysis of cultural, symbolic, and discursive practices. However, the authors of these five contributions do not attempt to reach a single position on the notion of the family; rather, by interlocking ethnographic and discourse-analytical methods and combining them with gender theory, they share a focus on the technologies, genealogies, policies, and regulations that participate crucially in the construction of family, gender, and bodies.

Imagined Family – How Family Is Made

In the organization of social interaction and the constitution of individuals, family and kinship are of prime significance across all cultures and epochs. That does not appear to have changed fundamentally in the socially differentiated, mobile, and globalized societies of late modernity. As the key orders of the social, and those with the greatest impact in everyday life, family and kinship constitute more than a formal classificatory system of social relationships and an order-endowing structure in the world's cultures: in Pierre Bourdieu's terms, they are "structuring structures", in other words "principles of the generation and structuring" of representations, practices, identities, and social forms (Bourdieu 1977: 72).

Against this background, our title, "Imagined Families", follows authors such as Deborah Bryceson and Ulla Vuorela (2002) in transposing Benedict Anderson's thesis of nationalism as imagined community (1983) onto the family, and thus directing attention to the ways that family is *made*: how it is negotiated, symbolically generated, and affirmed through everyday practice, but also how it is changed, for example through altered legal frameworks. In Euro-American societies, the order of the family has always been conceived of as something dual, both biological and social (König 1974: 61), and as centred on filiation and heterosexuality. The past few decades have seen numerous challenges to this understanding of family and kinship, which legitimizes and privileges consanguinity over other forms of long-term bonds and care and naturalizes the distinction between "natural" and "other" kinship. More recent thinking in kinship ethnology also reflects social transformations – especially altered gender relations, pluralized family formations, and the cultural consequences of migration and globalization, but also biotechnological developments such as reproductive medicine. Thus, current models of kinship emphasize the ways that family relationships are produced, revised, and lived within actual social processes (Carsten 2000; Faubion 2001). In her work on adoption practices, Signe Howell (2001) introduces the notion of "kinning", thus giving linguistic form to the processual and active character of "making kin". Similarly, the studies published by Beck et al. (2007) use the examples of transnational adoption and assisted reproductive technologies to show that the opposition between "natural" and "made" kin relationships is inexistent: instead, kinship is always and everywhere produced as a social form.

That "kin relationships are something that people make, and with which they do something" (Bourdieu 1990: 167) is also among the principal assumptions informing the contributions by Karen Körber, Gertrud Hüwelmeier, and Elisabeth Timm. All three authors are concerned, in differing ways, with present-day and historical dimensions of transnational familiarity; it is in this setting that they examine the constrictions and pitfalls of a Euro-American notion of family. Körber and Hüwelmeier pick up on current discussions around the relationship of gender, transnationalism, and family. On the one hand, they pursue an analytical perspective set out by Sarah Mahler and Patricia Pessar, focusing on a "gendered geography of power" (2001: 441) that aims to open up our awareness that "gender operates simultaneously on multiple spatial and social scales (e.g. the body, the family, the state) across transnational terrains" (ibid.: 445). On the other, they draw on studies that concentrate less on the material ties of reciprocal obligation in transnational families than on the cultural practices within and by means of which family attachments are experienced and moulded across time and space (Vuorela 2002; Baldassar, Baldock & Wilding 2007). Thus, Mary Chamberlain and Selma Leydesdorff (2004: 227–228) trace the special significance accorded to "memories and narratives" in diasporically dispersed families, as ways of enabling a shared understanding of family in circumstances of separation. Describing women's attempts to keep families living in separation physically and emotionally intact, Pierette Hondagneu-Sotelo and Ernestine Avila refer to transnational "circuits of affection, caring, and financial support" (1997: 550) – thereby naming the key dimensions addressed by numerous studies in recent years. All these investigations concur in relating the question of new forms and practices of familiarity to that of reconfigured gender relations in transnational families. Bridget Anderson (2001) and Aihwa Ong (1999), for example, both stress that an analysis of transnational social spaces cannot be restricted to the practices of the state, but must also address the politics of the body, the regulation of the private sphere and of family circumstances, and culturally hegemonic gender norms and discourses in both the sending and the receiving country (see also Hess and Radkowska-Walkowicz in this issue).

Karen Körber's contribution picks up on these debates. Through family biography interviews, she shows how transnational families use new communication technologies to produce familiarity across great distances and long periods of time. Two selected case studies of families, taken from European labour migrations of the 1960s and post-1990, reveal how the transformation of time-space organizational patterns can create a virtual proximity at a distance, enabling geographically fragmented families to forge new practices and forms of everyday togetherness that may endure for many years. This highlights the limits of a notion of family founded on spatial proximity and direct community, while also demonstrating that access to and use of new technologies is not something neutral, but is structured by relations of social inequality that unfold their specific effects in the context of migration regimes. In the European order of migration, an increasing feminization of migratory movements can be observed, the routes and practices of which are being progressively illegalized. This restrictive European policy has far-reaching consequences for the relationship between gender and family in transnational family configurations.

Giving a voice not only to the agents of migration themselves, but also to the "immobile" family members left behind, Körber's study identifies how both sides actively participate in sustaining transnational social and symbolic ties in the course of familial exchange processes. Transnational familiarity, the article shows, encompasses not only the relationship between adolescents and their parents, but more widely the lifelong relationship between people of different generations, which changes and redefines itself across the family's lifetime.

This observation connects Körber's study to Gertrud Hüwelmeier's. Hüwelmeier addresses the currently much-debated concept of transnational motherhood, but casts interesting new light on it from a historical and anthropological viewpoint: she investigates not biologically generated families, but kinship that is grounded in ritual in the framework of transnational women's congregations. Using multi-sited fieldwork, she traces the transformation of these relationships over time and space, showing that familial relations transcending national borders are not something new – in the past, without today's technological resources, it was already possible to maintain emotional presence and participation at a distance. In line with other historical studies of gender-specific practices of migration (Harasser 1996; Harzig 1997; Henkes 1998), Hüwelmeier's paper indicates that nuns, those "pioneers of female migration", were moving along transnational routes in the nineteenth century. Her research on the relationships of mother superiors to their daughters or "sisters" also refers to ethnographic studies of co-parenting. As well as revealing the ethnocentric narrowness of the Euro-American concept of family, this comparison underlines once more the inherently constructed character of "kinship" as a social form.

If Körber and Hüwelmeier query the notion of family as a biologically grounded and proximate social group, Elisabeth Timm tracks a further implicit norm of the Euro-American family. Her historically based study of popular genealogies, using the example of Austria, investigates a "cultural norm of settledness" (Merkel 2002: 233) that she finds inscribed in the genealogical practice of searching for, and constructing, family. Working from a micro perspective, she analyses the production of settledness through the case of Austrian parish registers, the *Matriken*. A focus on three moments, reaching from the Reformation via the interwar period into the digital present, shows how the fact of migration and mobility is negated across time and how the identification of "being *kin*" with "being *there*" has to be continually produced afresh. Timm traces how the process of grounding the family as the nucleus of the state and society has gone hand in hand with the process of localizing it and making it settled; against this, she posits the relational complementarity of mobility and immobility. As in Hüwelmeier's contribution, it again becomes obvious that transnationality is not a new phenomenon in historical terms. Timm's study contributes to a debate also found, in a different form, in Körber's: whether the opposition between mobile and immobile actors and ways of life does not itself obey an artificial binarism incapable of standing up to empirical examination.

Mobility, Gender, and Family – Policies, Regulations, and Technologies

The assumption of a settled, biologically grounded family based on experiences of intimacy and care is inextricable from notions of family and gender. Recent scholarship has often asked how far present-day transnational mobilities are changing family configurations in a gender-specific way. The gender significance of this question has also grown in that the narrative of mobility no longer takes concrete shape in the figure of the male breadwinner: women are now the ones on the move. Although women's migration is no historical innovation, as Hüwelmeier's contribution shows, the feminization of migration has attained new explosive force since the end of the twentieth century. This applies not only to the worldwide increase in the number of mobile women, but also to the global processes of economic restructuring, along with state and supra-state mobility regimes, that have resulted in feminized patterns and practices of migration (Anthias & Lazaridis 2000; Sassen 2000). Since the early 1990s, gender researchers have been observing this trend in the European area as well, noting that – particularly in the wake of the Europeanization of migration policy – migratory movements are experiencing a feminization of which the illegalization of migrant women is a crucial feature (Kofman & Sales 1998; see also Körber in this issue).

Sabine Hess starts from these debates in her study of the shift to governmentality in the European Union's migration regime. Using ethnographic and discourse-analytical methods, the author investigates the "anti-trafficking" dispositif – that is, the images and discourses of trafficking in women and forced prostitution that have made a major contribution to implementing, and now further refining, the political and legal constitution of the European border regime. As a participant observer over a substantial period, Hess took part in various EU round table disscussions in the field of migration policy, where participants in recent years have included not only politically nominated representatives and staff of the relevant regulatory bodies, but also members of NGOs, such as feminist activists. Hess draws on her many years of experience in the gender-sensitive research of border regimes to analyse the ambivalent effects of these new political practices. Underpinned by feminist discursive positions, they target the victimization of female migrants – with the result that ultimately even more restrictive controls of migration are legitimized. On the one hand, this case indicates how deeply the category of gender is inscribed in the procedures, technologies, articulations, and rationalities of the new European politics of migration; on the other, a degree of compatibility becomes evident between certain feminist positions and an increasingly rigid border-control policy, saying much about some approaches within feminist migration studies.

Hess shows that the Europeanization of migration policy can itself be understood as a transnationalization of politics. Her critical analysis of the anti-trafficking dispositif points to a structural dilemma of "Fortress Europe": migrating women can only be represented through the figure of the victim, so that their transnational practices and spatial mobilities are negated. The victimization of women invokes as its Other the image of the settled woman, tied to the home, who must stay at her husband's side if she is to venture into the public space or across the national frontier.

To this extent, female migrants disrupt the symbolic order of gender and the family and become the object of technologized and networked knowledge practices, deemed to require documentation and control. Control over women and their bodies is also the theme of the contribution by Magdalena Radkowska-Walkowicz, who, in a different nationally coded field of knowledge, discusses how biotechnological change in reproductive medicine is casting doubt on traditional conceptions of family and evoking highly contested images of familiarity.

Radkowska-Walkowicz investigates the Polish debate on in-vitro fertilization. Through discourse analysis, she evaluates statements by representatives of the Catholic Church, who oppose the right to extracorporeal fertilization to great media and public effect, and commentaries by women affected, who use an Internet platform to share their experiences of assisted reproductive technologies. The author reaches the apparently paradoxical conclusion that while public allegiance to the Catholic Church is still relatively intact in Poland, large parts of the population are in favour of the use of reproductive technologies. She argues that the seeming contradiction in fact dissolves once the shared core of the argument is identified: both sides are propounding the normative ideal of the heterosexual nuclear family. Whereas for the women affected, this ideal is realized only with the birth of a child (even one that has been artificially conceived), the Church defends the ideal per se, in the shape of the marriage vow, to curb potential transformations of the family that would also permit other familial forms.

In their contributions, Hess and Radkowska-Walkowicz come to rather similar conclusions. Both authors, though working in different fields of research, ask how bodies and gender are constructed with the help of policies, regulations, and technologies. In the case both of transnational European migration policy and of national discourse around the use of reproductive medicine, the political actors are confronted with developments that seem to entail the "danger" of lost boundaries and of the unconfined – developments, then, that seem to escape control. In one case it is the circulation of people, information, images, ideas, and products that crosscuts the state's attempts to reterritorialize, in the other biotechnology, enabling the separation of reproduction from heterosexual marriage, triggers a massive discursive campaign by the Catholic Church. At stake in both cases is the order of gender and the family, at the core of which is control over the female body, its spatial and corporeal circumscription.

Conclusions

The studies collected in this special issue approach the object of the family from various different directions. Through both historical and contemporary cases, they point out the restrictiveness of an ethnocentric concept of family, at the same time indicating the great adaptability of a social form whose downfall has been predicted so many times. The variety of approaches contributes to an understanding of family that may be both less normative and less crisis-ridden, instead directing our attention to cultural and symbolic practices by which and within which families are "made", experienced daily, lived, and transformed. At the same time, as a pivotal representation of social order with great impact in everyday life, the family is also the place where the gender order is negotiated and renegotiated. In the course of transnationalizing processes, therefore, the family is "the primary unit of regulation and the vehicle of state power" (Ong 1999: 71); it is the target of state and supra-state policies, the object of legal regulations, and firmly embedded in public discourses whose gendered images play a key part in the construction of family. In the context of the increasing transnationalization not only of family relationships, but also of political forms, this field of tension will continue to gain in importance for future research.

Note

1 The article was translated by Kate Sturge.

References

Anderson, B. 1983: *Imagined Communities: Reflections on the Origin and Spread of Nationalism.* London: Verso.

Anderson, B. 2001: Multiple Transnationalism: Space, the State and Human Relations. Working Paper WPTC-01-15, www.transcomm.ox.ac.uk/working%20papers/Anderson.pdf. Accessed June 14, 2012.

Anthias, F. & G. Lazaridis (eds.) 2000: *Gender and Migration in Southern Europe: Women on the Move.* Oxford: Berg.

Baldassar, L., C.V. Baldock & R. Wilding 2007: *Families Caring across Borders: Migration, Ageing and Transnational Caregiving.* London: Palgrave Macmillan.

Basch, L., N. Glick Schiller & C. Szanton Blanc 1994: *Nations Unbound: Transnational Projects, Postcolonial Predicaments, and Deterritorialized Nation-States.* New York: Gordon and Breach.

Beck S., N. Çil, S. Hess & M. Klotz (eds.) 2007: Verwandtschaft machen: Reproduktionstechnologien und Adoption in Deutschland und der Türkei. *Berliner Blätter: Ethnographische und ethnologische Beiträge* 42.

Beck, U. 2003: Das Meta-Machtspiel der Weltpolitik: Kritik des methodologischen Nationalismus. In: Armin Nassehi & Markus Schroer (eds.), *Der Begriff des Politischen. Soziale Welt: Sonderband 14.* Baden-Baden: Nomos Verlagsgesellschaft, pp. 45–70.

Bendix, R. & O. Löfgren (eds.) 2007: *Double Homes, Double Lives? Ethnologia Europaea: Journal of European Ethnology* 37:1–2.

Bourdieu, P. 1977: *Outline of a Theory of Practice.* Trans. R. Nice. Cambridge: Cambridge University Press.

Bourdieu, P. 1990: *The Logic of Practice.* Trans. R. Nice. Stanford, CA: Stanford University Press.

Bryceson, D.F. & U. Vuorela, 2002: Transnational Families in the Twenty-First Century. In: D. F. Bryceson & U. Vuorela (eds.), *The Transnational Family: New European Frontiers and Global Networks.* Oxford & New York: Berg, 3–30.

Carsten, J. (ed.) 2000: *Cultures of Relatedness: New Approaches to the Study of Kinship.* Cambridge: Cambridge University Press.

Chamberlain, M. & S. Leydesdorff 2004: Transnational Families: Memories and Narratives. *Global Networks* 4:3, 227–241.

Faubion, J.D. (ed.) 2001: *The Ethics of Kinship: Ethnographic Inquiries.* Lanham, MD: Rowman & Littlefield.

Harasser, C. 1996: *Von Dienstboten und Landarbeitern: Eine Bibliographie der (fast) vergessenen Berufe.* Innsbruck: Studien-Verlag.

Harzig, C. (ed.) 1997: *Peasant Maids, City Women: From the European Countryside to Urban America.* Ithaca, NY: Cornell University Press.

Henkes, B. 1998: *Heimat in Holland: Deutsche Dienstmädchen 1920–1950.* Straelen: Straelener Manuskripte.

Hondagneu-Sotelo, P. & E. Avila 1997: "I'm here, but I'm there": The Meanings of Latina Transnational Motherhood. *Gender and Society* 11:5, 548–571.

Howell, S. 2001: Self-Conscious Kinship: Some Contested Values in Norwegian Transnational Adoption. In: S. Franklin & S. McKinnon (eds.), *Relative Values: Reconfiguring Kinship Studies.* Durham, NC: Duke University Press, pp. 203–223.

Kofman, E. & R. Sales 1998: Migrant Women and Exclusion in Europe. *The European Journal of Women's Studies* 5:3–4, 381–398.

König, R. 1974: *Die Familie der Gegenwart.* Munich: Beck.

Lima, F.H. 2001: Transnational Families: Institutions of Transnational Social Space. In: L. Pries (ed.), *New Transnational Social Spaces: International Migration and Transnational Companies in the Early Twenty-First Century.* London: Routledge, pp. 77–93.

Mahler, S. & P.R. Pessar 2001: Gendered Geographies of Power: Analyzing Gender across Transnational Spaces. *Identities: Global Studies in Culture and Power* 7:4, 441–459.

Merkel, I. 2002: Außerhalb von Mittendrin: Individuum und Kultur in der zweiten Moderne. *Zeitschrift für Volkskunde* 98:II, 229–256.

Ong, A. 1999: *Flexible Citizenship: The Cultural Logic of Transnationality.* Durham, NC: Duke University Press.

Pries, L. (ed.) 2001: *New Transnational Social Spaces: International Migration and Transnational Companies in the Early Twenty-First Century.* London: Routledge.

Sassen, S. 2000: *Guests and Aliens*. New York: The New Press.

Sennett, R. 1998: *The Corrosion of Character: The Personal Consequences of Work in the New Capitalism*. New York: W.W. Norton.

Sørensen, N.N. & L.E. Guarnizo 2007: Transnational Family Life across the Atlantic: The Experience of Colombian and Dominican Migrants in Europe. In: N.N. Sørensen (ed.), *Living Across Worlds: Diaspora, Development and Transnational Engagement*. Geneva: International Organisation for Migration (IOM), 151–176.

Vertovec, S. 2009: *Transnationalism*. London: Routledge.

Vuorela, U. 2002: Transnational Families: Imagined and Real Communities. In: D.F. Bryceson & U. Vuorela (eds.), *The Transnational Family: New European Frontiers and Global Networks*. Oxford: Berg, pp. 63–82.

Karen Körber is a research fellow at the Jewish Museum Berlin. Her publications include books and articles on transnationalism, Jewish diaspora, migration and identity politics. A recent article is "Nähe auf Distanz: Transnationale Familien in der Gegenwart" (in Gertraud Marinelli-König & Alexander Preisinger, eds., 2011, *Zwischenräume: Migration und die Entgrenzung von Kulturen und Identitäten*. Bielefeld: Transcript).
(k.koerber@jmberlin.de)

Ina Merkel is Professor of European Ethnology and Cultural Studies at Philipps-University in Marburg, Germany. Her research focuses on the history of film, culture and consumption in the G.D.R., gender and transnational mobility. Her latest paper is on historical-critical methods of film analysis and will be published in 2013.
(merkeli@staff.uni-marburg.de)

SO FAR AND YET SO NEAR
Present-Day Transnational Families

Karen Körber

Through the expansion and development of communication technologies, transnational families are presently experiencing that they are close despite the great geographical distances between them. On the basis of a qualitative study with transnational families, I show that this virtual closeness at a distance brings out new practices of familiarity, on the one hand, but also produces conflicts and dilemmas, on the other. While the new technologies of closeness enable forms of everyday interactions over great distances, the compression of time and space does not take place in a vacuum. Instead, family members are positioned at interfaces of structures of difference and inequality, which decisively influence access to and use of the new technologies and which have far-reaching consequences for the shaping of transnational family configurations.[1]

Keywords: transnationalism, family, communication technologies, gender, migration regime

In his novel *A Tale of Love and Darkness* ([2002]2004), Israeli author Amos Oz described a recurring scene from his childhood in Jerusalem in the 1940s, vividly bringing back the reality of that time of a seemingly insurmountable distance, one which today seems like a stone's throw – that is, the distance between Tel Aviv and Jerusalem. In minute detail he described how his parents prepared for these telephone conversations that took place every few months with relatives in Tel Aviv. The call was first announced by letter, precisely fixing date and time, and then he and his parents would gather at the set time at the nearby pharmacy.

> [T]he conversation went something like this: ...
> "Yes, Arieh, hallo, it's Tsvi here, how are you?"
> "Everything is fine here. We're speaking from the pharmacy."
> "So are we. What's new?"
> "Nothing new here. How about at your end, Tsvi? Tell us how it's going."
> "Everything is OK. Nothing special to report. We're all well."
> "No news is good news. There's no news here either. We're all fine. How about you?"
> "We're fine too." ...
> And then the same thing all over again. How are you? What's new? ...
> And that was the whole conversation.
> (Oz [2002]2004: 11)

Descriptions like this, in which the elaborate preparations for the telephone calls assumed the character of a ritual that was at least as significant as the conversation itself, were also common in interviews of our research project with families that became transnational through the labour migration of part of the family in the 1960s and which report of how arduous and protracted efforts had been in the past to maintain contact over spatial distances.[2] With the mass expansion and rapid development of telecommunication technologies since the 1990s a fundamental shift can be observed, especially with respect to the ways people communicate over a distance. Whereas past generations commonly experienced that it could take months for news to reach them from far away, now family networks spread out over great distances can maintain regular and immediate contact with each other with the help of new technologies. Inexpensive telephone charges, mobile telephones, and the Internet have facilitated the rapid transfer of money, goods, and information, giving the impression that spatial barriers are steadily disappearing. Arjun Appadurai observed that today's world is characterized essentially by "objects in motion ... ideas and ideologies, people and goods, images and messages, technologies and techniques" (Appadurai 2001: 5). This seems to apply to the reality of transnational families in a special way, including the everyday experience of "time-space compression" (Harvey 1990: 240–242) as a result of the use of new technologies.

In the following I will examine the consequences of this shift and ask how families create familiarity across great distances. Within this context it is important to discuss the limits of the concept of family, among the crucial elements of which is the experience of shared time at a common location – in other words, spatial proximity and direct community. My empirical basis is a qualitative study of families whose transnational character developed in the 1950s and 1960s, and after 1990, within the scope of labour migration to Germany and Austria. Using selected cases from this sample I would like to show that the creation of familiarity in the families we studied is characterized by a tension involving a number of overlapping processes. For present-day transnational families the change in time-space organizational patterns is tied to the specific experience of feeling close also over great distances. This virtual closeness despite physical distance brings forth new practices that allow spatially fragmented families to create forms of everyday togetherness, thereby serving to increase the significance of familiarity as a value, longing, and myth, and allowing it in fact to be experienced and lived at times in various casual structures. Although this development appears at first glance to facilitate the project of living as a transnational family, upon closer scrutiny it becomes apparent that the compression of space and time can also bring out conflicts and dilemmas for family members. For one thing, members of transnational families are confronted with various problems deriving from the situation that increased options for accessibility also lead to increased expectations of being accessible. Furthermore, transnational communication does not take place in a vacuum. Family members are instead positioned at interfaces of structures based on difference and inequality that decisively influence access to and use of the new technologies. These complex, asymmetrical relations with respect to gender, ethnicity, nationality, and age develop their own specific influence within the context of migration regimes, whose mechanisms of incorporation and restrictive policies have consequences for the shaping of transnational family configurations. With respect to the families in our sample, the "mobility order" (Rogers 2004: 174) of the present European migration regime gains special significance in this context. The increasingly restrictive migration policies of the European Union, in particular Germany and Austria, are feminizing migratory movements, which produces a paradoxical experience as it were for female family members: apparently *unlimited* in their geographic mobility, they confront the *limitations* of the national migration regime, which in most cases allow them only unofficial and illegalized paths to the West (see article by Hess).

After a brief survey of the present state of research on transnational families, two cases from the sample shall serve to illustrate some of the problems and structural dilemmas that are connected to the experience of virtual proximity at a distance. Both of these examples are from a corpus of twenty-five families, with whose members – that is, parents and their (usually) grown children – biographical narrative interviews (Apitzsch 2003; Schütze 1983) were conducted. Corresponding to the labour recruitment agreements of the 1960s, families from Italy, Greece, Turkey, and the former Yugoslavia were selected. Also, families largely from Eastern Europe were interviewed, whose transnational life circumstances did not begin until the Iron Curtain fell after 1990. This included families from Ukraine, Belarus, Russia, Lithuania, and Slovenia. In addition we selected a small number of families that immigrated within the scope of labour migration and in doing so had to overcome incomparably great spatial distances. This group includes migrants from South Korea who were recruited in the 1960s as nurses, and women from Peru and Colombia, who have been working for a number of years in Germany and Austria as domestic workers. There are thus two groups of transnational families in the sample, which differ with respect to the duration of the migration process and the respective legal conditions for migration, as well as regarding the means of communication and transportation available for their endeavour to establish their family beyond national borders.[3]

Transnational Families: State of Research

Since the 1990s authors have observed that in the course of advancing globalization, more and more family forms are developing whose members spend their everyday lives separated from one another by great distances and national borders, but they nevertheless remain cohesive due to viable emotional and financial ties. Transnational families are by no means a new phenomenon, as historical studies show. Also in the past, immigrants from the Old World wrote letters to relatives reporting about their new home and sent money to cover the ocean passage (see also Thomas and Znaniecki [1918]1984; Yans-McLaughlin 1990). Studies in the countries of the Caribbean and Central and Latin America have for quite a while been drawing attention to a development in which migration becomes a central pattern for how families lead their lives, assuming the status of a social norm (Nyberg Sørensen & Fog Olwig 2002; Fog Olwig 2003).

At the same time expressions such as "transnational parenting" (Parrenas 2001: 62) and "long-distance mothering" (Gamburd 2000) provide evidence of current migration processes being characterized by qualitative and structural changes that become visible also (and precisely) in transnational families. This includes, for one thing, the feminization of migration since the 1980s, which challenges the symbolic family order and poses the question as to images and expectations of motherhood anew. While studies on migratory movements of women in the late nineteenth century already referred to gender-specific migration practices, the sphere of globalized domestic employment is today the most important labour market for women worldwide and with respect to hiring and recruitment practices it is considered to be better organized than ever before (Momsen 1999: 5; Lutz 2011). Furthermore, the new technologies allow members of transnational families "to be actively involved in everyday life there in fundamentally different ways than in the past" (Levitt 2001: 22). These developments have become the subject of studies that direct the attention to "distanced" models of familiarity, taking the changed time-space relationship into account.

In one of the first studies on transnational motherhood, Pierette Hondagneu-Sotelo and Ernestine Avila used the example of Latin American migrants in the United States to express – in their aptly titled essay "I'm here, but I'm there" – not only the longing of mothers for direct community but also the specific experience of creating new forms of closeness and intimacy as conveyed through regular telephone calls (Hondagneu-Sotelo & Avila 1997). American sociologist Rhacel Parrenas (2005), in her study of transnational families from the Philippines, treats the perspective of the children left behind. She analysed the constitution of gender in such transnational interactions, showing that the absent mothers not only assume the role of the male breadwinner in order to secure the livelihood of their families, but through emails and telephone calls they attempt to compensate for the gender-specific expectations on them for care. Parrenas observed that the practices of the women have served to redefine a concept of motherhood such that forms of material support are understood as expressions of maternal caregiving. Under the heading of transnational care, Loretta Baldassar et al. pursue the question of how the relationship between aging parents and their grown children is shaped against the background of great spatial distances (Baldassar, Baldock & Wilding 2007). In their study, the authors not only worked out "distant" practices of transnational care in family life, but also referred to a family network structure that is based on the principle of a "specific reciprocity" (Faist 2000: 106ff.).

In the present article I refer to these studies, therefore rejecting an understanding of transnationality that concentrates primarily on the mobile actors. I aim instead to show how in the course of exchange processes within the family both mobile and immobile family members actively participate in maintaining transnational social and symbolic ties (Brah 1996; Brennan 2004; Levitt & Glick Schiller 2004). I employ those approaches which do not view families as homogeneous units and instead look at how family relations are characterized by structural inequalities (Dreby 2006; Schmalzbauer 2004). Such a perspective views the family as a community of individuals, each with his or her own interests and experience. This also means that members select when, with whom, and in what way they maintain family ties. Attention is thus directed at those practices, strategies and negotiation processes through which family members "create familial space and network ties in terrain where affinal connections are relatively sparse" (Bryceson & Vuorela 2002: 11).

Whoever Emigrated "Was Simply Gone"

> Back then there was one shared telephone for the whole town and that's where my mother would call. My mother always collected 5-mark coins. When she called us she always went to a coin machine [i.e., a telephone booth], put in the 5-mark coins, and then called so someone would tell us. Then we'd come and she would call again. Mostly we talked about what was absolutely necessary.[4]

Such reports were common among our interviews with members of transnational families that were involved in labour migration in the 1960s. All conversation partners reported that private households in the respective countries of origin did not have telephone connections in the 1980s and that also those family members who had emigrated only rarely had their own telephones. Long distance calls were an expensive, public act. The main medium for communication was the letter, or a package with cassettes. This in turn was connected with waiting periods, which underscored the great geographical distance between members of the families. "That always took a long time, yes. It could take three to four weeks before you got an answer." Whoever emigrated "was simply gone, far away", as one of our interview partners summarized the family experience of these years. This also involved the gradual acknowledgement that what had begun as an exceptional, short-term situation, in many families changed to something "temporary that lasts" (Sayad 2004: 74), which stabilized, demanding new plans for organizing family life over great distances.

The family of Sophia Wassiliou, in her mid-forties and proprietor of a hairdressing salon in Frankfurt am Main, is such a case. Sophia's family came from a village near Thessaloniki, Greece. Her mother described life as characterized by the harsh conditions of agrarian life, of hardship and small yields, too little to feed a family. The labour migration seemed to be the final recourse, an act of necessity. The elder brothers of Sophia's father were the first to leave for Germany, then a brother of her mother. Recommended by his brother-in-law, Sophia's father was offered a job in a Volkswagen plant in northern Hesse as an unskilled labourer. He emigrated before the birth of his daughter, and his wife followed three years later, also to work in Germany. The three children remained in the village with their grandmother. When the parents realized that their economically successful return would take longer than they had expected, they brought their children to Germany as well. Because their workdays were long and hard, the children were often left to their own resources. Soon the two older brothers were sent back to relatives in

Greece so they could attend secondary school there. The family only got together during summer holidays in the village where they came from, in order to work on the project of building their own house.

> So there were certain years and then there was always a separation again. Good, so that's how things went all those years. And there were always tears, yes, always farewells and tears and farewells and tears.[5]

Similar to how Ayse Caglar (1997) analysed the situation of Turkish labour migrants, the myth of returning determined the everyday activities and family decisions in the life of the Wassiliou family. In social practice, the mentioning of the return took on the force of a key symbol: "It was always clear that somehow, sometime we would go to Greece. That was our family story."

Nevertheless, all three children started settling in as young adults in Germany. When family life seemed finally to shift to Germany for good after the sudden death of the father, the mother decided to return to the village she came from. This decision raised the painful question once again as to where and how they could set up a life they shared, a process which revealed the myth of return to be an illusion. In the interview, the daughter Sophia described her decision not to return, in which she referred to how different the circumstances of her life were from those of her parents:

> But it has become totally different for us. As soon as I realized that, I said: "OK, I can't leave here [Frankfurt] totally; I don't want to; what options do I have? Fly there often." And then I told my mother, "You will have to understand that somehow, that your children will come and go…" Yes, and now it has worked out so that basically we try to see each other as frequently as possible and, of course, through all these options – telephone, Internet – everything has become much easier.[6]

Sophia Wassiliou was referring here to a difference in the experience between the generations, which comes out especially in the different narratives that introduce the respective migration stories. Whereas the story of her mother carries qualities of an inevitable "either-or", the daughter experiences her family life at a distance more as a "both-and" (Kearney 1995: 558), in which everyday practice – virtual, communicative, and practical – makes it possible to overcome the distance and limitations without any effort. This description not only gives the impression that Sophia, in contrast to her mother, has a sense of belonging to more than one place, it also describes the conditions under which she decided to stay in Germany. Fate gives way to an active choice.

The narratives of the Wassiliou family reveal not only a change in perspective away from the shared notion of a remigration and towards awareness that the family already has numerous transnational references at its disposal. Their statements also reflect a specific experience of labour migrants of the 1960s who had come to West Germany as EU employees in the course of bilateral recruitment treaties. Sophia's parents were awarded legally regulated residential status, the right to choose their place of residence (right of mobility) and thus legally privileged status as compared with migrants from non-European Union countries. Since the German economy had an interest in trained workers, the planned rotation was suspended and family reunions in Germany were permitted. At the same time, Sophia's parents came from an economically depressed region in Greece and had had limited schooling – a fate they share with many labour migrants from EU countries in south-eastern Europe. Their economic status thus corresponded to that of the classical reserve army of labour in the country of origin. Although their income was much higher than what they would earn in Greece, it required that they accepted as a matter of course hard workdays with great sacrifice. This situation – similar to other families in the sample – led to children going back and forth between country of origin and country of destination. At first they remained in the country of origin with the grandmother; later the two sons were sent to Greek relatives so they could attend secondary school there. The parents' decision to put the children under the care of a network of relatives in the area of origin was not unusual at the time. Instead, it fits into an understanding of family that is based less on the nuclear family and much more on the extended family, in which care for the children is transferred also to other (mostly female) relatives (see Erel 2002). In the course of familiar chain migration, as in the case of the Wassiliou family, these care arrangements take on additional significance, since the great spatial and temporal distance requires a reliably functioning transnational family network. With this step Sophia's parents emphasized their intention to return, on the one hand, and they reacted to the social restrictions and discrimination they were confronted with in Germany, on the other. This included the experience that their adolescent children faced difficulties or were even denied higher schooling, which was why the parents decided that they should acquire this qualification in their country of origin (see Apitzsch & Siouti 2008: 98f.). The transnational living space that was established could, in its beginnings, also be seen as a reaction of the labour migrants to the exclusionary tendencies of the host society.

Compression of Time and Space

The changes that Sophia's family went through indicate, first of all, how the first generation's initial perspective on migration as one-time, temporary, and return-oriented often became a long-term, flexible, and intergenerational way of life for the family, located in various places both socially and culturally. In addition, Sophia's experiences also reflect the dynamic development of communications media and means of transportation, the "material infrastructure" of transnationalization, which according to Ludger Pries is what enables "the migrants to remain mentally present in their families and places of origin" in the first place (Pries 1998: 77).

Without exception, everyone interviewed in fact described that these developments greatly facilitated their family life at a distance, although there were differences among the interviewees in terms of both their respective options for access and the ensuing costs. In particular "cheap calls" (Vertovec 2004: 219), that is, the possibility to make inexpensive telephone calls worldwide, has changed the families' perception and underscored the impression of what Frances Cairncross characterized as the "death of distance" (1997: 27). Reports on the daily call "just because", in which someone could sometimes even learn of something "before everyone there heard about it", underlines the feeling that "I know everything that goes on there even though I am here". The progressing pregnancy of a daughter can be observed via webcam, and cousins can "chat" between Sydney, Frankfurt and Chicago on the Internet. But not only the ways and means of communication have changed. The possibility to exchange information frequently, spontaneously and informally generates a "virtual intimacy" (Wilding 2006) among the participants, which helps to make the physical absence lose significance, at least for the time being. Communication technologies researcher Christian Licoppe came to similar conclusions in his studies, in which he described: "Communication technologies, instead of being used (however unsuccessfully) to compensate for the absence of our close ones, are exploited to provide a continuous pattern of mediated interactions that combine into connected relationships' in which the boundaries between absence and presence eventually get blurred" (Licoppe 2004: 136). Most of the mediated interactions thus lead not only to a compression of time and space, but give the impression of shared time and space despite the physical distance. This experience of simultaneity over great geographical distances is an essential factor, enabling transnational families, as "imagined communities" (Anderson 1983; Vuorela 2002: 63), to create and maintain shared notions and narratives of cohesion and belonging.

Taking a closer look at how the increase in mediated interactions developed within the families we studied, it is apparent that the communication technologies available were not used by all participants to the same extent. While contact to the older generation is generally maintained by telephone, the middle and younger generations use especially the Internet – that is, email – in addition to telephone and mobile phone, in their communications.

We hear from each other regularly, also the cousins, etc. ... So now I actually have much more contact with them than my parents. And through Facebook I have ... the contact is maintained, like, I don't know, by exchanging pictures or whatever, and talking a little and sending messages; that usually is kept up through Facebook.[7]

What at first glance signals only a change in medium, turns out when looking closer to be a change that also has consequences for the ways family members refer to one another. First, the increased use of the Internet means that information can be passed on within the shortest possible time to a large number of people. Thus the circle of people who can potentially be informed of "family matters" and who feel connected is expanded. In particular among members of the younger generation the Internet has created new forms and forums for coming together through the various social networks such as Facebook. Here, independent communication between peers is possible over great geographic distances, which is significant in order to maintain a sense of familiarity. Also, the medium of Internet has increased the number of male participants in family communication, since they are generally more willing to send an email than to pick up the telephone. Both developments contribute to the fact that two different patterns can increasingly be observed within families. Both for letters that had been written in the past and for the telephone, which increasingly replaced letter-writing, it was and is primarily women who maintain this communication:

The women talk to each other on the phone much more often and that is really like: My mama picks up the phone and then her sister will be called, and then the other sister, and the aunt, and everything is discussed with one another.[8]

Such descriptions, which give female relatives a key function in terms of gathering and passing on information, refer to a network with one person at the centre who is responsible for exchanging and directing transnational communication. Through media such as the Internet and email, parallel networks are emerging, "in which communications proceed simultaneously in more or less all directions" (Urry 2003: 160). The structures of these media appear to be looser and less binding, but at the same time they involve a larger circle of participants who in different ways can participate in or help shape family events.

From a historical perspective we are thus dealing with a unique extent of closeness created through communication, which results in a new problem for the members of transnational families in our sample. The virtual closeness over a distance corresponds to the insight that one's own actions remain indirect, conveyed via media, and – for example in the case of a family crisis – are no substitute for co-presence. This experience produces new dilemmas for members of transnational families, which go hand in hand with the availability of new technologies. When in many cases distance no longer represents an insurmountable barrier, then one's own absence no longer assumes the character of fate, but instead increasingly becomes an act of decision-making. If, when and under what conditions family members get together is thus the subject of negotiations of what comprises family obligations and responsibilities (Urry 2003: 169). In other words, the increased opportunities to be accessible also lead to increased expectations of accessibility.

Sophia Wassiliou also shared this experience. Similar to other people we interviewed, she stressed the close contact with her birth family. Through inexpensive telephone tariffs and the Internet she can communicate daily with her mother and relatives. The expansion of means of transportation – in particular inexpensive air travel – has multiplied the options for travelling very quickly to her hometown in Greece. At the same time her descriptions also present an unspoken problem: Sophia knows that she will not be there if something happens to her mother. The daily calls and the detailed knowledge of the various flight connections stand for her promise to be there as fast as possible in case of a crisis. When she was told that her grandmother in Greece lay on her deathbed, she had to admit that in reality such a promise could always fail.

And I tried to still get a ticket and it was just not possible. And I had already prepared myself for it ... to say goodbye to her and it was just impossible, no matter what ticket I had taken, even though we are in Frankfurt and I would've had to fly via Athens and then, well, I never would have made it. ... And that made me totally crazy, because I thought, I just can't believe it![9]

Although Sophia Wassiliou looked into various travel routes, she did not make it there in time. Her frustration and anger is an expression of a series of dilemmas that emerge through access to "time- and space-compressing technologies". One of them is that the technological changes and facilitated access have served to increase mutual expectations and commitments within transnational families. Furthermore, this change can also lead to a reassessment of the migration process itself. If long-term processes of immigration and emigration give way to virtual and spatial interrelations that can be set up individually and flexibly, then the standards for assessing life at a distance also gradually change. The guilty conscience that one senses from Sophia's account traces back to a self-attribution in which she assessed her own absence as the consequence of an individual decision that she could have also made differently. But whereas Sophia and her relatives enjoy freedom of movement within the legal space of Europe, flexible and mobile interrelations in many cases are also an expression of restrictive European immigration policies, whose border regimes separate the demand for immigrant labour from the workers' social reproduction, thereby largely contributing to the transnationalization of families.

Virtual Closeness at a Distance

One example of this is the story of Ingrida Einars. Ingrida, 38 years old, is from Kaunas, Lithuania. She has been living and working in Frankfurt am Main since 1998, although her eighteen-year-old daughter Danuta stayed in Kaunas with her grandparents. Like the Wassiliou family, Ingrida had planned to spend one or at most two years in Germany. However, the legal conditions of her migration are fundamentally different from the basic conditions of the recruitment measures of the 1960s. Whereas the Wassiliou parents received legally regulated residential status in the course of so-called guest worker migration, which provided for their children to later join them, Ingrida is subject to the restrictive requirements that the countries of the European Union, and especially Germany and Austria, implemented in the 1990s through the Schengen agreement. Not only does this treaty provide for a stepwise system of selective immigration controls both internally and externally, it limits in principle the right of people from Eastern Europe to move and reside freely and abolished the right to settle – with few exceptions – almost entirely (Bade 2003: 288–290). British sociologists Eleonore Kofman and Rosemarie Sales have determined that the few remaining legal forms of labour migration address primarily the migration of men, whereas migrating women are increasingly forced to resort to unofficial means (Kofman & Sales 1998). The disproportionate illegalization of the migration of women has led to specifically female migration patterns and job opportunities developing especially within the so-called low-skilled and informalized service sector. Aside from the sex industry, it is predominately work in private households – that is, the unregulated and informalized area of domestic help – that is available to most female migrants as a chance for employment (see Anthias & Lazaridis 2000). This was also the case for Ingrida Einars. Until Lithuania joined the EU in 2004 she was eligible for a three-month tourist visa, and after 2004 a bilateral treaty between Germany and Lithuania abolished the visa requirement for tourists. Ingrida Einars was able to enter Germany but she had no work permit. She worked illegally and unregistered as a seamstress in a sweatshop together with other Eastern European women. Later she took on various cleaning jobs, and not until 2009 did she register her own cleaning services as a business. Her irregular status has led to her not being able to have her daughter join her, especially since the restrictive German legislation provides for neither the right for her child to attend school nor sufficient rights to adequate healthcare. Similar to the account of Mirjana

Morokvasic (1999), Ingrida left her home in order to be able to maintain it. Migration made possible for her what she could not accomplish at home: to earn a livelihood for herself and her daughter and to renovate the house in Kaunas where Danuta and her grandparents live. In the interview Ingrida described her own lifestyle as torn: "I have one foot here and one foot there." This statement expresses not only her longing for a life together with her daughter, but also the fact that she has been living with a man for several years in Frankfurt – a situation that her birth family does not approve of and which continues to stabilize the circumstance of separation.

At the same time, Ingrida's statement is evidence – similar to those in the studies on transnational motherhood (Parrenas 2005) – also of her attempt to be there for her daughter even over a distance and to provide both emotional and material care. Unlike the families involved in labour migration in the 1960s, Ingrida Einars can compensate for the geographical separation from her family through daily use of new communications media. Over the years she has built up a complex network of conversation partners who help her participate from a distance in the family life "at home". Via telephone, Internet and Skype she communicates regularly with her daughter, her parents and her sister, whose family lives next door. If acute financial problems arise, she can transfer money almost immediately. If her parents complain about their granddaughter, she tries to assuage the situation from a distance, occasionally asking her sister to help out. Ingrida keeps abreast of Danuta's school achievements, not only through her daughter directly, but also through the school's Internet portal, where absent parents like Ingrida can see their children's grades from a distance. In addition, she and Danuta's teacher communicate by email about Danuta's progress in school. What at first sounds like a success story of modern communication technologies must be qualified when looking closer at how this communication is organized in practice. Ingrida's parents have both been suffering for years from a hearing disability that makes talking on the phone very difficult. Both parents can write but have had very little practice so that written contact is in fact not really possible. In the initial period of back-and-forth migration, Ingrida was therefore only able to have contact with her young daughter and her sister, who occasionally served as mediators between her and her parents. Not until the family in Kaunas gained access to a computer, webcam, and an Internet connection was it possible for Ingrida to communicate with her parents via Skype from a "call shop" in Frankfurt. Now she is able to use her partner's computer. Since Ingrida's parents are not very proficient at using the computer, they need to rely on their granddaughter to prepare the necessary computer set-up for them to be able to communicate with Ingrida using the keyboard, individual words, and sign language. This laboured communication is even more difficult due to interruptions in the connection and deficient picture quality. Despite these problems, Skype and webcams have in fact made it possible for Ingrida and her parents to have direct contact with each other.

Whereas in this case the technological innovations are a necessary prerequisite for the communication, they have also given rise to an opposite effect when Ingrida Einars tries to contact her daughter. When Danuta entered puberty Ingrida was confronted via Skype and webcam with the (not unusual) changes her daughter was going through: nail polish, dyed hair, and a lip piercing made Ingrida fear that her daughter might go astray, causing her to seriously consider returning to Kaunas, a thought she later abandoned. Mother and daughter decided instead to change the medium of their communication. Their daily exchange now takes place via email, since both of them discovered that the webcam and computer telephone conversations created a closeness that they had difficulty dealing with emotionally from a distance.

> We write. Whenever we talk we end up arguing. Always, almost every time we talk, I give some kind of sermon and she raises her voice a bit when she responds and that's it. Then it just takes off from there. But when we write I don't hear her tone, since it doesn't come through the writing. And that's better.[10]

Conflict-laden conversations between parents and their pubescent children are an everyday part of family life, whether they are interacting under the same roof or over a great distance. While the conflict in a face-to-face situation can be carried out by, for example, slamming doors and avoiding each other's glance at meals until the waves of escalation begin to ebb, in this case mother and daughter have taken a course that is much more rational. Since the goal of communication from a distance is to maintain communication per se, it requires controlling anger and curbing emotions in order to avoid potential conflict; otherwise the escalation can lead only to ending the conversation and, with that, all contact.

Ingrida Einars's story is exemplary for a series of experiences shared also by other interviewees, including the knowledge that family interactions can indeed be carried out via the Internet and telephone, but the indirectness and mediatization of the contact also changes the quality of the relationship. The virtual closeness can generate emotions that as perceived by family members cannot be adequately dealt with through the new communication technologies. The dilemma of the illusion of closeness produces not only disappointed expectations among the conversation partners, but can also lead to reflections on how to deal with the corresponding media. This can involve weighing considerations of the possible emotional repercussions of a short-term "virtual intimacy" against the long-term goal of successfully maintaining contact. The decision of family members as to which of the available media might seem best suited for communicating with each other can also be understood as an attempt to appropriately fathom the relationship between closeness and spatial distance.

This leads to another experience shared by members of transnational families. Using media such as mobile telephones and the Internet they continually become involved in difficult family situations that nevertheless take place *elsewhere*. As Ingrida Einars's example shows, she is directly available but can only indirectly take action, a situation that she experiences with emotional ambivalence. The new technologies make it possible for her to do whatever she – in agreement with her family – decides is necessary. Almost immediately she can put through a bank transfer or share ideas and information, but she is not there in person. This leads to a feeling of tension that also comes from a sense of asynchrony, namely, of being close to the absent person virtually, whereas one's actions are bound together, as Norbert Elias described it, in extended "chains of action", which have been "lengthened" in the course of interdependent transnational contexts (Elias 2000: 370). As Ingrida's example shows, her scope of action had been considerably expanded, yet at the same time she cannot anticipate the outcome of her actions. This awareness increasingly pressures individuals to "take account of the effects of his or her own or other people's actions on a whole series of links in the social chain" (ibid.: 370), but without losing the insight that in the end they do not regain control of their intended actions.

The dilemma that has emerged for migrant women in our sample is especially apparent regarding matters of distributing money in transnational families. Similar to Ingrida Einars's case, also in other families a large share of the earnings of the migrant women is used to support their family network in their region of origin. An attempt is made to control the distribution of the funds from a distance by transferring money to one particular person in the place of origin who then makes decisions regarding the further distribution there. As a rule this contact is a female relative, such as their own daughter or a sister in the family (see Gamburd 2000; Parrenas 2005). The migrants can, however, never really check whether or not their money transfers are used as they intended. Also, the chain of family obligations and problems does not end, as can also be seen in the example of Ingrida Einars. From the costs to renovate and maintain the house to financing the daughter's education and the parents' visits to the doctor, new demands and emergencies continue to arise, which prolong the migrant's stay in Germany in order to earn the necessary money. Conversely, Ingrida Einars is dependant on the support of the family network, especially with respect to caring for her daughter. This "moral economy of family loyalties" (Lutz 2008: 161) leads to close, often also burdensome, emotional and mental ties with the region of origin, which at the same time makes it all the more difficult to take advantage of opportunities to establish one's own life in the place of destination.

These accounts clearly show that the use of new communication technologies does not take place in a vacuum, but that the compression of space and time is embedded in a "power geometry" (Massey 1993) characterized by structures of social inequality that exert a determining influence on the positioning of the individual family members. Access to these technologies presupposes that the parties involved are either financially in a position to acquire the necessary equipment or that a local infrastructure exists, such as "call shops", which offer inexpensive opportunities to have contact. Family members are thus confronted both with economic constraints that can limit transnational contact (Mahler 1998) and with the unequal distribution of resources worldwide or the existence or lack of varying technological infrastructures in urban areas such as Frankfurt am Main and Kaunas.

In addition to the fact that the respective economic and technological accessibility of transnational communications media has far-reaching consequences for the success of this communication, the example of the Einars family indicates additional factors of social inequality that greatly determine the actual options and abilities of the individual participants in the communications. The new technologies thus enable contact between Ingrida and her family in principle, but this communication also displays an asymmetry that determines its form. Whereas Ingrida's daughter was too young during the first few years of Ingrida's migration to independently engage in contact with her absent mother, the grandparents had to painfully admit that, due to their physical disabilities and insufficient technological savvy, they did not always have the necessary means or unobstructed access at their disposal to be able to enjoy unrestricted use of these new technologies (see also Baldassar 2007).

Conclusions

The two cases of Sophia Wassiliou and Ingrida Einars do not only reflect a short narrative on the compression of time and space, they also illustrate the different realities of labour migration in the 1960s and 1990s. Both families have developed forms of familiarity at a distance which, for one thing, make the great technological leaps apparent and, for another, show how the different legal conditions for migration offer the families a framework to refer to in shaping their own transnational experiment. The case of the Wassiliou family is exemplary for how the specific positioning of the EU labour migrants in the 1960s influenced the family structure. Unlike the case of Ingrida Einers, the parents of Sophia Wassiliou were recruited and then given permanent residential status that provided for the right to move and reside freely and the right to reunite the family by allowing other family members to join them. This legally privileged position was combined with an economic status in which the migrants were better off than in their country of origin, yet they were confronted with tendencies in the host country to close itself off to immigrants, which caused the family to take advantage of transnational family networks to arrange for the extended family to participate in caregiving in the country of origin.

Sophia Wassiliou's family has a citizenship that allows family members to develop multi-local reference points within the European sphere. Ingrida Einars's situation, however, illustrates the development of European migration policies that reflect a dependence on migrant labour, on the one hand, but which are increasingly restrictive towards them, on the other. This development goes hand in hand with a political and legal practice leading to a feminization and illegalization of migratory movements, as also experienced by Ingrida Einars. Her irregular employment as a domestic worker long denied her the opportunity to bring her daughter to join her in Germany. In contrast to the Wassiliou family, however, she had greater spatial mobility from the very beginning of her migration and was able to maintain contact to her family in Lithuania by virtual means. Present-day communication technologies allowed her to develop everyday practices and routines of transnational motherhood while assuring her financial support of the family. At the same time, however, she has been denied the opportunity to develop any lasting prospects for a future in Germany, since both the legal regulations for migration in the country of destination and the continuing financial demands of her family in the country of origin hamper such a project.

These two examples show how a concept of familiarity that remains tied to face-to-face relationships at close proximity ignores the ways in which new technologies create closeness and how the related practices make it possible to create and maintain a family lifestyle spanning great geographical distances. At the same time this clearly shows that participation in this process is essentially characterized by the individuals' (unequal) social positioning, which largely determines the respective opportunities to use these technologies. This applies not only to family members who physically engage in the cross-border mobility, but also to those who remain at the places of origin, because they too actively help shape the transnational relations. Against this background, members of transnational families experience the new technologies as a relief, on the one hand, since they enable everyday interactions in which familiarity can be experienced. On the other hand, along with the increased options for crossing virtual and spatial boundaries quickly and flexibly, the evaluating standards with respect to the decision for a life-at-a-distance have changed. While migration used to be connected with the burden of necessity, today's mobile lifestyles seem more and more to be an act of choice, taking wishes to shape one's own life into account. What is subjectively perceived as a process of individualization, however, is the outcome of a European immigration regime that produces flexible and mobile labour, but which places the responsibility for the consequences of these constraints on the migrants themselves.

Notes

1 The article was translated by Allison Brown.

2 The Transnational Familiarity research project (Prof. Ina Merkel, Dr. Karen Körber, Mag. Polina Kirjanenko) was conducted from 2008 to 2011 at the Institute for European Ethnology/Cultural Studies at the Philipps University, Marburg. It received funding from the German Research Foundation (DFG).

3 The interviews were conducted in Frankfurt am Main and in the Rhine-Main region, as well as in Vienna. These cities and regions have been affected by processes of migration and mobility for decades: The share of the population with a migration background in Vienna is roughly 32 percent of the overall population; the figure is 39.5 percent for Frankfurt am Main, and 38 percent in the Rhine-Main region. Through contacts to immigrant organizations, cultural and religious associations, and schools, which served as networks and hubs, we were able to gain access to the field, finding the families for our sample through the snowball effect. The interviews were conducted in either German or Russian and in isolated cases interpreters were used. Because limited research funding was available, we first interviewed members of the families living in the greater Frankfurt area or in Vienna and then those family members who shuttled regularly between Germany or Austria and their respective country of origin, or those who were visiting in Frankfurt or Vienna. Finally, a group interview with the family was carried out. We also gathered data using the methodology of participant observation to determine how family members organized their transnational communication. In addition, we participated in both private family celebrations and religious services and festivals as well as activities organized by immigrant organizations, in which the families were present in various different configurations. The interviews were transcribed and then evaluated on the basis of hermeneutic processes (Fischer-Rosenthal & Rosenthal 1997). Thus patterns of action and interpretation were reconstructed in order to reveal those – often invisible – "structures of intricately networked state, legal, and cultural transitions, which provided a biographical orientation for the individuals and represented a shared experience for them" (Apitzsch 2003: 69).

4 Interview with Wassilis K. on 11 May 2009 in Frankfurt am Main, transcript, p. 5.

5 Interview with Sophia Wassiliou on 10 February 2010 in Frankfurt am Main, transcript, p. 3.

6 Ibid., transcript, p. 5.

7 Interview with Raina S. on 12 October 2010 in Wiesbaden, transcript, p. 9.

8 Ibid., transcript, p. 8.

9 Interview with Sophia Wassiliou on 10 February 2010 in Frankfurt am Main, transcript, p. 17.

10 Interview with Ingrida Einars on 16 December 2010 in Frankfurt am Main, transcript, p. 15.

References

Anderson, B. 1983: *Imagined Communities: Reflections on the Origin and Spread of Nationalism.* London: Verso.

Anthias, F. & G. Lazaridis (eds.) 2000: *Gender and Migration in Southern Europe: Women on the Move.* Oxford & New York: Berg.

Apitzsch, U. 2003: Migrationsbiographien als Orte transnationaler Räume. In: U. Apitzsch & M.M. Jansen (eds.), *Migration, Biographie und Geschlechterverhältnisse.* Münster: Westfälisches Dampfboot, pp. 65–80.

Apitzsch U. & I. Siouti 2008: Transnationale Biographien. In: G. Homfeldt, W. Schröer & C. Schweppe (eds.), *Soziale Arbeit und Transnationalität: Herausforderungen eines spannungsreichen Bezugs.* Weinheim: Juventa, pp. 97–111.

Appadurai, A.J. 2001: Grassroots Globalization and the Research Imagination. In: A.J. Appadurai (ed.), *Globalization.* Durham, NC: Duke University Press, pp. 1–21.

Bade, K. 2003: *Migration in European History.* Trans. A. Brown. Oxford: Blackwell.

Baldassar, L. 2007: Transnational Families and Aged Care: The Mobility of Care and the Migrancy of Ageing. *Journal of Ethnic and Migration Studies* 33:2, 275–297.

Baldassar, L., C.V. Baldock & R. Wilding 2007: *Families Caring Across Borders: Migration, Ageing and Transnational Caregiving.* Houndmills, UK: Palgrave Macmillan.

Brah, A. 1996: *Cartographies of Diaspora: Contesting Identities.* London: Routledge.

Brennan, D. 2004: *What's Love Got to Do with it? Transnational Desires and Sex Tourism in the Dominican Republic.* Durham, NC: Duke University Press.

Bryceson, D.F. & U. Vuorela, 2002: Transnational Families in the Twenty-First Century. In: D. F. Bryceson & U. Vuorela (eds.), *The Transnational Family: New European Frontiers and Global Networks.* Oxford & New York: Berg, pp. 3–30.

Caglar, A. 1997: Hyphenated Identities and the Limits of 'Culture': Some Methodological Queries. In: P. Werbner & T. Madood (eds.), *The Politics of Multiculturalism in the New Europe: Racism, Identity, Community.* London: Zed Publications.

Cairncross, F. 1997: *The Death of Distance.* London: Orion.

Dreby, J. 2006: Honor and Virtue: Mexican Parenting in the Transnational Context. *Gender and Society* 20, 32–60.

Elias, N. 2000: *The Civilizing Process.* Trans. E. Jephcott, rev. ed. Oxford: Blackwell.

Erel, U. 2002: Reconceptualizing Motherhood: Experiences of Migrant Women from Turkey Living in Germany: In: D.F. Bryceson & U. Vuorela (eds.), *The Transnational Family: New European Frontiers and Global Networks.* Oxford & New York: Berg, pp. 127–146.

Faist, T. 2000: *The Volume and Dynamics of International Migration and Transnational Social Spaces.* Oxford: Clarendon.

Fischer-Rosenthal, W. & G. Rosenthal 1997: Narrationsanalyse biografischer Selbstpräsentation. In: R. Hitzler & A. Honer (eds.), *Sozialwissenschaftliche Hermeneutik: Eine Einführung.* Opladen: Leske + Budrich, pp. 133–164.

Fog Olwig, K. 2003: 'Transnational' Socio-Cultural Systems and Ethnographic Research: Views from an Extended Field Site. *International Migration Review* 37:3, 787–811.

Gamburd, M.R. 2000: *The Kitchen Spoon's Handle: Transnationalism and Sri Lanka's Migrant Housemaids.* Ithaca, NY & London: Cornell University Press.

Harvey, D. 1990: *The Condition of Postmodernity: An Enquiry into the Origins of Cultural Change.* Oxford & Malden, MA: Blackwell.

Hondagneu-Sotelo, P. & E. Avila 1997: 'I'm here, but I'm there': The Meanings of Latina Transnational Motherhood. *Gender and Society* 11:5, 548–571.

Kearney, M. 1995: The Local and the Global: The Anthropology of Globalization and Transnationalism. *Annual Review of Anthropology* 24, 547–565.

Kofman E. & R. Sales 1998: Migrant Women and Exclusion in Europe. *The European Journal of Women's Studies* 5:3–4, 381–398.

Levitt, P. 2001: *The Transnational Villagers.* Berkeley: University of California Press.

Levitt, P. & N. Glick Schiller 2004: Conceptualizing Simultaneity: Theorizing Society from a Transnational Social Field Perspective. *International Migration Review* 38:3, 1002–39.

Licoppe, C. 2004: 'Connected' Presence: The Emergence of a New Repertoire for Managing Social Relationships in a Changing Communication Technoscape. *Environment and Planning D: Society and Space* 22, 135–156.

Lutz, H. 2008: *Vom Weltmarkt in den Privathaushalt: Die neuen Dienstmädchen im Zeitalter der Globalisierung.* Opladen: Budrich.

Lutz, H. 2011: *The New Maids: Transnational Women and the Care Economy.* Trans. D. Shannon. London & New York: Zed.

Mahler, S. 1998: Theoretical and Empirical Contributions: Towards a Research Agenda for Transnationalism. In: M.P. Smith & L.E. Guarnizo (eds.), *Transnationalism from Below.* New Brunswick, NJ: Transaction Publishers, pp. 64–100.

Massey, D. 1993: Power-Geometry and a Progressive Sense of Place. In: J. Bird, B. Curtis, T. Putnam, G. Robertson & L. Tickner (eds.), *Mapping the Futures: Local Cultures, Global Change*, London: Routledge, pp. 59–69.

Momsen, J. Henshall 1999: Maids on the Move. In: J. Henshall Momsen (ed.), *Gender, Migration and Domestic Service.* London & New York: Routledge.

Morokvasic, M. 1999: La mobilité transnationale comme ressource: Les cas des migrants de l'Europe de l'Est. *Cultures et Conflits* 33–34, 105–122.

Nyberg Sørensen, N. & K. Fog Olwig 2002: *Work and Migration: Life and Livelihood in a Globalizing World.* London & New York: Routledge.

Oz, A. (2002) 2004: *A Tale of Love and Darkness*. Trans. N. de Lange. London & New York: Harcourt.

Parrenas, R.S. 2001: *Servants of Globalization: Women, Migration and Domestic Work*. Stanford: Stanford University Press.

Parrenas, R.S. 2005: *Children of Global Migration: Transnational Families and Gendered Woes*. Stanford: Stanford University Press.

Pries, L. 1998: Transnationale soziale Räume: Theoretisch-empirische Skizze am Beispiel der Arbeitswanderungen Mexiko–USA. In: U. Beck (ed.), *Perspektiven der Weltgesellschaft*. Frankfurt am Main, pp. 55–87.

Rogers, A. 2004: A European Space for Transnationalism? In: P. Jackson et al. (eds.), *Transnational Spaces*. London: Routledge, pp. 164–182.

Sayad, A. 2004: *The Suffering of the Immigrant*. Trans. D. Macey. Cambridge & Malden, MA: Polity Press.

Schmalzbauer, L. 2004: Searching for Wages and Mothering from Afar: The Case of Honduran Transnational Families. *Journal of Marriage and Family* 66, 1317–31.

Schütze, F. 1983: Biographieforschung und narratives Interview. *Neue Praxis* 3, 283–293.

Thomas, W.I. & F. Znaniecki (1918)1984: *The Polish Peasant in Europe and America*. Ed. E. Zaretsky. Chicago: University of Illinois Press.

Urry, J. 2003: Networks, Travel and Talk. *British Journal of Sociology* 54:2, 155–175.

Vertovec, S. 2004: Cheap Calls: The Social Glue of Migrant Transnationalism. *Global Networks* 4:2, 219–224.

Vuorela, U. 2002: Transnational Families: Imagined and Real Communities. In: D.F. Bryceson & U. Vuorela (eds.), *The Transnational Family: New European Frontiers and Global Networks*. Oxford & New York: Berg, pp. 63–82.

Wilding, R. 2006: Virtual Intimacies. *Global Network* 6:2, 125–142.

Yans-McLaughlin, V. (ed.) 1990: *Immigration Reconsidered: History, Sociology, and Politics*. Oxford & New York: Oxford University Press.

Karen Körber is a research fellow at the Jewish Museum Berlin. Her publications include books and articles on transnationalism, Jewish diaspora, migration and identity politics. A recent article is “Nähe auf Distanz: Transnationale Familien in der Gegenwart” (in Gertraud Marinelli-König & Alexander Preisinger, eds., 2011, *Zwischenräume: Migration und die Entgrenzung von Kulturen und Identitäten*. Bielefeld: Transcript).
(k.koerber@jmberlin.de)

"THE DAUGHTERS HAVE GROWN UP"
Transnational Motherhood, Migration and Gender among Catholic Nuns

Gertrud Hüwelmeier

This article explores transnational spiritual motherhood in women's congregations from a historical and anthropological perspective, considering the question as to how ideas of motherhood have changed across geographic borders and over an extended period of time. Within a religious context, kinship terms (mother, sister, daughter) are based not on biological, but on ritual relationships. In the past, social contact to biological parents and to the family of origin was reduced to a minimum or cut off entirely when a young woman entered a religious congregation. In view of the *transnationalization of convent life* and the accompanying increased mobility of Catholic sisters, this presents new challenges for many religious orders.

Keywords: transnational motherhood, Catholic nuns, migration, mobility, Europe, United States

As early as the nineteenth century, especially due to the migration movements from Europe to the United States, thousands of Catholic nuns were separated from their mother houses, and thus also from their "mothers", the founders of the respective women's congregations. Despite the spatial separation, the sisters were pioneers of female migration, maintaining transnational connections to their places of origin on the other side of the Atlantic. As spiritual mothers, the founders of these communities worried about their "daughters" living so far away.

Transnational motherhood is by no means a phenomenon of the twenty-first century. Although a growing number of mothers presently live separated from their children (Hondagneu-Sotelo & Avila 1997; Hoang & Yeoh 2011; Hüwelmeier 2013a), motherhood across geographic and cultural borders existed in earlier centuries and in various different societies, including mobile Catholic sisters, whom I have referred to as pioneers of female migration (Hüwelmeier 2005a; Hüwelmeier 2005b). Based on ethnographic fieldwork with the Poor Handmaids of Jesus Christ (PHJC), a globally interconnected women's congregation, I will illustrate how ideas of spiritual and social motherhood have changed over the course of a 150-year period and across continents.[1] In line with Carling, Menjivar and Schmalzbauer (2012: 192), I argue that physical absence is compatible with social and emotional presence and participation.

In the first part of this article I will sketch new approaches to transnational motherhood, a phenomenon that is gaining significance in view of recent migration movements and new communication technologies. This also involves re-evaluating the traveling activities of women who had already crossed geographic and territorial boundaries in the nineteenth and early twentieth centuries, long before anthropological research started speaking of globalization or global flows (Appadurai 1996; Hannerz 1996). I will then discuss the dynamic relationship between gender, migration and mobility. Further, I describe the bidding of farewell to "mothers" by focusing on traveling nuns, and depict tensions and conflicts between "mothers", "co-mothers" and "daughters" beyond borders. Transatlantic communication is also a main aspect of the historical and anthropological perspective on transnational motherhood.

Based on multi-sited ethnography, in the next section I will discuss the processes of transformation and the new way of looking at social motherhood in women's congregations since the 1960s. Hierarchy and power relations were increasingly questioned in Catholic religious orders as well as in other "total institutions" (Goffman 1961). The women's movement, students' movement and the young Indian and African women who joined women's congregations with a "Western" orientation in the 1960s all contributed to cracking the image of dominant mother superiors.

Co-parenthood and Transnational Motherhood

My understanding of transnational motherhood is not reduced to the relationship of mothers living in the diaspora to their minor-age children in the country of origin. Instead, I view the concept of transnational motherhood as an enduring relationship between people of different generations in different countries. Thus it is independent of age and can also exist among adults (see also Åkesson, Carling & Drotbohm 2012: 239). My analysis of transnational connections between Catholic nuns and their "mothers" focuses on social and spiritual motherhood as a kind of fictive or ritual kinship relation. Configurations of co-parenthood have long had great significance in anthropology, in particular with regard to the expansion of social and political networks, such as *kivrelik* in the Turkish context (Kudat-Sertel 1971: 37) or *compadrazgo*, a relationship between parents and godparents that is maintained in Spain and in many Latin American countries (Mintz & Wolf 1950). In addition to biological parents, co-parents also assume responsibility for children or adolescents. It is not unusual for co-parents to live at different locations. Esther Goody (1982) has shown that many children in West Africa do not grow up in their families of origin, but are brought to relatives or friends living elsewhere, who then raise the children. Sometimes these "new" parents live in different countries or even continents. Older siblings can also assume responsibility. In some African countries, for example – as a consequence of AIDS/HIV – orphans grow up in households run by other children. In these child-headed households, older siblings or underage relatives take on the role of the mother (Wolf 2010).

Practices of co-parenthood are as well known in European countries. From the mountainous regions of Austria, for example, into the 1930s "illegitimate" children of servants and maids, working as farm laborers, were not allowed to remain living with their parents if the parents did not want to risk losing their place of employment. Thus parents sought other options and asked "foster" parents to take care of their children. In general, foster parents (*Zieheltern*) were couples, friends or relatives, who either had their own children but needed more workers or were without children and subsequently had no heir for the farm. Foster parents often lived nearby, either in the next valley or a few hours away on foot, but without means of transportation the walking distances were a difficult endeavor. Another kind of co-parenthood is known from the so-called Swabian children. With their parents' consent children between five and fourteen were sent from the Tyrol and Vorarlberg areas of Austria to work as maids and servants for farmers they did not know in Upper Swabia (Lampert 1996).

Children who travel on their own, without parents or co-parents, are today looked after as unaccompanied minors by state institutions in European societies. The majority of minors not living with their parents, however, live with co-parents. In my current research on transnational Vietnamese families in Berlin, some children and adolescents below eighteen live with relatives who have already resided in Germany for some time. Their parents in Vietnam want them to have a better life than their own and entrust them in the migration context to the care of their uncles, aunts, or older cousins. Young women from Vietnam who work as domestic workers or nannies in Germany make up another group. On the one hand these are situations in which minors are exploited, since many of these women are irregular migrants and totally dependent on their "employers". On the other hand, this offers young women from Vietnam their only chance to leave their country of origin and live in Germany "without papers", with the possibility of finding new, more long-term prospects.

Gender, Migration and Mobility

In many societies, female migrants have ideas of "good motherhood" that are characterized by caring practices for their children. Due to the mobility of mothers, relatives such as the father, uncle and aunt or grandparents take care of the children (Erel 2002). Mothers who leave their families behind to work as nurses or domestic workers (Liebelt 2011) are able to stay in contact with their partners and children thanks to modern communication technologies. In the late 1980s these options were still very limited, in socialist societies in particular. For example, many female Vietnamese contract workers in East Germany (GDR) lived separated from their families in Vietnam (Hüwelmeier 2013a). Thousands of mothers and fathers had to leave their children behind in Vietnam. Due to bilateral agreements between the Socialist Republic of Vietnam and East Germany, contract workers were not permitted to bring their children with them. Whereas in the early 1980s state-owned Vietnamese companies started "delegating" primarily "singles", that is, unmarried people, to Russia, East Germany and other socialist countries, in the late 1980s the Socialist Republic of Vietnam had to resort to sending married people (with children who had to be left in Vietnam) in order to cover the increased demand for labor in "socialist brother countries". By sending just one spouse, there was a high probability that this person would return to the home country and not stay in the GDR. Already at that time some parents tried to bring their children into East Germany from Vietnam (Hüwelmeier 2013a), but these efforts failed due to bureaucratic obstacles and the state control. Not only mothers, but also fathers suffered from spending years living away from their children and spouse. Furthermore, as Hoang and Yeoh mentioned, notions of masculinity change when fathers have sole responsibility for raising their children (Hoang & Yeoh 2011).

Migrants, both men and women, will continue to care for the emotional and physical well-being of their children. In particular, they try to provide money for them to receive good education and/or training (Åkesson, Carling & Drotbohm 2012: 239). In cases of female migration, financial responsibility for the children often lies with the mothers, who also send remittances for the rest of the family. Simultaneously, mothers are primary caretakers for their children. In many cases, mothers have daily contact with their children, talking on the phone or via Skype, discussing school problems, the latest fashion news or conflicts with friends.

Traveling Nuns

Romanticizing and idealizing notions of motherhood in Western European societies can be traced back to the bourgeois milieu of the nineteenth century. Women in religious congregations are an excellent example of the fragility of such ideas. Female Catholic congregations in particular opened doors for many young women to live out their own ideas of professional work beyond the bourgeois perceptions of the family and without the protective hand of a father or husband. At the same time they could organize their daily lives as well as their religious lives in a community with other women. In women's congregations that were founded around 1850, Catholic sisters who became active nuns (i.e., not contemplative), made a clear decision for professional work as a nurse, a midwife, a teacher, and against the ideal of the bourgeois housewife and mother (Hüwelmeier 2004; Meiwes 2000).

One of the most pressing responsibilities of the

"good mothers" who founded women's congregations was to provide for their "daughters" to receive qualified training once they had bid a final farewell to their families of origin. Qualified specialists were urgently needed as home nurses and later as nurses in newly established hospitals (Meiwes 2008). As teachers and carers in nursery schools, women religious assumed the task of partly replacing biological mothers: Women working as industrial workers could thus earn a living because the sisters cared for and raised their children. This is why the Poor Handmaids of Jesus Christ (PHJC) had already migrated in the last three decades of the nineteenth century from Germany to the working-class districts of London. They followed German migrants who had found work in London, and taught their children. Other PHJC sisters lived and worked in villages in the Westerwald region, north of Frankfurt am Main, caring for children who were left alone at home during the day because their mothers had to work in the fields. The fathers left the villages to work as seasonal labor migrants (Hüwelmeier 2000) and did not return to their homes until late autumn. A considerable number of sisters became co-mothers, which thus enabled many women to contribute to the family's livelihood as factory workers or smallholders. Still, some Catholic sisters left Europe and traveled to the United States as early as the nineteenth century.

Among the many women who migrated from Europe to the United States in the second half of the nineteenth century were thousands of Catholic nuns. I cannot go into detail here about their motivation for emigrating, how they experienced their departure or their impressions upon arriving and becoming incorporated into the host society (Hüwelmeier 2005b), as the subject of this article is constructions of motherhood in transnational settings. The theoretical question, however, is not directed at the process of migration as a unidirectional movement; instead, I would like to concentrate on recent concepts of transnational migration and maintaining contact between two or more countries (Hüwelmeier 2010, 2009a, 2009b, 2008a, 2008b; Gabaccia 2000).

Since most of the women's congregations that were founded in Europe in the nineteenth century still exist today, it is relevant to ask how cross-border relations have been maintained over several generations. As early as 1850 Catholic sisters left their hometowns in Europe, finding their own way in American society, which was totally foreign to them, largely without any male support. Priests and bishops were often not present at all in very remote rural areas. Male representatives of the Catholic Church, however, played a prominent role in sending the first sisters on their journey. From a gender perspective, the concept of transnational motherhood poses the question whether women religious, frequently perceived as "daughters" by female founders of the congregations, enjoyed greater independence from their "mothers" in Europe while living abroad. Recent debate and empirical research on transnationalism have shown that theories on migration that focus on assimilation and adaptation to the host society must be criticized for not adequately taking into account the everyday experiences of migrants (Levitt & Glick Schiller 2004). It has instead turned out that individuals and groups who left their home countries for either voluntary or coerced migration still participate in activities in their society of origin, whether by participating in political issues, by trading, by founding and supporting religious networks (Levitt 2007; Hüwelmeier 2011) or by maintaining regular, long-term contact with their extended networks of relatives. In any case, farewells as rituals of separation are among the emotional experiences of migrants. In the following, I will first describe the departure of the "daughters" from the female founder of the PHJC. Then I will explore how motherhood is maintained beyond national borders and discuss the tensions that may emerge between spiritual mother (the female founder), spiritual co-mothers, and "new daughters".

Separation from the Spiritual Mother

As early as 1868 the first sisters of the PHJC crossed the Atlantic to the United States, as migration from Europe to North America brought a great demand for nurses and teachers among the German population settled there. Katharina Kasper, founder of the PHJC and referred to as "Mother", encouraged her "children", as she called the sisters, to build new branches in the United States. She nevertheless had a close and at the same time very responsible relationship with them. The way she personally said goodbye to her "daughters" is evidence of her emotional attachment. She even traveled with them to the port in France, from where they set sail for the United States. Eight nuns from Germany were accompanied to Le Havre (France) by the Reverend Mother, which is how she was referred to in virtually all texts from that time. It was not planned that the "children" would return. Katharina Kasper reported to the sisters in the German mother house on the departure of the eight as follows:

> When we said goodbye at the port, we promised to greet them one more time at the waterfront, where they again received priestly blessings from several priests, and the sisters had to sing: Guide us through the waves. And then it went into the open sea, and the poor children were allowed to cry. But, my beloved sisters, what a moving sight it was, the great sea, the terrible waves, the quick departure of the ship. The poor sisters were out of sight. Now I too could cry and watch the ship for a long time, until we could not see it anymore...[2]

This letter expresses her sadness that the "children" were no longer nearby, possibly also the idea that she would never see them again. In addition, the author reveals something to her readers about her emotions, which kept her standing there watching until she could no longer see her departing daughters (Hüwelmeier 2005a). Only then did she allow her tears to flow. It was presumably embarrassing for her to cry in the presence of her "children". This text passage is exemplary of the significance of the emotional implications of life in a transnational setting, which, as Louise Ryan remarked (Ryan 2011), has not yet been thoroughly researched.

Cross-Border Relations

Arrival in the United States was not only characterized by new living and working conditions, but the sisters also had to learn the language of the country. Further, they had to understand a different political culture and develop a modified concept of hierarchy in their small communities. What kind of relationship did the "daughters" maintain to the "mother" in Germany? Who were their contact persons in the United States? Who made decisions? How did power relations function among women?

Maintaining the social and political order of any religious order is based on compliance with the constitutions and the vows of poverty, chastity and obedience taken (Hüwelmeier 2004). Superiors were and are appointed to monitor the upholding of the congregation, with a house superior for each local community, a regional superior for the respective region, a provincial superior for the province and at the highest level authority was exercised by the Spiritual Mother, founder of the religious congregation, and later by her successors, the General Superiors. Already in the nineteenth century, regional and provincial superiors frequently traveled back and forth in their respective "domains", regularly visiting the scattered convents of the sisters. The chronicles show numerous references to these journeys, which sometimes lasted several days or even weeks (Hüwelmeier 2008b).

Due to the difficulty and expense of travel, transatlantic meetings were rather rare in the nineteenth century. Only on special occasions were delegations from the mother house in Germany sent to the United States. In 1872 a sister from Germany arrived as a visitor to Fort Wayne, Indiana, along with six other sisters who were to remain in the United States as "reinforcements". As representative of the Reverend Mother the sister inspected all US branches and simultaneously assumed office as provincial superior in the United States. The incumbent provincial superior then returned to Germany. In subsequent years more and more branches were founded in the United States, thus increasing the travels of the provincial superior.

From 28th March until 10th April the Reverend Sisters Secunda accompanied by Sister Hyacintha visited the branches in Ashland and New Ulm. On 20th April the Rev. Sister Secunda traveled to Chicago .... From 1st to 12th May the Rev. Sister Secunda stayed in the branch houses of Germantown, Carlyle and Trenton....[3]

Striking about this quote is the designation of the highest authority, the spiritual co-mother in the United States, as "Reverend Sister". Reverend Sister is distinguished from Reverend Mother in that the former had assumed a position of power in the United States, whereas the Reverend Mother, as founder of the community in Europe, was in charge of all branches. To safeguard the power and authority of the Generalate in Europe, close contact between the US branches and the German mother house was indispensable. Transatlantic relations and the maintenance of the "German spirit" of the PHJC in the United States were guaranteed, first of all, through the "reinforcements" sent from Germany. But German sisters in the United States also paid visits to Germany. Although these trips were few and far between, they helped create and maintain a transnational consciousness, strengthening the community's collective identity.

On 19th May the Reverend Sister Secunda, together with Sisters Hyacintha, Suitberta and Anasthasia, took a trip to visit the beloved mother house in Dernbach. After a pleasant crossing the sisters were greeted upon their arrival at the mother house with heartfelt love and joy by the Reverend Mother and the reverend assistants and sisters and showered with all possible attention. They were most joyous to find the Reverend Mother even healthier and heartier than her age and previous strenuous efforts would have let them anticipate. After the spiritual exercises and the holding of the general chapter, the sisters returned to America. Sister Suitberta remained according to her wishes in Europe, and in turn three novices were sent with the others to America. On 2nd August the sisters arrived safe and sound back at the provincial mother house in Fort Wayne, where they were most cordially received by the sisters.[4]

This passage illustrates that transnational connections were not unidirectional, but encompassed two or more countries. In the nineteenth century sisters in women's congregations in Germany established not only transatlantic meetings and contact, but in addition also built up branches in the Netherlands and England.

When "Daughters" Leave

Not all "daughters" living in the United States wanted to uphold the "German spirit" of the community. Some strove to break off from the German mother house and found their own community. One German provincial superior was called back to Germany in the early 1880s because she had made some decisions independently, without the approval of the Mother (Hüwelmeier 2005a). In some cases the leadership took drastic measures and dismissed some sisters, although they had been members of the community for many years.

In 1889 we experienced a very regrettable incident, namely, the necessity to dismiss a sister who had already been a member of the congregation for eighteen years. After Sister Klara had already often caused disturbances of the peace, conducted herself improperly towards her Mother Superior and finally had tried to talk other sisters into leaving the congregation for the purpose of founding a new community, the Reverend Sister Secunda thought it would be best in avoiding any greater damage to present the case to the Most Reverend Bishop. He decided that Sister Klara had to be dismissed, which then happened on 6th March.[5]

The text passage indicates that in some cases the "Father", represented in the figure of the bishop, was consulted. This was not always the case, as there were times when gender conflicts beyond borders, between spiritual mothers and fathers – that is, between women as founders of congregations and bishops – seemed insurmountable (Hüwelmeier

2005a). In addition to cross-border gender conflicts between "parents" there was also tension among German sisters in the United States. Some of them feared that the young American sisters who joined the congregation would deviate from the "German" course and, with support of the provincial superior, establish a separate community in the United States. This can ultimately be referred to as transnational "sibling conflicts" or generational conflicts.

Communication beyond Borders

Communication between parents and their children living far apart from each other is "intimately linked with communication technologies" (Carling, Menjivar & Schmalzbauer 2012: 204). This also applies to transnational sisters and their "mothers". In the nineteenth century relationships were kept up beyond borders especially by letter writing and later via telegrams. Although the "Mother", General Superior of the PHJC, could not visit the branches in the United States for health reasons, she traveled to America several times per day in her prayers. These spiritual journeys strengthened the bonds between her and her "daughters". In the letters that she sent to the United States, she expressed her regrets that she could not be there in person, but at the same time she assured her "children" that she was always thinking about them. She urged them to obey the rules, that is, the constitutions, and to remain good *Handmaids of Jesus Christ.*

> Although we are physically separated, through our sacred profession and the spirit of the poor handmaids of Jesus Christ we are very closely united with one another, so that no one can speak of a separation due to the ocean.[6]

Through her letters she maintained not only continuous contact, but also attempted to create a united community by emphasizing the collectivity and a shared consciousness. Even if the founder of the women's congregation was not able personally to get to know the United States, she, like her "children", was part of a "transnational social field" (Levitt & Glick Schiller 2004), thus belonging to the large group of people whose lives are influenced by the migration of people close to them and by the upholding of social relations and emotional ties to those living far away.

Tension arose time and again over decades between German general superiors and American provincial superiors. But the geographic distance between the United States and Europe was too great for the German Generalate to be able to exert any sustained influence on the "daughters" in the United States over several generations and an extended period of time. German-American sisters, especially since the First World War and the start of anti-German sentiments in the United States, led relatively independent lives on the other side of the ocean. Not until the 1960s did transatlantic relations experience a kind of revival.

"The Daughters Have Grown Up"

After the Second Vatican Council (1962–65) introduced the reform process in the Catholic Church, cautious protest initially emerged in the American provinces with regard to the dominance of the German mother house. For decades, as I discovered during my ethnographic fieldwork with American sisters, attempts were made again and again to contain the German influence. After 1965 the major discussion on the issue of the habit and civilian dress was sparked in many religious congregations in the United States, whereas in Germany the debate was conducted on the quiet. American and also Dutch sisters told me that they have long since lived in their home countries wearing civilian clothing and without a habit, although this was not permitted by the German General Superior (who into the 1970s was still referred to as "Mother"). When they traveled to Germany, however, to visit the Reverend Mother and participate in conferences of the community, they brought their habit with them and changed clothes in the aeroplane. They would put on their headpiece as soon as they arrived at the mother house.

When in the course of my fieldwork in the 1990s I asked a superior in Germany why the term "Mother" was abandoned in the 1970s, she explained not without pride that "the daughters have grown up". In her view it was no longer appropriate for superiors to treat adult women in a patronizing manner. Many sisters had entered the congregation in the 1950s and around the period of Vatican II with great hopes for change in the Catholic Church and thus also in women's congregations. They wanted to articulate and discuss their own ideas of living together in a religious community. In this article I cannot go into the diversity of processes of democratization in many convents, but the debate on the habit was just a small part of it (Hüwelmeier 2004).

The arrival of Indian sisters in Germany between 1963 and 1970, traveling in several cohorts, had a far more sustained influence. Most of their German peers referred to them as "children" who needed protection, as young women who should not be overburdened or given any responsibility whatsoever. After the Indian sisters had lived and worked in Germany for more than ten years, they returned to India to found new branches. They did not travel alone, however, but were accompanied by a German "mother" who took care of all the arrangements, especially maintaining contact with the German mother house. In the 1970s that was not an easy matter. Sister Maria, as I call her here, was appointed a Superior by the Generalate; she was not elected by the Indian sisters. In Bangalore, India, she purchased real estate with the financial backing of the German mother house, collected donations and had a large building built that accommodated all the sisters in India. As "mother" she felt responsible for the well-being of the Indian sisters as well as for the growth of the community in India. Many new convents were opened between 1970 and 2000 throughout India. Indian sisters built schools, orphanages, boarding schools and specialized tuberculosis hospitals. In particular they actively supported women's and children's rights.

Since the 1990s the Indian sisters have become increasingly self-confident, but even many years after returning to India they did not become independent. They still relied on financial support from the German mother house and Sister Maria still held a leadership position, watching over the hygiene regulations in the main convent, and disapproving of the Indian sisters' eating with their hands. German meals were always cooked especially for her. Even though she was very outspoken regarding the affairs of the PHJC in India, Indian sisters imagined themselves not as "daughters", but as independent women who were treated patronizingly now and then. After prolonged debate over many years within the entire community of the congregation, Indian sisters were ultimately granted greater independence from the mother house in Germany. In 2000 they founded their own "province". In other words, since that time they elect their own leadership teams, but like all the other provinces they continue to be under the auspices of the Generalate, which has meanwhile become international, with its headquarters in Germany. After all, the Indian daughters, too, have grown up.

Conclusion: Transnationalization of Convent Life

The call of Vatican II to renew or "modernize" the Catholic Church contributed in many women's congregations to a new focus in their social work, namely to a greater involvement in so-called developing countries. Many of the communities established in Europe in the nineteenth century had not perceived themselves as a missionary order. However, this changed after Vatican II, when a number of women's congregations invited women from Asia, Africa and Latin America to join their communities.

In the following decades the multi-ethnic presence contributed to a transformation of everyday life in the convents, to a new orientation in the work of the sisters and generally to a process that I have referred to as the *transnationalization of convent life* (Hüwelmeier 2013b). With that I mean the creation and maintenance of social and religious networks beyond geographic and cultural borders. Crossing cultural spaces generates new mobilities and greatly influences the traveling activities of sisters, many of whom had previously never been to Asia or Africa. Finally, the transnationalization of convent life has contributed to the abandonment of the concept of the mother. Processes of breaking down hierarchies can be observed in many convents and processes of democratization in women's congregations, in which particularly women from non-European societies are granted an equal voice, making the concept of the mother superfluous and at the same time strengthening the idea of sisterhood.

Presently, more and more convents are made up of women from diverse ethnic, national and linguistic backgrounds. In India, small communities are consciously mixed with sisters of different ages, languages, and countries of origin. These ways of living together, according to sisters, contribute to better mutual understanding. Ultimately the sisters create what they refer to as "lived internationalism". For these reasons they no longer need spiritual mothers, since they have all grown up.

The biological parents of Catholic sisters have recently received increased attention. If a mother or father is sick or dying, the sisters are encouraged by the leadership team to travel to their hometowns, also for extended periods of time. Whereas a hundred and fifty years ago nuns either broke off contact with their parents entirely or reduced it to a minimum, sisters now assume that the emotional contact to biological parents and siblings is generally beneficial and positive for convent life. Sisters from India working in Germany regularly spend their holidays in India in order to visit their mother, father, and other relatives. In this way they do not differ at all from many women in transnational families who, depending on their financial options, take trips to their places of origin to care for their sick or aging parents.

Notes

1 This article is based on multi-sited fieldwork in a transnational women's congregation. Empirical research for the Transnational Religion project was conducted between 2000 and 2005, financed by the German Research Foundation (DFG, Transnational Religious Networks, HU 1019/2-1 and HU 1019/2-2). Based on historical documents from various archives and anthropological fieldwork in convents in Germany, the Netherlands, England, the United States and India, I examined the creation and maintenance of cross-border relations in the past and present.

2 Letter by Katharina Kasper of 15 August 1868. Archives of the PHJC mother house in Dernbach, Westerwald. In: Gottfriedis Amend, ADJC 2001, 73.

3 Chronicle of the American province. Archives of the ADJC (PHJC), Dernbach mother house, entry: 1889.

4 Chronicle of the American province. Archives of the ADJC (PHJC), Dernbach mother house, entry: 1889.

5 Chronicle of the American province. Archives of the ADJC (PHJC), Dernbach mother house, entry: 1889.

6 Letter by Katharina Kasper of 17 December 1887. In: Gottfriedis Amend, ADJC 2001, 389.

References

Åkesson, Lisa, Jørgen Carling & Heike Drotbohm 2012: Mobility, Moralities and Motherhood: Navigating the Contingencies of Cape Verdean Lives. *Journal of Ethnic and Migration Studies* 38:2, 237–260.

Amend, Gottfriedis, for the Generalate of the Poor Handmaids of Jesus Christ (ADJC), 2001: *Katharina Kasper – Gründerin der Kongregation der Armen Dienstmägde Jesu Christi. Schriften*, vol. 1: Erste Regeln und eigenhändige Briefe. Kevelaer: Verlag Butzon & Bercker.

Appadurai, Arjun 1996: *Modernity at Large: Cultural Dimensions of Globalization.* Minneapolis, MN: University of Minnesota Press.

Carling, Jørgen, Cecilia Menjivar & Leah Schmalzbauer 2012: Central Themes in the Study of Transnational Parenthood. *Journal of Ethnic and Migration Studies* 38:2, 191–217.

Erel, Umet 2002: Reconceptualizing Motherhood: Experiences of Migrant Women from Turkey Living in Germany. In: Deborah F. Bryceson & Ulla Vuorola (eds.), *The Transnational Family: New European Frontiers and Global Networks.* Oxford & New York: Berg, pp. 127–146.

Gabaccia, Donna R. 2000: *Italy's Many Diasporas.* London: University College London Press.

Goffman, Erving 1961: *Asylums: Essays on the Social Situation of Mental Patients and Other Inmates.* Chicago: Aldine Publishing.

Goody, Esther N. 1982: *Parenthood and Social Reproduction: Fostering and Occupational Roles in West Africa.* Cambridge: Cambridge University Press.

Hannerz, Ulf 1996: *Transnational Connections: Culture, People, Places.* London: Routledge.

Hoang, Lan Anh & Brenda S.A. Yeoh 2011: Breadwinning Wives and 'Left-Behind' Husbands: Men and Masculinities in the Vietnamese Transnational Family. *Gender & Society* 25:6, 717–739.

Hondagneu-Sotelo, Pierette & Ernestine Avila 1997: 'I'm here, but I'm there': The Meanings of Latina Transnational Motherhood. *Gender & Society* 11:5, 548–571.

Hüwelmeier, Gertrud 2000: Gendered Houses: Kinship, Class and Identity in a German Village. In: Victoria Ana Goddard (ed.), *Gender, Agency and Change: Anthropological Perspectives.* London: Routledge, pp. 122–141.

Hüwelmeier, Gertrud 2004: *Närrinnen Gottes: Lebenswelten von Ordensfrauen.* Münster: Waxmann Verlag.

Hüwelmeier, Gertrud 2005a: Ordensfrauen unterwegs: Transnationalismus, Gender und Religion. *Historische Anthropologie* 13:1, 91–110.

Hüwelmeier, Gertrud 2005b: 'Nach Amerika!' Schwestern ohne Grenzen. *L'Homme: Europäische Zeitschrift für Feministische Geschichtswissenschaft* 16:2, 97–115.

Hüwelmeier, Gertrud 2008a: Formations of the Religious Self-Becoming 'Women in Christ' in a Globalizing World. In: Heike Bock, Jörg Feuchter & Michi Knecht (eds.), *Religion and Its Other: Secular and Sacral Concepts and Practices in Interaction*. Frankfurt am Main & New York: Campus, pp. 199–211.

Hüwelmeier, Gertrud 2008b: Nonnen auf Reisen – Transnationale Verflechtungen. In: Susann Baller, Michael Pesek, Ruth Schilling & Ines Stolpe (eds.), *Die Ankunft des Anderen*. Frankfurt a. M. & New York: Campus, pp. 226–233.

Hüwelmeier, Gertrud 2009a: Global Sisterhood: Transnational Perspectives on Gender and Religion. In: Ann Braude & Hanna Herzog (eds.), *Gendering Religion and Politics: Untangling Modernities*. New York: Palgrave Macmillan, pp. 173–190.

Hüwelmeier, Gertrud 2009b: Women's Congregations as Transnational Social Security Networks. In: Carolin Leutloff-Grandits, Anja Peleikis & Tatjana Thelen (eds.), *Social Security in Religious Networks: Anthropological Perspectives on New Risks and Ambivalences*. Oxford & New York: Berghahn, pp. 187–205.

Hüwelmeier, Gertrud 2010: Female Believers on the Move: Gender and Religion in Vietnamese Pentecostal Networks in Germany. In: Glenda Lynna Anne Tibe Bonifacio & Vivienne Angeles (eds.), *Gender, Religion and Migration: Pathways of Integration*. Lanham, MD: Lexington Books, pp. 115–131.

Hüwelmeier, Gertrud 2011: Socialist Cosmopolitanism Meets Global Pentecostalism: Charismatic Christianity among Vietnamese Migrants in Germany. In: Tsypylma Darieva, Nina Glick Schiller & Sandra Gruner-Domic (eds.), *Cosmopolitan Sociability: Locating Transnational Religious and Diasporic Networks. Ethnic and Racial Studies* (Special Issue) 34:3, 436–453.

Hüwelmeier, Gertrud 2013a: The 'Children of Uncle Ho' – Socialist Cosmopolitans in East Germany. In: Katrin Hansing & Maxim Matusevich (eds.), Socialist Migrations during the Cold War. Basingstoke: Palgrave Macmillan (forthcoming).

Hüwelmeier, Gertrud 2013b: 'Our future will be in India': Traveling Nuns between Europe and South Asia. In: Ester Gallo (ed.), Migration and Religion in Europe: Comparative Perspectives on South Asian Experiences. Farnham: Ashgate (forthcoming).

Kudat-Sertel, Ayse 1971: Ritual Kinship in Eastern Turkey. *Anthropological Quarterly* 44, 37–50.

Lampert, Regina 1996: *Die Schwabengängerin*, ed. Bernhard Tschofen. Zürich: Limmat.

Levitt, Peggy 2007: *God Needs No Passport*. New York: The New Press.

Levitt, Peggy & Nina Glick Schiller 2004: Conceptualizing Simultaneity: A Transnational Social Field Perspective on Society. *International Migration Review* 38, 1002–1039.

Liebelt, Claudia 2011: *Caring for the Holy Land: Transnational Filipina Domestic Workers in the Israeli Migration Regime*. Oxford & New York: Berghahn.

Meiwes, Relinde 2000: *Arbeiterinnen des Herrn: Katholische Frauenkongregationen im 19. Jahrhundert*. Frankfurt am Main & New York: Campus.

Meiwes, Relinde 2008: Katholische Frauenkongregationen und die Krankenpflege im 19. Jahrhundert. *L'Homme: Europäische Zeitschrift für Feministische Geschichtswissenschaft* 19:1, 39–60.

Mintz, Sidney W. & Eric R. Wolf 1950: An Analysis of Ritual Co-Parenthood (Compadrazgo). *Southwestern Journal of Anthropology* 6:4, 341–368.

Ryan, Louise 2011: Transnational Relations: Family Migration among Recent Polish Migrants in London. *International Migration* 49:2, 80–103.

Wolf, Angelika 2010: Orphans' Ties – Belonging and Relatedness in Child-Headed Households in Malawi. In: Hansjörg Dilger & Ute Luig (eds.), *Morality, Hope and Grief: Anthropologies of Aids in Africa*. New York & Oxford: Berghahn, pp. 292–311.

Gertrud Hüwelmeier is an anthropologist and a senior research fellow at Humboldt University, Berlin. She is the Director of the research project The Global Bazaar: Markets as Places of Economic and Social Inclusion, funded by the German Research Foundation. Her publications include articles on transnationalism, religion, gender, postsocialism, cosmopolitanism and global Pentecostal networks. Her most recent book, edited with Kristine Krause (2010), is *Traveling Spirits – Migrants, Markets and Mobilities* (London: Routledge).
(ghuewelmeier@yahoo.de)

GROUNDING THE FAMILY
Locality and its Discontents in Popular Genealogy

Elisabeth Timm

This paper discusses the grounding of the family in popular genealogy today. It applies a historical and comparative approach to the use of parish registers in three empirical cases from Austria. This use consists in a continued process of rooting the family locally, while simultaneously delocalizing it through the digital connection of data kept separate by the Catholic Church for many centuries. Grounding the family is thus a complex articulation of the modern discourse of settledness, closely bound up with a popular historical culture able to access archival sources directly for the first time in history. The paper questions the category of "imagined families", which may marginalize this popular practice of producing kinship and perpetuate the essentialist notion of otherwise "authentic" (e.g. juridical, social, biological) families.[1]

Keywords: genealogy, family, migration, archives, Austria

> Hello and good day to you, as a new member of this list I'd like to introduce myself briefly, my name is Georg Jochum, 64 years old and I live in Barsinghausen which is near Hanover. (...) My forebears came from Graben/Karlsruhe and seem to be spread across all of northern Europe. That's why I joined this list, because bearers of my name also ended up in Vienna. But it seems that the JOCHUM family in Vienna has died out. (...) Maybe one of the list members has the family name JOCHUM in their files, I would be grateful if you could get in touch. Greetings from the far north. Georg (Jochum)[2]

Posted on an email discussion list in 2011, this email is a dense and complex articulation of the relationship between family and locality in popular genealogy today: the genealogist introduces his family, defined in patrilineal and historical terms, through its surname; he locates it in one (and only one) place, but also finds himself confronted with migration, leading him to begin his search at many locations. That is, he is aware of the history of the production and processing of genealogical data recorded by the state, communes, and churches over the last several centuries. A virtual place that enables him to access this data is the "austria" mailing list, a German-language forum open to everyone researching "in all the southern areas that belonged to the Habsburg monarchy up to 1918". Mailing lists like this one are interfaces between the localization of the family and its de-localization. The names of the lists correspond to the political, geographical, and ethnicized contours of Old Europe, with an "austria list", a "bavaria", "sudeten", "gottschee", "slovakia", "westphalia", "prussia", "switzerland", "poland", and other lists. Yet at the same time, the users of the lists disclaim this historical world, because their databases generate a digital kinship that is no longer represented within this national, ethnic, and geographical order.

Genealogical sources have always arisen in relation to place. As Foucault (2007: 555–583) has shown, from the seventeenth century onward statistics emerged as a new form of government and "population" became an object of knowledge for the state, but long before that – starting with the Council of Trent in the mid-sixteenth century – the Roman Catholic Church had begun to keep parish registers: records of births, marriages, and deaths that registered their objects in relation to place. Popular genealogy today uses this historical data and operates with this knowledge (in this case, the "distribution" of the "forebears", or the idea that if I have ancestors in Vienna, I must network within the "austria" list that specializes in the southern Habsburg monarchy). For this reason, I argue here, popular genealogy grounds the family – both founds it and ties it to locality – not *in* Austria but *with* Austria. Yet at the very same time, it also delocalizes the family (the family name will be found in the "files" of some list member), reassembling it in new emplacements that are generated not by the technologies of rule but by the individual ("my forebears came from Graben/Karlsruhe"). At first sight, the label "imagined families" thus seems to capture neatly the notion of family that is at work in popular genealogy. However, on closer examination it becomes clear that such a definition would establish a problematic distinction – problematic because it asserts that the state of being "imagined" is limited only to particular families, and because it would have only essentializing responses to the question of what a non-"imagined" family might be.

In this paper, I use the example of the production and utilization of parish registers in Austrian popular genealogy to examine how family and locality are at once connected and unbound. I show that the place where a family "comes from" or "originates" (thus the semantics in this field) always combines a dynamics of ontology with one of atopia. Every genealogical practice gives rise to both moves: the ontologizing deployment of locality as the first foundation of the family being researched, and the atopic pursuit of the family beyond the locality-bound sources. I conclude that a distinction between "imagined" and "actual" does not account for the family of popular genealogy. This becomes particularly apparent in the interplay of location and dislocation that is continually produced by the epistemic medium of the parish register.

Research on Popular Genealogy: Findings and Perspectives

In the classical phase of anthropology, genealogies were not only an object of study but also an instrument of analysis. After the crisis in the anthropology of kinship, this object attracted new interest and new perspectives, from both "new kinship studies" (e.g., Bouquet 1996; Franklin & McKinnon 2001) and its critics (for German-language ethnology, see Schnegg et al. 2010).[3] In contrast, European ethnology and folklore studies paid almost no attention to popular genealogy until very recently (with some exceptions, e.g., Byron 1998). The scattered early studies on popular genealogy in Euro-American ethnology's societies of origin were carried out by historians and sociologists (e.g., Burguière 1997; Hareven 1978) or by French or Anglo-American anthropologists (e.g., Ayoub 1966; Sagnes 1995; Segalen & Michelat 1990). This work indicates that local references and their political frames, such as the nation state, are utilized by popular genealogy activists in differing ways. They may be accentuated and selected, which is usually read by researchers as a way of producing and safeguarding "identity" (Angelidou 2001: 11; Caron 2002; Segalen & Michelat 1990: 208). For this approach, it is a short step – probably too short – from popular genealogy to "identity", because the genealogical format is methodologically posited as a cultural form with an established, inherent effect. This contrasts with approaches that do not formulate "identity" as a given, defined and defining magnitude in their investigations of popular historical culture (Byron 1998; Edwards 1998: esp. 148, 155, 157f., 161). In his study of the genealogical emplacement of the Irish diaspora in the United States, Byron (1998: 27) reflects upon "ethnic identity" in multiple ways: firstly as an "empty vessel" both produced and invoked in the social context, which needs to be interrogated using a critical theory of the subject; secondly, as regards the evaluation of ethnographically collected data, he asks whether it is in fact feasible to infer a collective self-location ("ethnic identity") from the empirical material (ibid.: 33f.); and thirdly, he questions the empirical findings in methodological terms: "That we were a research team from Ireland interested in their Irish connections and their sense of Irishness undoubtedly influenced what our informants told us" (ibid.: 34; for a similar methodological reflection, see Edwards 1998: 155). Malkki (1992: 25) pinpoints the problem of the methodological coupling of "genealogy" and "identity" by noting that it rests upon "deeply territorializing concepts of identity".

The present paper picks up and advances this latter perspective, which takes the equation of genealogy and locality as its object of study. I argue that the territorialization of kinship knowledge is not, and has not been, a predetermined feature of genealogy or of genealogical research. Rather, the identification of "being *kin*" with "being *there*" has had to be constantly produced and secured afresh – in fact, this is a case of the production of settledness.[4] It has been studied in some detail within the history of ideas and political thought, as the socially conservative ideological pairing of family and locality among nineteenth-century political theorists of society like Wilhelm Heinrich Riehl (1855) and Frédéric Le Play (1855). These two scholars grounded the family in blood, in the patriarchal order, with nature, and via property ownership. Jacques Donzelot's (1979) discourse analysis has shown how the "policing of families", and especially "familializing the popular strata", in the second half of the nineteenth century was spatially fixed and literally emplaced through its crucial grounding in architecture.[5] Pierre Bourdieu (2005) traced in detail the resulting Fordist social order that finally supplied the lower social strata with homes of their own as well, localizing them in bourgeois respectability but also putting them under economic pressure and chaining them to their "house". Research on the Parisian bourgeoisie of the present day indicates the extent to which an assumed genealogical and spatial locality forms part of the symbolic capital of these families.[6] Since a genealogy of settledness has not yet been written,[7] these case studies must suffice to hint at the extraordinarily momentous establishment of settledness for, and by means of, the modern Euro-American family in the modern era.

Presenting three case studies from a micro-perspective, in the following I will show how genealogical practices can articulate the family again and again as the sum of locations and dislocations.

A Genealogy of Grounding Family in and with the Parish Registers

My argument in all three cases proceeds from written, materialized sources of popular genealogy: parish registers, in Germany called *Kirchenbücher* and in Austria *Matriken*. It would be easy enough to classify this written record in one of two ways. Either, as Goody (2000) argues, the parish registers are instruments with which the Catholic Church pursued its economic interests (i.e., safeguarding legacies) by keeping track of kinship relations, enforced the canonical prohibitions on marriage, and by these means contributed to the replacement of kin-based, extended, and spatially dispersed social formations by the small, home-based "European family". Or the parish registers' function may be interpreted analogously with Foucault's (2007) thesis of the emergence of state statistics from the sixteenth century on as part of a new technology of power that produced "population": as a means of government which the Catholic Church used to flank its pastoral techniques and tie them to territory, and the causes and effects of which cannot be explained by economic interests alone.

However, rather than trying to fit the parish registers into one of these hypotheses, I prefer to discuss the different ways they have been handled by genealogy. I think of the empirical sources not as representations of hidden forces of history (such as economics or power), but as "actants" in the sense of Latour's (1996) actor-network theory – in other words, as virtual or material participants that develop their own logic and their own dynamic within the genealogical procedure. The three cases of genealogical practice I have selected exemplify the fact that "settledness" is not a given, and that "migration" is not its other. Instead, it will become clear that mobility and immobility can only be adequately understood as relational complements. The three examples are taken from Austria (I will come back to the problems of this localizing statement); they are small segments from my more extensive study on the cultural anthropology of popular genealogy. I arrange the cases not chronologically, but in the order that they made their appearance in my research. By choosing this arrangement, I am also suggesting a potential relationship between ethnographical and historiographical approaches to popular genealogy: is it possible to identify historical links or formal peculiarities without organizing these as a linear array, but also without essentializing them by detaching them from history?

I firstly show how Catholic priests in Bavaria and Styria between the wars invented a *Volksgenealogie*, "folk genealogy" – and, in their study of the parish registers, were taken aback by migration. In politically agitated times, they had hoped to extract a sense of stability from these monolocally organized genealogies, yet such stability was precisely what the sources refused to supply.

I then go back several centuries, to the period of the Reformation and the beginning of the parish registers. Later used by priests as their sources, the registers began life as sources *produced* by priests. Genealogy here is a way of fixing the kinship knowledge of the Catholic Church's canon law, a technology for dealing with migration. My study of the sources demonstrates that the parish registers, as the key materials of genealogical research, originated in part from a confrontation with migration.

Finally, I turn to popular genealogy today, and specifically the ways that its networking, data, and knowledge formats ground and, simultaneously, digitally dislocate the family. In these genealogical practices, emplacing the family is both the objective and the means of the research – for without knowledge of the church, state, and communal record-keeping that divided people up by place and by rule, it is impossible to pick up traces in the archives and find the desired documents. Where migration interrupted the processing of kinship knowledge into the parish registers, today's popular genealogy is collectively working to close the gaps, as becomes particularly clear in the case of the project to create a digital "marriage index".

Producing and Using Church Registers: Three Examples

1. Styria, 1919: Priests Grounding the Family

In the mid-nineteenth century, the history of the countryside had already come to the attention of scholars, *Heimatpfleger* or "nurturers of local life", and of social policy-makers in the context of urbanization and industrialization. As the weapon of choice against the "flight from the land" (the term itself was a political battle cry), ideas of agrarian romanticism arose that also contributed to the formation and expansion of folklorist interests in this period. Agrarian romanticism's interest in the rural space and its history, gathering pace since the mid-century, had also embraced genealogies.[8] In many European countries in the late nineteenth century, priests and ministers began isolated genealogical studies in towns and villages, taking their own parish as their object and starting point. Between the First and Second World War such projects, especially in Styria and in Bavaria, were drawn together under the heading of *Volksgenealogie* or "folk genealogy". The political basis of this movement's argument was partly the notion of *Heimatschutz*, "protecting the homeland". Its advocates' energetic agitation was often largely dismissed by the local population, as Judson (2006) has shown for the case of nationalist language policy in Styria. This may be one reason why ever new arguments had to be sought, as here in the case of "folk genealogy", where a family imagined in deeply historical terms was set up in opposition to the "flight from the land".

When the Styrian priest and theologian Konrad Brandner started his genealogical research in 1919, he turned first to the registers of the parish of Haus, the oldest volume of which is a register of baptisms begun in 1586.[9] In making this decision, he was going back to the earliest accessible point not only historically (even now, no older parish registers have been found to survive in Styria; see the compilation in Ruhri 1997: 123–138), but also biographically: Brandner had started his pastoral service in August 1905 to August 1907 as a chaplain at the Ennstal parish of Haus. He had no overview of the state of the sources, but judged the parish registers to be reliable evidence of a long-standing affinity between family and settledness. His key objective was to influence the rural population: "Genealogy now shows them [the inhabitants of Styria] in a documentary manner how long and where their family has been settled (...). This awareness will without doubt increase love for the homeland and spin threads between the past and the present" (Brandner 1920: 9).[10]

In his vision of popular genealogy as a brake on migration, Brandner assumed that an agrarian economy correlates with geographical immobility (Brandner 1926). However, the "folk genealogists" did not succeed in proving this claim. The correspondence of the priests carrying out genealogical research hints at a perplexity arising from the sources: many of their research reports and reflections on the innovative project of a folk genealogy discuss migration, and there are also specific assessments such as the following: "This study may, at least, indicate that even in such inhospitable regions, the 'internal migration of the peoples' is far from insignificant" (Felber 1927b: 10; see also Felber 1927a). But the genealogists did not allow such findings to shake their postulate of sedentarism, and the assertion that families from the villages had been immobile for many centuries remained intact. Interested in people's *Bodenständigkeit*, their autochthony or "rootedness in the soil", Brandner concentrated on the cases that supported this fantasy (Brandner 1926). He noted the predominant finding that most of the families showed no such *Bodenständigkeit*:

> When I considered this result, I saw that among them there are many genealogical tables that cover only two or three generations. (...) They thus stand, so to speak, as fragments of a lineage in folk genealogy; in many cases these will only have been fragments split off from larger lineages in other locations. (Brandner 1926: col. 227)

Here Brandner identifies and isolates the empirical findings that counter the thesis of *Bodenständigkeit* – he qualifies the quantitatively prevailing cases as a "fragment", something "split off". Methodologically, he thus makes settledness an Archimedean point that permits him to register migration while leaving *Bodenständigkeit* untouched. At times Brandner gave very explicit form to this profile of his genealogies, marked both by a new collapse of boundaries and by new demarcations: "Of course, only persons born in Styria could be considered for the genealogy, in other words also many people who live outside Styria; however, on the other hand, many persons living in Styria would not be included in the genealogy because they were not born there" (ibid.: col. 228).

Even the *völkisch* protagonists of folk genealogy did initially take note of the migration that appeared in the sources. For example, having completely transferred the information in the registers from 1650 to the present for his 650-soul parish to a card index and arranged it into descendancy lists, Josef Demleitner – a Bavarian priest who later achieved fame through his guide to genealogical research or *Sippenkunde* ("clan lore") in the context of the Nuremberg Laws (Demleitner & Roth 1935, 1936) – wrote the following in a letter to his Styrian colleague Brandner in January 1926:

> When I looked through various parish registers in the area this year for a local-history study on the Thirty Years' War, I found that, particularly in the 1650–1680 period, a tremendous number of strangers settled in the area through marriage. At least the tenth part of all weddings are to foreigners. At any rate, as folk genealogy advances, some attention must be paid to the question of population exchange.

The folk genealogists' surprise at migration articulates the grounding of the family with great precision: they had worked their way through the records of the Catholic Church in the sure conviction of finding settledness there. The settled ideal that the priests intended to find in the parish registers reflects the discourse of a sedentary Europe. The correspondence demonstrates how the folk genealogists, searching for *Heimat* and aiming to produce the region in a combination of temporal constancy and spatial immobility, came up against a mobile history. At first, the priests reacted to this confrontation with surprise and curiosity; even an ideologue like Josef Demleitner did not immediately resort to denying this rupture of the nationalist ideal of centuries-old, secluded rural localities, home to enclosed families and clans. There is an element of tragicomedy in the way that these pastors, facing the depopulation of the villages, sat down at the sources to build bonds to the locality in support of settledness and love of *Heimat*, only to be confronted with and disappointed by the internal European migration of the past three centuries.

In the correspondence of folk genealogists of the early interwar years, the researchers still responded to the registers' indications of migration using the tools of debate and argumentation. Just a few years later, that space no longer existed. The compulsory genealogy that the Nazi state imposed through the Nuremberg Laws of 1935 (Ehrenreich 2007; Pegelow 2006) depended on forgetting the knowledge of migration that folk genealogy had addressed. When Georg Grüll, "Gausachbearbeiter für Sippenkunde im Gau Oberdonau" ("Regional Officer for Clan Lore in the Upper Danube Region"), organized the card-indexing of the parish registers in the early 1940s, settledness had already become a methodological essential. In point 8 of his 1941 "Instructions for card-indexing the Linz parish registers", he required the indexing staff to fill out the marriage cards as follows:

> The place of origin of A and B [i.e. the bridal couple] need only be included if it differs from the place of residence of the parents. (...) In a rooted [*bodenständig*] population, this field will as a rule remain empty, because the bridegroom's and the bride's place of origin will accord with that of their parents.[11]

In the Nazi period, settledness appears as the ideal of an identity between descendancy and alliance.[12] Nazi genealogy no longer expects to find any disparity between the two, and logically enough the regional genealogical officer signals an "empty field" in this segment of the data record. The empty space is there to prove that no rupture has occurred: that is the *völkisch* grounding of the family.

This conclusion is not new; it has already been set out in analyses of the ideology of "blood and soil". However, the present micro-perspective on the genealogical utilization of historical sources shows how close the nationalist "folk genealogists" came to quite different evidence. Consulting the parish registers, they were using sources for the grounding of the family that had been created in the sixteenth century to localize kinship knowledge, but which nevertheless passed on manifold evidence of the disengagement of family and locality, as I shall now show.

2. *Styria, 1563: Priests Producing Sources*

The sources used by the folk genealogists were almost exclusively parish registers, and even today these books are key sources for popular genealogy. The history of such documents, and of the knowledge practices from which they emerged, is closely bound up with far-reaching political, religious, and social conflicts in Europe over the past five centuries. In the sixteenth century, parish registers were developed by technologies of power that could no longer make use of older forms of personal documentation – the medieval lists of townsmen or nobility, for example – because of their estates-based profile. Whereas older techniques for documenting populations were socially segregated and specific (each listing, for example, only townspeople or only nobles), parish registers were socially undefined from the very start.

The existence of parish registers in the Catholic Church goes back to the Council of Trent, 1545–1563 (for the case of Styria, see Ruhri 1997: 109–111; see also the following points). The Council's decree *Tametsi* of 11 November 1563 required all parishes to keep registers of baptisms and marriages. With this, the Catholic Church's documentation of the population was founded upon the documentation of the population-as-Catholic: the objects of the parish register were initially neither birth nor death but two Catholic sacraments, baptism and marriage. Parish priests were charged with entering the data and preserving the registers, in the shape of books or loose-leaf collections. Entries included the names of the bridal couple and the witnesses along with the day and place of the wedding, or for baptisms the names of the infant and its godparents.

The decree *Tametsi* is the founding document of the Tridentine marriage. It was the Catholic Church's reaction to religious, political, and social upheavals in the sixteenth century that sprang from many different sources: Reformation and Counter-Reformation, increased mobility, new family structures and lifestyles resulting from changes in urban life, and an altered form of statehood that no longer rested on the person and family of the monarch. The new registers also responded to the everyday conflicts arising from the practice of "clandestine marriage" in the sense of marriage without a specific ecclesiastical form – the marriage format that had previously dominated in quantitative terms, except among the nobility and burghers, most of whose marriages were recorded by notaries and therefore, as in Roman law, functioned contractually, as agreements, rather than spiritually, as sacraments (Zarri 2001: 344f.). The Council of Trent decree turned the private matter of marriage, an undertaking between two individuals, into a public, formalized, written, clericalized, and sacralized act (ibid.: 361), and made priests the crucial figures in what may be described as a "disciplining" of the family (ibid.: 364f.).

Zarri (ibid.: 362; see also the following points) additionally interprets the parish registers as a means of creating a legally unequivocal definition of the domestic community in the context of growing conflicts around children born out of wedlock. But most relevant to the question addressed here, the localization of family, is the fact that the parish registers were first and foremost a technology for disciplining lower-status and mobile population groups. Increasing mobility threatened to hollow out the epistemological foundations for enforcing Catholic canon law, oral communication; the Church responded by switching to the written word. However, the parish registers did not completely replace oral tradition, for the regulations surrounding the Tridentine marriage also required the reading of banns, in other words the public announcement of a marriage among the congregation before the wedding. This targeted and prescribed scanning of unwritten kinship knowledge at the occasion of the wedding was intended to supply information about any impediments to marriage, namely family relationships that precluded marriage under canon law. The Church was not willing or able to rely upon the kinship knowledge it had itself recorded in written form. Publishing the banns was the technology that riveted together local kinship knowledge and practices – "habitual kinship" – with the "official kinship" (Lanzinger & Saurer 2007) of the parish registers.[13]

The development of record-keeping was continued with Paul V's Rituale Romanum of 17 June 1614, which prescribed the compilation of registers of confirmations and deaths (or rather funerals); these registers were also to include information on the family of the person involved. On 20 February 1784, the Habsburg Emperor Joseph II issued an edict making the keeping of parish registers a state duty, although he devolved this to the churches and state-recognized religious communities (Ruhri 1997: 108, 119). One consequence of this was the standardization of entries through the use of pre-printed tabular forms (Becker 1989). But whereas the German Empire established state civil registers in 1874, in Austria the parish registers remained the only documentation of this kind until 1938. State documentation has only existed in Austria since 1 August 1938 (the introduction of civil marriage) and 1 January 1939 (the establishment of civil registry offices).

In various historical contexts throughout Europe, long before the creation of a system of state civil registration, conflicts frequently arose around the right of access to the parish registers, as did calls for them to be taken into state hands. The Council of Trent had authorized priests to administer the parish registers, and they held on to that responsibility. The keeping of registers did not begin immediately in all parishes; there is evidence in the case of Styria, for example, that this sometimes took several decades and rebukes from the bishop. However, when a parish register was set up, priests quickly took up their role as guardians of the archive. Once the volumes came into existence, what Latour calls their "programme of action" began to unfold: mediating between locality and movement, and between connection and separation. Within that field of tension the priests acted as archontes, as the high officials and custodians of the archives, who constantly developed new ways to combine the collection and sealing of knowledge in the books with the publication of knowledge and opening of the books.[14]

The registers always physically remained within the parishes, and this sedentary aspect both expresses and explains the fact that it was nearly the middle of the twentieth century before kinship knowledge could be produced from the parish registers that was not separated out and tied to a particular location. When Catholic priests in the interwar period began, as I have described, to use these volumes as historical sources for their "folk genealogy", that move displays typical elements of an innovative utilization, and is not a distinctive feature of the history of Church documentation. In her genealogical study of files, legal historian Cornelia Vismann (2008) shows that well into the sixteenth century, the processing of the state and municipal administrations' files consisted in either using them within the chancery or storing them – they were not yet deployed as historical sources, and "it took a long time for the practice of referring to old files to assert itself" (ibid.: 99). The Catholic Church in Austria had not even centralized the storage of parish registers, which is why the folk genealogists had to work on the registers of their own specific parishes. Even the diocesan archives that have now taken on the parish registers do not hold them as property, but preserve them in trust for the parishes (thus Ruhri 1997: 122, on the diocesan archives in Graz-Seckau). In fact, even today a clear distinction between chancery and archive has not yet been established in the parishes.

The most recent utilization of the parish registers, present-day popular genealogy, leapfrogs that distinction by digitizing the data to create an open archive. In its indexes and databases, simple search runs can close many of the gaps in kin connections that were opened by the local storage of the parish registers and by their localization of kinship in many different ways. Although this present-day use of the parish registers initially also arises from a desire to identify a particular family and to ground it historically in a single location, there are two further products of popular genealogy's indices and mailing lists: on the one hand new relays that for the first time delocalize kinship knowledge, and on the other a popular historical culture with direct access to archival material.

3. The Net, 2007: The Marriage Index

Present-day genealogical research – which must rely on the parish registers if it is to reach back over centuries – always starts, like the email cited at the opening of this article, with a place: "My family comes from ...". However, later this spontaneous logic of place is often frustrated. The researcher comes up against too many "blanks" – *tote Punkte*, "dead points", in the German genealogical jargon – so that church records from other parishes have to be consulted in order to trace further connections and set up new relays. The converse of "the blanks" is "serendipity" (*Zufallsfund*), the chance discovery of an individual in the register of a parish where he or she was not resident (for example in a marriage or godparenthood entry). Using mailing lists and the Internet, popular genealogy today brings the "blanks" into contact with the "serendipities", so that kin connections can be traced beyond the records that are localized by parish.

To be sure, these techniques are not the first attempts to overcome the locality of kinship knowledge. Popular genealogy worldwide has focused particularly on the Mormons' efforts to microfilm and centralize parish registers, which began as early as the 1930s.[15] The Salt Lake City vault where these microfiches are stored is regarded in popular genealogy as a "mythic place" (Sagnes 1995), partly because of its association with the practice of baptism for the dead, but, among those active in genealogical circles, also as a "disputed paradise" (Richau 2007). It is a place that for many centuries did not exist because the church registers, scattered by parish, never documented every connection. The Mormon archive in Utah is a kind of super-locale for the grounding of the family. Yet it dates from an era that was able to bring together the parish registers materially, as microfilm, but not informationally. That would be achieved only by today's newest generation of popular genealogy, which switched from the analogue mode of centralizing material sources into the digital mode of data without locality. I will now discuss how popular genealogy is collectively producing this unseparated kinship knowledge, using the example of a "marriage index".

Several years ago, I interviewed Herr Noggler.[16] He is a well-known activist of popular genealogy in Austria, and is one of those who organize and network activities (in associations, mailing lists, and web portals) and advance the field through methodological innovation. His work is not limited to research on his "family"; rather, he develops forms and formats of digitizing the historical source material that enable linkages far beyond what was available to him when he first began to research his "family history". It is a notable feature of this type of popular genealogist that his innovations are developed inductively, out of his confrontation with problems of researching "my family" in the parish registers:

> It's a regional peculiarity that for baptisms the mother's maiden name isn't included, and that makes it difficult, and for marriages, if the parents' names are not included, then it really gets problematic. If it only says that bridegroom and bride married, then that's a problem, but I have – if you want some idea of numbers – I have found 560 or 570 of my paternal line, mainly – not only – in Lower Austria, and more than 200 from my grandfather's line in the Bohemian Forest or round about 200, and for those of my grandmother it's now about 140. But that's also because registers are missing there, we've now even begun, with a few colleagues, to completely transcribe the registers of Liebental – that's the main relevant parish in Austrian Silesia (...) and to draw up tables of names (...). You wouldn't believe what there is lying around in the archives, tons of material, mostly not indexed (...).

"For marriages", "if it only says that bridegroom and bride married", then the genealogist is confronted with a "blank", a "dead point": alongside the names of the bridal couple, he finds no reference to their place of residence or birth, and thus cannot go to the parish archives of that locality to research their family background. In a case like this, his search for his genealogy comes to a stop. But Herr Noggler thinks beyond the locality of kinship that the parish registers present him with: his comment "mostly not indexed" implies that he could find many more connections if the material were arranged in a different way, if it were switchable as data. Herr Noggler has put that insight into practice, playing an active part in the association "Familia Austria", which he also helped to found.[17] Of the association's many and various activities – networking genealogical activists and creating cooperative, collaborative structures to digitize data from historical sources (these might be written sources in archives, or gravestones carrying personal data) – the marriage index[18] is of particular relevance for the grounding of the family in popular genealogy. The index's presentation clearly shows the inductive procedure applied when networking the data. Popular genealogy may start out from research on "my family", but that search soon generates very different dynamics:

> Marriage index
> Almost every genealogist and family researcher has been there: you find the baptism of a forebear some time in the sixteenth, seventeenth, or eighteenth century, but the wedding of the baby's parents and the parents' birth or baptism entries are nowhere to be found, even though you know their names. First you search the registers of the surrounding parishes (...). But then in most cases there is nothing else you can do!
> You will now only be able to make progress if, by a lucky chance, you discover the parents' marriage somewhere after all. Some colleagues then invest years of work in complicated name analyses, bombard the parishes of whole regions with enquiries, and put together extensive studies of migration in the period concerned. But most of these cases unfortunately remain unresolved.
> This is where our MARRIAGE INDEX initiative comes in.
> Working together with, if possible, all the parishes in former Austria Hungary, we are drawing up name indexes of the marriage registers, or collecting indexes that have already been made, and making this data accessible in a shared searchable database.
> (...)
> Our aim is to make it possible to track down ancestors who have moved across long distances (and whose origin is not named at their place of destination).

In the genealogical project "marriage index", both the family's settledness and its de-localization materialize. Today, the first step is still to assume the emplacement of familial reproduction – which is why the genealogists work concentrically outwards from the baptismal location of the "forebear". But because most genealogists in these circles have now acquired very sophisticated historical knowledge (in the history of administration, social history and the history of rule) as well as skill in the use and critique of sources, particularly through the case-specific exchanges in mailing lists, they now wish to address the problem in a more thorough-going way. The marriage index realizes a delocalized kinship on the basis of the very parish registers that were created to localize the family. Where the historical sources are silent because they divide up kinship knowledge by place, the digital mode makes them speak again. Within a few clicks searching the index, a "blank" or "dead point" can become a potent relay. It is true that this move is once again linked to the restrictive grounding of a – "my" – family: as Herr Noggler put it in the interview, "my mother is descended from Sudeten Germans". But this topographical ontology is not a logical consequence of the data researched or the atopic linkages that Herr Noggler himself helped bring into being. Rather, it is a practical consequence of the suspicion of ontology that fuels the research.

Conclusion: Grounding the Family and Losing Locality

These three cases of the genealogical handling of parish registers indicate the complexity of the dynamics associated with the grounding of the family. In the history of genealogy, the parish registers are an extremely dynamic epistemic medium, on the one hand producing settledness and migration as complements while, on the other, creating connections between them.

Rather than grounding its family *in* Austria, popular genealogy grounds it *with* Austria – locality functions both as the ontological grounds of the family and as the medium of research. But in this encounter with the sources, objectives and outcomes ultimately emerge that the researchers had not intended: the genealogists develop a pleasure in tracking down information, in source criticism, in historical and critical evaluation of their data, in their growing knowledge of European history. In parallel to its location and dislocation of the family, popular genealogy also brings forth a historical culture. This vernacular historiography emerges not via the mediating authorities of public cultural and educational efforts, but in direct contact with the archives. This is why Tyler (2005) emphasizes the emancipatory thrust of popular genealogy today, while Hackstaff (2009: 178) refers to a "democratization of genealogy". Direct, unmediated access to the sources is a specific enjoyment that arises precisely from the problems encountered in research. It rests not on a positivist reading of the sources, but on an open process of interrogating one's own research results, and on the knowledge that there are also research situations (for example in the case of homonymy) where it is not possible to move forward. In her ethnography of US genealogical associations, Hackstaff (ibid.) has described this attitude as "analytic realism". It is, though, striking that this criminological pleasure in working on sources does not supersede the grounding of the family but, on the contrary, is inextricably connected with it. It is only the imagining of a monolocally situated family and the attempt to verify this which leads to the navigation through the archives – a navigation by means of which popular genealogy simultaneously reconstructs historical migrations and digitally erases them.

The question now arises whether this grounding of the family is specific to the Austrian situation. Because few case studies on popular genealogy have so far been carried out, this cannot be answered with certainty; but historical emplacement is always involved in popular genealogy. It is worth noting that many studies on the United States describe popular genealogy as working with a combination of historical sources and genetic testing (Hackstaff 2009; Nash 2004; Nelson 2008). This may be partly due to the particular questions such studies pose – certainly, Tucker's (2009) ethnography, focusing primarily on the relationship between public and private archives, does not confirm the hypothesis that genetic kinship is central to US popular genealogy. There do seem to be some features specific to popular genealogy referencing Scotland and Ireland and to black genealogies: the political and economic momentum of the heritage industry and a sophisticated "roots tourism" sector (Basu 2005; Basu 2006; Gilroy 1997; Legrand 2006; Schramm 2008) – formations that have not been recorded for genealogy relating to other countries, at least in Europe. Critically upturning the question of the national specificity of popular genealogies today, one might conclude that the question itself does not so much address cultural differences as pursue a "methodological nationalism" (Wimmer & Glick Schiller 2002). Within which popular genealogy should we classify, for example, an activist living in Australia who is researching his ancestors in Europe by means of the "austria", "slovakia", and "switzerland" mailing lists, archive visits, and databases? Just as popular genealogy is unsettled by historical migration as it searches for unequivocal localizations of its family, the digital mode of current popular genealogy's networking and information exchange is antagonistic to an anthropological form of questioning that focuses on the national specificity of popular genealogies.

I also doubt that "imagined" adequately describes the specific kinship whose grounds popular genealogy both seeks and disrupts in the course of its encounter with the parish registers and other sources in its databases. The ligature between family and place is not an "idea" or "mental image" external or subordinate to an otherwise authentic (e.g. social, juridical, genetic) kinship. Rather, grounding the family causes an ontological unrest that is what produces the kinship of popular genealogy in the first place. Therefore, my comparative discussion of the genealogical production and utilization of the parish registers since the sixteenth century stresses that locating the family is always associated with dislocating the family. Unlike an intellectual or political history of settledness, the perspective of cultural anthropology can face up to the finding that knowledge about the discontents of locality is not simply the result of academic research, but itself part of the field it studies.

Notes

1 The article was translated by Kate Sturge. I thank her for the thorough discussion concerning translations from historical sources. Also, I would like to thank the four anonymous reviewers for their critique and valuable suggestions regarding the first version of this article.

2 Austria-L, 23 September 2011 (names anonymized), http://list.genealogy.net/mm/listinfo/austria-l (accessed March 28, 2012). Here and throughout, translations from German are by Kate Sturge.

3 These new perspectives on genealogy must be placed in the context of increasing anthropological research on family and kinship (for selected European states, see the extensive historical and contemporary, quantitative and qualitative comparative studies by Beck et al. 2007; Grandits 2010; Heady & Kohli 2010; Heady & Schweitzer 2010; Knecht, Klotz & Beck 2012; Segalen 2012).

4 The "transnationality" of kinship is not a recent phenomenon. As has been sufficiently demonstrated, kinship was never something immovable, either in the city or in the village or provinces: labour and economic forms (e.g., transhumant shepherds), markets and commerce, natural disasters, pilgrimages and wars, the science and technology of ecclesiastical and secular powers (such as visitations, tax collection, population censuses), and not least emotional yearnings have always given rise to mobility, including in pre- and early modern Europe. Although there were certainly variations, with different regions experiencing more or less mobility, it is clear that the narrow horizons and immobility of the village were inventions of the nineteenth century – carefully crafted ideals that seemed to promise some contemporaries an element of stability in the maelstrom of manufacturing's dizzying pace.

5 Social housing construction in the nineteenth century calculated the space required very precisely, the objective being "to design a housing unit small enough that no 'outsider' would be able to live in it, yet large enough for the parents to have a space separate from their children, so that they might watch over them in their occupations without being observed in their own intimate play" (Donzelot 1979: 42). One figure of this discourse was the vagrant, who for "roughly ten years (1890–1900)" became the "universal of mental pathology" and a "special category" for the legal system (ibid.: 130).

6 "One does not search for one's roots; they are there, forming part of one" (Le Wita 1994: 120f.). Le Wita argues that the Parisian bourgeoisie's forms of housing and property – a town house, a country house – function not only as economic capital but also as symbolic capital, because they index the respectability of sedentary life in relation to the mobility of migration: "The existence of family seats places the bourgeois at the opposite pole from the migrant. His urban way of life is not made up of wrenching breaks or splits. He knows nothing of exploded kindred, the separation of the generations, weekends spent in the grey monotony of Paris or the suburbs with the children entrusted to their schools' outdoor centres" (ibid.: 35f.).

7 Deleuze and Guattari's nomadic utopia *A Thousand Plateaus* (1992) may be read as this kind of a genealogy of settledness – albeit one that is so obligated to the atopic that it cannot bring forth its nascently empirical approaches in the shape of recognizable "fields".

8 For example as peasant family histories or "family books", intended to help preserve ties to the agrarian lifeworld and working environment. Indications of this can be found in, for example, Wilhelm Heinrich Riehl's *Land und Leute* [Land and people] (1851), which recommends drawing up peasant family chronicles; in *Die Familie* [The family] (1855) Riehl calls for bourgeois family chronicles to be compiled.

9 Diocesan archives Graz-Seckau, Graz, Personalakten

Priester, Dr. Konrad Brandner. Unless otherwise mentioned, this is the source of all information on Brandner in the following and all the documents cited.

10 In fact Konrad Brandner was aware of the existence of similar interests. He explicitly mentions, for example, the "efforts of folklorists", which he wishes to supplement through his project (Brandner 1920).

11 Upper Austrian Archives Linz, Arbeitsbund für österreichische Familienkunde [Working Group for Austrian Family Lore], box 9, Georg Grüll: "Arbeitsanleitung für die Verkartung der Linzer Kirchenbücher" [Instructions for card-indexing the Linz parish registers], November 1941.

12 In popular genealogy, this ideal resulted in a distinct genre, the *Ortsfamilienbuch* or village genealogy. These family registers are not simply one more component in the "grey literature" of this field; rather, they function as important interfaces between popular and scholarly genealogy or demography, because their use saves time compared with the extremely time-consuming research on the original parish registers. This certainly applies to the historical and demographic research carried out by the Cambridge Group for the History of Population and Social Structure (Knodel 1975, 1988; Knodel & Shorter 1976). As can be seen in the example of Styrian folk genealogy, the compilers of these village genealogies (later also called *Ortssippenbücher*) were not so much collectors as editors of the material. For an example of source criticism on migration in an older form of the genre, the *Familienbuch* or "family book", see Lanzinger (2003).

13 However, it would be wrong to conclude that the introduction of the written form resulted in a straightforward implementation of canonical and legal provisions. The parish registers were compilations, open to interpretation, and all those involved (married couples and their relatives, representatives of state and church authorities) pursued flexible strategies and their own distinct interests when producing and deploying them (Lanzinger 2003, 2006, 2007).

14 In a late-eighteenth-century example, when the district authorities demanded access to baptismal registers in order to identify potential conscripts the pastors refused. They feared that making public the paternity of children born out of wedlock, recorded in the registers, would result in conflicts. In this case, the solution was to draw up a separate and confidential register, the *liber arcanum*, to document the baptisms of children born out of wedlock (Ruhri 1997: 117).

15 On genealogical research by the Mormons, see Mehr's overview (1992) and Richau's (2007) critical account from popular genealogy.

16 Interview with Herr Noggler, Vienna, May 5, 2007.

17 This association has no physical home. Some of its most active members have been working together for many years to digitize archival genealogical data without ever having met in person (interview with Herr Noggler, Vienna, May 5, 2007; interview with Frau Eschenbach, Vienna, March 16, 2009). As a result, the web portal does not indicate activity in "real life": it is itself the association. www.familia-austria.at (accessed February 10, 2012).

18 All the following quotations are taken from www.familia-austria.at/projekte/hzindex_projekt.php (accessed February 10, 2012).

References

Angelidou, A. 2001: "Qu'est-ce qui nous rassemble ici?" Mémoire généalogique, histoire locale et construction de l'identité dans un village contemporain. Regard sur la Bulgarie voisine. *Strates* 10, http://strates.revues.org/document50.html?format=print. Accessed January 1, 2006.

Ayoub, M.R. 1966: The Family Reunion. *Ethnology: An International Journal of Cultural and Social Anthropology* V:4, 415–433.

Basu, P. 2005: Macpherson Country: Genealogical Identities, Spatial Histories and the Scottish Diasporic Clanscape. *Cultural Geographies* 12:2, 123–150.

Basu, P. 2006: *Highland Homecomings: Genealogy and Heritage Tourism in the Scottish Diaspora.* London: Routledge.

Beck, S., N. Çil, S. Hess, M. Klotz & M. Knecht (eds.) 2007: Verwandtschaft machen: Reproduktionstechnologien und Adoption in Deutschland und der Türkei. *Berliner Blätter: Ethnographische und ethnologische Beiträge* 42.

Becker, P. 1989: *Leben, Lieben, Sterben: Die Analyse von Kirchenbüchern.* St. Katharinen: Scripta Mercaturae.

Bouquet, M. 1996: Family Trees and their Affinities: The Visual Imperative of the Genealogical Diagram. *The Journal of the Royal Anthropological Institute* 2:1, 43–66.

Bourdieu, P. 2005: The House Market. In: *The Social Structures of the Economy*. Trans. C. Turner. Cambridge: Polity Press.

Brandner, K. 1920: Die Bevölkerung der Pfarre Weichselboden in Steiermark. Genealogisch dargestellt. Nebst einigen Gedanken über die Schaffung einer steirischen Volksgenealogie. *Jahresbericht des Fürstbischöflichen Gymnasiums am Seckauer Diözesan-Knabenseminar Carolinum-Augustineum in Graz am Schlusse des Schuljahres 1919/20.*

Brandner, K. 1926: Über Volksgenealogie. *Familiengeschichtliche Blätter* 24, 225–228, 293–296.

Burguière, A. 1997: La généalogie. In: P. Nora (ed.), *Les Lieux de mémoire*, Vol. III. Paris: Gallimard.

Byron, R. 1998: Ethnicity and Generation: On "Feeling

Irish" in Contemporary America. *Ethnologia Europaea* 28:1, 27–36.

Caron, C.-I. 2002: La narration généalogique en Amérique du Nord francophone: Un moteur de la construction identitaire. *Éthnologies comparées* 4, 1–19, http://alor.univ-montp3.fr/cerce/r4/c.i.c.htm. Accessed March 27, 2012.

Deleuze, G. & F. Guattari 1992: *A Thousand Plateaus: Capitalism and Schizophrenia*. Trans. B. Massumi. London: Continuum.

Demleitner, J. & A. Roth 1935: *Der Weg zur Volksgenealogie: Anleitung zur übersichtlichen Darstellung des sippenkundlichen Inhalts der Kirchenbücher in Familienbüchern*. Munich: Oldenbourg.

Demleitner, J. & A. Roth 1936: *Der Weg zur Volksgenealogie: Anleitung zur übersichtlichen Darstellung des sippenkundlichen Inhalts der Kirchenbücher in Familienbüchern*. 2nd, rev. ed. Munich: Oldenbourg.

Donzelot, J. 1979: *The Policing of Families*. With a foreword by Gilles Deleuze. Trans. R. Hurley. New York: Pantheon.

Edwards, J. 1998: The Need for a "Bit of History": Place and Past in English Identity. In: N. Lovell (ed.), *Locality and Belonging*. London: Routledge.

Ehrenreich, E. 2007: *The Nazi Ancestral Proof: Genealogy, Racial Science, and the Final Solution*. Bloomington: Indiana University Press.

Felber, F. 1927a: Fremde Zuwanderer in der Gebirgspfarre St. Johann am Tauern im 19. Jahrhundert. *Mitteilungen über die steirische Volksgenealogie* 6 (January 1927), 2–6.

Felber, F. 1927b: Fremde Zuwanderer in der Gebirgspfarre St. Johann am Tauern im 19. Jahrhundert. *Mitteilungen über die steirische Volksgenealogie* 7 (July 1927), 6–10.

Foucault, M. 2007: *Security, Territory, Population: Lectures at the Collège de France 1977–1978*. Trans. G. Burchell. Basingstoke: Palgrave Macmillan.

Franklin, S. & S. McKinnon (eds.) 2001: *Relative Values: Reconfiguring Kinship Studies*. Durham, NC: Duke University Press.

Gilroy, P. 1997: Diaspora and the Detours of Identity. In: K. Woodward (ed.), *Identity and Difference*. London: Sage.

Goody, J. 2000: *The European Family: An Historico-Anthropological Essay*. Cambridge: Blackwell.

Grandits, H. (ed.) 2010: *The Century of Welfare: Eight Countries*. Vol. 1 of *Family, Kinship and State in Contemporary Europe*. Frankfurt/Main: Campus.

Hackstaff, K.B. 2009: Who Are We? Genealogists Negotiating Ethno-Racial Identities. *Qualitative Sociology* 32, 173–194.

Hareven, T. 1978: The Search for Generational Memory: Tribal Rites in Industrial Society. *Daedalus* 107:4, 137–149.

Heady, P. & M. Kohli (eds.) 2010: *Perspectives on Theory and Policy*. Vol. 3 of *Family, Kinship and State in Contemporary Europe*. Frankfurt/Main: Campus.

Heady, P. & P. Schweitzer (eds.) 2010: *The View from Below: Nineteen Localities*. Vol. 2 of *Family, Kinship and State in Contemporary Europe*. Frankfurt/Main: Campus.

Judson, P. 2006: *Guardians of the Nation: Activists on the Language Frontiers of Imperial Austria*. Cambridge, MA: Harvard University Press.

Knecht, M., M. Klotz & S. Beck (eds.). 2012: *Reproductive Technologies as Global Form: Ethnographies of Knowledge, Practices, and Transnational Encounters*. Frankfurt/Main: Campus.

Knodel, J.E. 1975: Ortssippenbücher als Quelle für die Historische Demographie. *Geschichte und Gesellschaft* 1, 288–324.

Knodel, J.E. 1988: *Demographic Behavior in the Past: A Study of Fourteen German Village Populations in the Eighteenth and Nineteenth Centuries*. Cambridge: Cambridge University Press.

Knodel, J.E. & E. Shorter 1976: The Reliability of Family Reconstitution Data in German Village Genealogies (*Ortssippenbücher*). *Annales de démographie historique*, 115–154.

Lanzinger, M. 2003: *Das gesicherte Erbe: Heirat in lokalen und familialen Kontexten. Innichen 1700–1900*. Vienna: Böhlau.

Lanzinger, M. 2006: Heiratskontrakte – intermediär: Als Form der Vermittlung zwischen gesetztem Recht, sozialen Normen und individuellen Interessen. In: A. Klampfl (ed.), *Normativität und soziale Praxis: Gesellschaftspolitische und historische Beiträge*. Vienna: Turia & Kant.

Lanzinger, M. 2007: Umkämpft, verhandelt und vermittelt. Verwandtenehen in der katholischen Dispenspraxis des 19. Jahrhunderts. In: M. Lanzinger & E. Saurer (eds.), *Politiken der Verwandtschaft: Beziehungsnetze, Geschlecht und Recht*. Vienna: V&R unipress.

Lanzinger, M. & E. Saurer 2007: Politiken der Verwandtschaft: Einleitung. In: M. Lanzinger & E. Saurer (eds.), *Politiken der Verwandtschaft: Beziehungsnetze, Geschlecht und Recht*. Vienna: V&R unipress.

Latour, B. 1996: On Actor-Network Theory: A Few Clarifications. *Soziale Welt* 47:4, 369–382.

Legrand, C. 2006: Tourisme des racines et confrontations identitaires dans l'Irlande des migrations. *Diasporas: Histoire et sociétés* 8, 162–171.

Le Play, F. 1855: *Les Ouvriers Européens: Études sur les travaux, la vie domestique et la condition morale des populations ouvrières de l'Europe, précédées d'un exposé de la méthode d'observation*. Paris: Imp. Impériale.

Le Wita, B. 1994: *French Bourgeois Culture*. Trans. J.A. Underwood. Cambridge: Cambridge University Press.

Malkki, L. 1992: National Geographic: The Rooting of

Peoples and the Territorialization of National Identity among Scholars and Refugees. *Current Anthropology* 7, 24–44.

Mehr, K. 1992: International Activities and Services of the Genealogical Society of Utah. *Archivum* 37, 148–157.

Nash, C. 2004: Genetic Kinship. *Cultural Studies* 18:1, 1–33.

Nelson, A. 2008: Bio Science: Genetic Genealogy Testing and the Pursuit of African Ancestry. *Social Studies of Science* 38:5, 759–783.

Pegelow, T. 2006: Determining "People of German Blood", "Jews" and "Mischlinge": The Reich Kinship Office and the Competing Discourses and Powers of Nazism, 1941–1943. *Contemporary European History* 15, 43–65.

Richau, M. 2007: Die Mormonen – ein umstrittenes Paradies für Familienforscher. *Der Herold: Vierteljahrsschrift für Heraldik, Genealogie und verwandte Wissenschaften* 50:4, 225–237.

Riehl, W.H. 1851: *Land und Leute.* Vol. 1 of *Die Naturgeschichte des Volkes als Grundlage einer deutschen Sozial-Politik.* Stuttgart: J.G. Cotta.

Riehl, W.H. 1855: *Die Familie.* Vol. 3 of *Die Naturgeschichte des Volkes als Grundlage einer deutschen Sozial-Politik.* Stuttgart: J.G. Cotta.

Ruhri, A. 1997: Die pfarrlichen Altmatriken in der Steiermark. *Mitteilungen des Steiermärkischen Landesarchivs* 47, 107–138.

Sagnes, S. 1995: De terre et de sang: La passion généalogique. *Terrain* 25, 125–145.

Schnegg, M., J. Pauli, B. Beer & E. Alber 2010: Verwandtschaft heute: Positionen, Ergebnisse, Forschungsperspektiven. In: E. Alber, B. Beer, J. Pauli & M. Schnegg (eds.), *Verwandtschaft heute: Positionen, Ergebnisse und Perspektiven.* Berlin: Reimer.

Schramm, K. 2008: *Struggling over the Past: The Politics of Heritage and Homecoming in Ghana.* Walnut Creek, CA: Left Coast Press.

Segalen, M. (ed.) 2012: Parentés et paternités en Europe. *Éthnologie Française* 42:1.

Segalen, M. & C. Michelat 1990: L'amour de la généalogie. In: M. Segalen (ed.), *Jeux de familles.* Paris: Presses du CNRS.

Tucker, S.N. 2009: *The Most Public of All History: Family History and Heritage Albums in the Transmission of Records.* Ph.D. thesis, University of Amsterdam, http://dare.uva.nl/record/325290. Accessed March 30, 2012.

Tyler, K. 2005. The Genealogical Imagination: The Inheritance of Interracial Identities. *The Sociological Review* 53, 475–494.

Vismann, C. 2008: *Files: Law and Media Technology.* Trans. G. Winthrop-Young. Stanford: Stanford University Press.

Wimmer, A. & N. Glick Schiller 2002: Methodological Nationalism and the Study of Migration. *Archives Européennes de Sociologie* 43, 217–240.

Zarri, G. 2001: Die tridentinische Ehe. In: P. Prodi & W. Reinhard (eds.), *Das Konzil von Trient und die Moderne.* Berlin: Duncker und Humblot.

Elisabeth Timm is Professor of Cultural Anthropology/Folklore Studies at the Department of Folklore Studies/European Ethnology, University of Münster (Germany). Her research interests focus on family and kinship, and comparative approaches integrating historical and contemporary anthropology. Her latest article (with Kathrina Dankl, Tena Mimica, Lukasz Nieradzik and Karin Schneider), "Fault Lines of Participation: An Ethnography Translated into an Exhibition on Family and Kinship" (*Museum & Society*, 2013), combines kinship studies and museum studies.
(Elisabeth.Timm@uni-muenster.de)

HOW GENDERED IS THE EUROPEAN MIGRATION REGIME?

A Feminist Analysis of the Anti-Trafficking Apparatus

Sabine Hess

Based on a two-year ethnographic research project on the making of European migration policy, this article explores the ways in which gender is deeply inscribed in the articulations, practices, and rationalities of the new European migration regime. It focuses on the area of "anti-trafficking" policies at national and transnational levels, showing how and why an "anti-trafficking dispositif" has been created over the last twenty years. Anti-trafficking policy, which targets women in particular, has become one of the main pillars of a restrictive, Europeanized migration and border regime. The article offers theoretical and methodological approaches to this gendering of migration policy, and asks what such a co-optation of feminist discourses and practices means for reflexive feminist cultural theory, research, and practice.

Keywords: border regime, anti-trafficking, gender, ethnographic regime analyses

Unaccustomed Alliances: Round Tables on the Trafficking of Women

I am standing in front of a five-star hotel at the outskirts of Istanbul, only a few minutes from the airport, waiting for my lift. Once again I had endured a two-day political spectacle together with delegates from governments, secret service organizations, the European Union, international and supranational organizations such as Europol, the Organization for Security and Co-operation in Europe (OSCE), and the International Organization for Migration together with national and local non-government organizations (NGOs). For the past six months I had been doing ethnographic fieldwork, applying a multi-sited approach, on policy development within the so-called Budapest Process[1] – a series of ongoing conferences and workshops begun in 1991 on the implementation of EU migration and border policies in areas outside of EU jurisdiction – and held the role of "independent researcher", that peculiar person who somehow belonged at the far end of the table (see Hess 2009, 2010). The Budapest Process and the ICMPD, the International Centre for Migration Policy Development located in Vienna,[2] which acted as Secretariat for the Process, had caught my attention many years earlier as a key political institution in the area of migration and border management. The ICMPD informs EU Member States, especially new Member States, about policies in these areas and also targeted adjacent countries through workshops and "capacity building programmes" (see Düvell 2002; Hess 2009; Georgi 2007; Geiger & Pécoud 2010).

Hosted by Turkey, a broad cross-section of very different organizations – including the Budapest Process, the ICMPD, the United Nation Office of Drugs and Crime (UNODC) and the Black Sea Economic Cooperation Organization (BSEC) – had extended the invitation to the Istanbul conference. The issue at hand was "Trafficking in the Black Sea Region" (UN.GIFT 2007). Surprisingly, despite their diverse interests, the participating institutions had reached a formulaic compromise to rally around the issue of "anti-trafficking", which meant that in the end funds would flow in this direction. Also surprising were the two foci on which participating actors had been able to agree after numerous rounds of negotiation: 1) "*transnational cooperation* between law enforcement and NGOs for the referral of *victims of trafficking*" and 2) "data collection and *information management*" (emphasis by the author).

In my eyes, this conference provided an extraordinary example of the far-reaching impacts and effects of the anti-trafficking discourse (re)produced for years by the EU, the USA, and many international intergovernmental organizations – as well as by regional and local NGOs. At this conference, interagency alliances could be observed that had previously been considered impossible in this region. Concurrently, spaces of possibility had also been opened to an unforeseen extent for formerly marginalized groups and positions, and for the discourses of non-government organizations. For example, estranged but nonetheless at the same table sat the chief of the Jandarma, Turkey's paramilitary law enforcement unit, and representatives of the country's two feminist battered women's shelters. They discussed the limits and difficulties of their therapeutic social work, whereby all NGO representatives repeatedly identified restrictive migration management policies as a major cause of the problem. The OSCE delegate also held an impassioned speech and, after distancing herself from the term "illegal migration" in a very differentiated manner, made clear that restrictive immigration policies and tightened border controls pushed more and more women into the hands of so-called human traffickers[3] in their efforts to cross the borders as "irregular migrants".[4]

After completing the departure process, once on the plane I wrote in my fieldbook: "The grotesqueries born out of European governance policy are incredible!" As an example: with me in the Jandarma's VW van being driven to the airport were two battered women's shelter workers, clearly anxious and fidgeting nervously in their seats. When we got out I asked them about the cause of their discomfort, and they answered that such vans usually brought them to another destination – namely into police custody after participating in demonstrations. In the context of anti-trafficking policy, these women are now committed members of civil society and not only sit with, but also co-operate with the very same law enforcement institutions. They are unequal actors in the field of anti-trafficking policy, although they understand full well the negative impact of restrictive border policies. Increasingly these alliances, although entry into them may be merely strategic, piqued my interest. In the course of my research on European migration and border policy (2004–2009), I ran into them on the community, regional, and European level – in particular in the context of anti-trafficking policy. I wanted to better understand these alliances and take a closer look at this style of setting government policy. I was further interested in the role and function of anti-trafficking policy for the European border regime from a gender theoretical and cultural anthropological perspective. My ethnographic and discourse analysis research therefore focuses on the European context.

The key focal point of this research interest is the international policy field of anti- or counter-trafficking in human beings – especially in women – in the main because it is this migration policy terrain that "works" with discursive positions situated within feminism and women's rights. It is a field which over the past fifteen years has stepped out of the political niche of the international women's movement and become a dominant apparatus within European and globalized migration management. Not only does it legitimize the discourse of tightening migration control, it provides a foundation for this discourse and has a massive public impact. For example, "MTV" and another music TV channel "Viva" take part in international campaigns against human trafficking and trafficking in women, and international celebrities such as Angelina Jolie act as international extraordinary ambassadors (MTV 2012; http://news.change.org/stories/latest-big-names-in-human-trafficking-fight-liu-streep-jolie).[5] This discourse has also freed very large sums of money for the international fight against organized crime and produced new coalitions of actors such as the one outlined above in which – under the aegis of governments – members of civil society, feminist NGOs, international organizations such as the omnipresent International Organization for Migration (IOM), and national and supranational law enforcement and secret service agencies gather around the same table. Even if the IOM and the International Labour Organization (ILO) have made attempts in the past few years to expand the discourse to include all forms of the exploitation of labour, at the centre of the anti-trafficking apparatus are still the images and discourses of trafficking in women and forced prostitution. Like almost no other international policy area, it focuses on the female body and female sexuality – in particular on the topos of the helpless female "victim".[6] For this reason, an analysis of the anti-trafficking apparatus can also reveal how deeply the category of gender is inscribed in the procedures, technologies, articulations, and rationales of modern European migration policy.

Based on Michel Foucault's ideas, I speak of the "anti-trafficking apparatus" (*dispositif*).[7] Foucault, in Reiner Keller's estimation, introduced the concept of the apparatus following his discourse theory work in order to connect studies of the said with studies of the unsaid: of materials, infrastructures, and institutional actions (Keller 2008: 93ff.). In this vein, I am interested in an analysis of the linkages of policies and discourses, especially of their rationales and their impact in terms of power and discourses of truth. I am also concerned with the function and relevancy of these linkages in relation to European migration policy. To this end, I look at the way in which the apparatus of "anti-trafficking policy" plays a central role in policies governing tightening border controls and the externalization of the European border regime. It shall become clear that the current turn towards "governance" within the migration regime is also built upon these discourses of victimization and uses discursive positions of the human rights' and women's movements in its argumentation (see also Hess & Karakayali 2007). I shall also show how new governmental political practices and discourses are connected to this apparatus – such as the politics of round-table meetings – with very ambivalent effects on, among other things, feminist political practices. I am particularly interested in understanding how discourses of women's rights – in particular positions against violence against women – came to fit so well with the restrictive rationalities of the border regime. This leads me to ask in the final section what it means when feminist theory and practice act on the terrain of migration and border policy. I also try to pinpoint those discursive positions – including research on women and migration – which help(ed) produce this adaptability.[8]

In the following I draw mostly from the interdisciplinary approach of Anglophone queer and gender-aware research on immigration and border management such as the work of Bridget Anderson (2009) and Rutvica Andrijašević (2009, 2010), as well as from Foucauldian and post-colonial debates on the refashioning of Europe. I also draw from the results of my own research on European migration and border policy such as the work mentioned above (Hess 2009, 2011), the interdisciplinary research project Transit Migration (2003–2005), and research conducted within the Network of Critical Migration and Border Regime Research (Hess & Kasparek 2010). Within the framework of the collaborative Transit Migration research project[9], we conducted ethnographic research at the southern and eastern borders of the EU on the Europeanization of migration policy. Building on this research, we developed what we called an "ethnographic border regime analysis" (Hess & Tsianos 2007). This ethnographic border regime analysis connects more recent approaches to ethnographic field research – in particular variants of multi-sited ethnography (Marcus 1998) – with genealogical and discourse analysis approaches (Hess & Tsianos 2010). In terms of content and theory, it attempts to look at the developments of migration policy from the perspective of migrants' movements and also to develop a form of praxeological policy research capable of analysing "doing border" (see Hess, Karakayali & Tsianos 2009; Ferguson & Gupta 2005; Shore & Wright 1997). In our Transit Migration fieldwork, we identified the discourse of asylum and the discourse of anti-trafficking – and the actors and practices associated with them – as the central discursive and legitimizing pillars of European migration and border management policy. Eva Bahl and Marina Ginal, in their ethnographic research on the local adaptation of anti-trafficking policy in Munich, Germany, were able to show how this discourse has a strong normative effect on what could be expressed and what was unspeakable. For example, it makes it almost impossible to talk about migrant sex work unless it can be subsumed under the topos of sex trafficking and forced prostitution (see Bahl, Ginal & Hess 2010).[10]

However, before going into the interplay of the Europeanization of immigration policy and the discourse on trafficking in women, I would like to first outline the genesis of the anti-trafficking apparatus. Below I sketch its varying disciplinary components and dominant dichotomous discursive strategy in an attempt to identify the factors leading to the "boom" in this sector.

Genesis of the Anti-Trafficking Apparatus

There are very few other political discourses and arenas of praxis in which the female migrant body is so explicitly the central object not only of numerous discourses and fears, but also of exploitative relations, of violence, and of a package of quite contradictory countermeasures. It is at the centre of feminist anti-violence politics advocated by activists who have successfully devoted decades to creating a public scandal of the issues of forced prostitution and sex trafficking of women and to promoting feminist protective measures developed to provide concrete support and care. These support practices run the gamut from charitable church measures to radical feminist and anti-racist approaches, from abolitionist to empowerment positions (see Andrijašević 2010: 2, 14f.; Karakayali 2008), and are clearly divisible according to whether migrant women are given the status of objects or subjects/active agents (see, e.g., Lindqvist 2007).

Historical research on the genesis of the discourse of human trafficking such as Serhat Karakayali's work on the politics of irregular migration (2008) or Eval Bahl, Marina Ginal, Bernd Kasparek's joint work on urban migration policy discourses (2009) reveal through their reconstructions a series of thematic shifts and, in Germany, three clear time periods: In the first period at the beginning of the twentieth century, as mass immigration into and out of Germany was the order of the day, the discourse was widespread and also focused in the main on immigrant women. Warnings about the danger of forced prostitution were published in leaflets and on posters. During this period for example, the *Bahnhofsmission* (church travellers' aid association) was founded for the protection of young women travelling alone (see Hess 2005). This discourse again became virulent in the 1960s and 1970s at the height of labour migration in the context of the so-called guest worker (*Gastarbeiter*) system. However, in this period, neither the immigration of women nor the sex industry was at the centre of the narrativization. Rather the conditions of self-organized and irregular labour migration were criticized. Working conditions in factories and on construction sites were termed "slavery" and the exploitative practices of labour recruitment agencies were condemned as "human trafficking". Serhat Karakayali points out that at this time too, left-wing poeple – advocated in this case mostly by trade unions – portrayed the situation as a scandal in order to give the discourse more impact (2008: 235). Anti-trafficking discourse died down again in the 1980s as Germany presented itself as a "non-immigration country" and reappeared in the 1990s as a discourse about women as debates increased on the increase of immigration, in particular from Eastern Europe and the global South.

The renewed interest in this issue by policy makers in the 1990s was the fruit of decades of campaigning by feminist and women's groups to have sex trafficking taken seriously. The struggle against the trafficking of women and children and the struggle against forced prostitution, closely linked on the discursive level, were placed on the political agenda in particular because of the focus on these issues at the UN human rights conference in Vienna in 1993 and the UN World Conference on Women in Beijing in 1995 (Schwenken 2006; Düvell 2002). On the EU level, the political scientist Helen Schwenken (2006: 111) has underscored the importance of what she termed the "velvet triangle" of so-called femocrats (feminist bureaucrats), scientists, and activists/lobbyists in establishing this discourse in the 1990s. The European Union, after receiving the mandate to become active in the areas of justice and home affairs and legal issue in the treaties of Maastricht (1992) and Amsterdam (1995), worked closely together with NGOs and other lobby groups and profited from their expertise and knowledge. These new EU structures gave political women's networks in particular a chance to establish a hegemony for their positions – mostly through the Women's Office (later the Equal Opportunity Unit) – especially if these positions were presented as gender equality issues. The issue of trafficking in women profited greatly from this window of opportunity and feminist groups were increasingly able to put it on the political agenda during this period.

The first EU action programme against trafficking in human beings was the 1996 STOP programme (Commission of the European Union 1996). In this programme, the EU stresses that it brings together a broad spectrum of actors including "universities, NGOs, police and immigration services, government and parliaments" (ibid.). The next communication about the programme also underscored the broad spectrum and heterogeneity of the actors with whom the EU commission was able to work in this area, naming in particular cooperation with "non-member countries and specialised organisations" (Commission of the European Union 1998). This communication refers to other action programmes and forums within which the issue had been dealt with in the previous years:

> The fight against trafficking in human beings has also been tackled in the United Nations (special Protocol to the International Convention against Organised Transnational Crime), the G8 (action plan), the Council of Europe, the International Organisation for Migrants (IOM) (regional surveys and information campaigns), Interpol, the Organisation for Security and Cooperation in Europe (OSCE) and in the context of the transatlantic dialogue. (Ibid.)

A further EU action programme, Daphne, ensued in 2000 (Commission of the European Union 2000). Daphne provided funding for NGOs that offered support to women and children who had been victims of trafficking. And two years later, in 2002, the Council of the European Union adopted a framework decision to establish a common legal framework on human trafficking within the Member States (Council of the European Union 2002).[11] Daphne I and II were extremely instrumental in strengthening the anti-trafficking discourse and the relevant actors. Where no NGOs had previously existed, they were created and, as our research within the Transit Migration project showed for the example of Turkey and the Balkan states, influence was exerted on the political programmes of existing NGOs. In an interview with the Berlin anti-racism organization *AntirassismusBüro*, Marion Böker from the Federal Association against Trafficking in Women and Violence against Women in the Migration Process (KOK) criticized the fact that the EU's grant programmes contributed greatly to splits in the NGO community between those initiatives which were willing to work together with the EU on victim protection measures and round table politics and those that rejected cooperation or collaboration with government law enforcement agencies and therefore did not receive financial aid (Böker 2004).

Concretely, within EU migration and border policies, two arenas of political practice emerged in the area of anti-trafficking policies. This can be seen in other areas of the world as well, for example in the so-called Bali Process in the Asia-Pacific region. Anti-trafficking politics thus act in an arena of high-profile politics of representation, and establish a very specific regime of the gaze of the female body. Concurrently, especially in the area of security, these policies are enacted as a part of the overall increasing efforts to combat irregular migration and organized crime.

We should first examine the politics of visualization which create a racialized and sexualized regime of the gaze and has a negative impact in particular in female migrants' home countries, because it places the migration of women in general under the moral misgivings surrounding prostitution and stigmatizes women's migration as, among other things, a risk which cannot be taken (see Hess 2005). This takes place mostly within so-called awareness-raising or educational campaigns that warn of the dangers of human trafficking on large billboards and other advertising media in the home countries. The International Organisation for Migration (IOM), one of the few global all-around agencies in the field of migration control, is particularly active in this area (Düvell 2002; Georgi 2010).[12] Rutvica Andrijašević conducted an analysis of the images used by the IOM in their 2001–2002 campaign in the Baltic States. As in other IOM campaigns, this Baltic campaign made use of images of usually naked female bodies posed as victims. One poster, for example, portrays a half-naked female body hanging in the air on hooks and ropes. These images are meant to warn potential migrants of the dangers of migration and prostitution (Andrijašević 2005). IOM's Head of Mass Information put it as follows:

> The nakedness was meant to show the helplessness and vulnerability of trafficked women. The hooks are visual metaphors used to convey an essential aspect of trafficking, namely the manipulation and exploitation to which trafficked women are subjected (...). Most trafficked women find themselves treated as slaves with no control of their lives whatsoever. This is the idea we wanted to convey. (Cited in ibid.: 35–37)

Stressing the dangers of migration, in Rutvica Andrijašević's analysis, is meant to keep women away from informal labour migration and "implies that the safest option is to remain home" (ibid.: 31). Furthermore, Andrijašević shows that the male voyeuristic gaze is inherent to these images, constructed as they are of women's suffering and victimized bodies. This degrades them to objects of voyeuristic eroticization, thereby reproducing the stereotype of Eastern European women as "beautiful victims". In light of this, Andrijašević shows that the campaign is not about, but rather against, women and women's migration and transports the message: stay at home!

Global anti-trafficking policy, alongside large public relation campaigns such as this one – campaigns in which Viva and MTV also sometimes participate – has otherwise been rooted mostly in the terrain of security and migration management policy. Combating sex trafficking takes place mostly in connection with the fight against organized crime, thus correlating the two. The UN protocol, considered the central document of anti-trafficking policy, illustrates the way in which sex trafficking was made into a security issue. The protocol was celebrated – also by feminist activists – as a milestone in bringing the issue onto the official European and global political agenda. The so-called *Palermo Protocol* was adopted by the United Nations Office on Drugs and Crime in 2003 as a supplement to the broader Convention against Transnational Organized Crime (UNODC 2004). It is thus primarily a political instrument to improve international cooperation and develop a new international legal regime in the fight against organized crime. The protocol differentiates between trafficking (forced trade) and smuggling (voluntary migration). On the one hand this is laudable, because it allows for differentiated interpretations – not all transport and information services in this area should be automatically defined as "trafficking". On the other hand, the Convention strengthens and formalizes the central dichotomy between voluntary migration and force which characterizes this discourse. Christina Hahn conducted a reconstructive discourse analysis of the positions of various NGO-affiliated lobby groups in this area. She showed how abolitionist positions increasingly gained hegemony that treated women migrants, especially sex workers, as defenceless victims without a voice (Hahn 2007).

However, biographically-oriented ethnographic research in this area has shown that the reality of these women is different. In their daily lives, voluntary actions and direct and structural violence intersect in contradictory manners and are judged and negotiated in myriad ways, both in migrants' interpretations and in their actions. Ramona Lenz for example, in her study of mostly Filipina and Eastern European sex workers in Cyprus, shows how these women arrived in the country on their own with an official artist visa and only later, as a result of having no rights, drifted into relations characterized by dependency and coercion (Lenz 2009). On the other hand, women interviewed by Rutvica Andrijašević for her study about Eastern European sex workers in Italy, describe how they chose to work as prostitutes and themselves turned to trafficking networks and at the same time say they were forced. Nevertheless, the women interviewed in this study clearly developed strategies to deal with dependency and coercion (see Andrijašević 2010).

Boom Sector Sex Trafficking: Migration Policy as a Catalyst

Numerous studies have shown that over the past years, demand has increased for sexualized and racialized women's bodies and emotion-laden sexualized work in the context of globalization and economic restructuring (see Andrijašević 2010: 5ff.; Hochschild 1983). Feminist scholars search for the causes in the heteronormative, patriarchal, capitalist, and racialized world order. Sex trafficking, the trade of women and children for the purpose of sexual exploitation, is now, according to international law enforcement agencies such as Europol, the fastest growing criminal sector. After the drug and arms trade it is also, according to some, the third most profitable sector (see for example Andrijašević 2010: 7). However, since statistics are problematic in this area,[13] because of the informal character of the phenomenon and the different statistical methods used by different authorities, the authors of the study "Human Trafficking in Germany" cite Europol as follows:

> Europol assumes that "hundreds of thousands" of victims are trafficked into the EU Member States each year for the purpose of sexual exploitation and labour exploitation and notes that the number of victims has increased considerably over the past few years. (Cited in Folmer & Rabe 2009: 20)

Feminist studies with a biographical and ethnological orientation have pointed out that stereotypes of the impoverished woman from the global South and East together with increased male demand in the North create a push-pull model that does not do justice to the complexity of this field, which is not only economic, but also social, cultural, and political. These studies show that subjective, emotional, and ethical aspects such as the women's own ideas about sexuality and a better life as well as their rationalizations must be given more importance in order to place more weight on the agency of the migrant women themselves (see for example Andrijašević 2010: 12; Hess 2005).

Andrijašević also shows how the spread of the sector is connected to the general increase in underpaid labour in deregulated and informal sectors following the flexibilization of labour policies in the Western and Northern countries. This went hand in hand with an increased demand for an inexpensive and flexible female migrant labour force, leading to the feminization of migration which can be observed in many southern and eastern countries (see for example Anthias & Lazaridis 2000). However, for most of these migrants, because of restrictive immigration and labour policies in most EU countries – and in connection with racialized images of (still) female (domestic) workers – the only field open to them is the large field of caretaking; including care for the sick and elderly, cleaning and ironing, domestic and childcare services, and also sex work (see Lutz 2007). This labour segment of the three Cs (cooking, cleaning, caring)[14] is very gender-specific. It often falls under the "private" sphere and is thus not subject to public scrutiny or formalized labour contracts (ibid.). Ethnographic and biographical research has shown that this is also a factor which migrants often use to their advantage (see Hess 2005; Lutz 2007).

Alongside these subjective biographical and political-economic factors, researchers also point out a genuinely political regulatory factor which has led to the increase in the nexus of migration-trafficking-sex work: official European immigration policy itself. Without this regulatory influence, which to this day can only be described as restrictive and gendered, the phenomenon of sex trafficking could not possibly be as widespread as it is today. For example, most countries allow very little official immigration and immigration laws reflect a view of migration as a male undertaking focused on male labour (see Hess 2005). Feminist and queer research on migration has been able to demonstrate the way in which immigration policy is based on heteronormative concepts of gender and sexuality, in particular that of the dependent wife who is not herself actively seeking migrant status. Policies geared towards the reunification of families or regulations granting the right of residence as a result of marriage – two ways in which women often gain legal immigrant status – reproduce heterosexual patterns and female dependency (Kofmann & Sales 1998; Andrijašević 2009: 394). Because of these immigration and labour market policies, women migrants are overrepresented in precarious and informal migration and labour sectors. In the end, policies that grant only few residency and work permits – which are moreover temporary and uncertain – create marginalized groups of migrants without any meaningful access to the formal labour market and without recourse to law. Within this logical framework, "illegal" immigrants are not an abnormality or an outgrowth of the system, but rather a constructed, regulatory category of immigration.

In order to further this restrictive migration policy, which creates hierarchies and puts migrants in precarious situations, over the past two decades European border management has been harmonized and continually intensified using diverse (military) apparatuses and practices of knowledge and technology. Images of drowned immigrants in the Strait of Gibraltar and the Aegean and Libyan Sea or of military patrol boats belonging to the European border control agency Frontex are only the apex of a technological/military apparatus that, in the name of "migration management", works towards the selection of immigrants to maximize benefits (see Ghosh 1997; for a critical analysis see also Mezzadra 2009; Geiger & Pécoud 2010; Hess & Kasparek 2010). In sum, it can be said that it is European immigration and border management policies themselves – as has been acknowledged at EU conferences as well – which have helped further the phenomenon of sex trafficking, because migrants are dependent upon the services of trafficking and smuggler organizations in order to cross the border at all. When migrants do manage to cross the external borders,[15] immigration policy paired with nationalist, racist labour market policies[16] and heterosexist gender policies push women towards informal (sex) work sectors and produce dependencies and disenfranchisement.

The European Border Regime and the Role of Anti-Trafficking Policies

In the public mind, the Europeanization of migration policy is closely connected to the name of a small village in Luxembourg. In Schengen, five Member States of what was then the European Community, including Germany, met in 1985 on a multi-lateral level and outside of EU structures to establish a common market. As a so-called compensatory measure, they agreed to shift border controls to the outer borders and to harmonize policies regarding refugees, foreigners, and visa practices. But it took over ten years before the Schengen Agreement became official EU policy in the 1998 Treaty of Amsterdam (see Hess & Tsianos 2007; Hess 2010).[17] Although the harmonization of EU migration policies is a sluggish process, harmonization and consensual immigration control practices can be observed, known in EU jargon as "integrated border management" (see Geiger & Pécoud 2010).

A central characteristic of this policy is the externalization and internalization of borders. "Borders" have now been placed far beyond the actual borders of the EU and have also been defined within EU territory, producing flexible, fragmented border areas and border corridors which are enacted in a highly technocratic manner (Walters 2002; Tsianos 2008). On the European Commission level, this transformation of the border regime is expressed discursively and operatively through a focus on "migratory routes" (see Commission of the European Union 2007). The Commission's 2007 communication states: "However, applying the Global Approach to the Eastern and South-Eastern regions neighbouring the EU according to the concept of 'migratory routes' also requires consideration of countries of origin and transit further afield" (ibid.: 247). This approach no longer focuses on the crossing of national borderlines, rather it is the migratory movement itself – in particular the routes taken by migrants – that is at the centre of these control policies. This leads to a massive imperial extension of European immigration policy into migrants' home countries. In this context, the discourse on smugglers and human traffickers takes on a key operative function that is not limited to exposing and shutting down smuggling rings and human trafficking routes. This act of putting immigrants under general suspicion, or rather the linkage of migration and criminality, provides regulatory bodies with the legitimation they need to detain all migrants and interrogate them – using violence at times – about their routes. Pro Asyl has documented this practice in Greece (Pro Asyl 2008). In this way, large data sets are generated and visualizations of migration patterns are produced such as the so-called i-Map, a digital map of migration routes created by Europol, Frontex, the United Nation High Commissioner (UNHCR), the UNODC, and the ICMPD (see i-Map 2012).

Even if the harmonization of EU migration policy has faced many setbacks (see Birsl 2005), the Europeanization of migration management has nevertheless developed an internal dynamic. As we were able to show in our research project Transit Migration, this can be traced in the main to the formation and activities of innumerable international, regional, and local actors who both support and flank government policies, and who are also miles ahead of them and are following their own political agendas. This multiplication of actors is known in international border studies as "privatization", and is called the politics of "remote control". European border policy is thus also made outside of government institutions and far from national borders (see Lahav & Guiraudon 2000; Guiraudon 2001). Within Transit Migration, we termed this process "NGOization" in order to make clear that this method of governmental policymaking takes place mostly through and in cooperation with NGOs, and itself takes on elements of an activist repertoire (see Hess & Karakayali 2007).

The two largest intergovernmental organizations in this field are the UNHCR, whose existence goes back to the Geneva Convention on Refugees (see Ratfisch & Scheel 2010), and the above-mentioned IOM. In contrast to the UNHCR, the IOM has no foundation in international law, although it makes great efforts to performatively generate such a foundation. As our ethnographic research in Transit Migration made clear, the exploitation and hegemonization of the anti-trafficking discourse played a key role in the IOM's ability to secure its dominant position in the global arena. Combatting human trafficking is, alongside refugee policy, one of very few areas of migration policy which uses a discourse promising protection and is pushed forward in the main by the USA (see US Department of State 2012), which in turn set the course of the IOM. As we have seen in the example of the Istanbul conference, anti-trafficking discourse is also reproduced by further large and small institutional actors in the migration management arena from the OSCE to small NGOs on the local level (see Migmap 2006).

New European Governance – Turning the Border Regime into a Human Rights Issue

This multiplication of key players and inter-agency cooperation correlates directly with changes in the European Commission's political practice as laid out in detail in the White Paper on European Governance (Commission of the European Union 2001). As a response to global challenges, the Commission writes, politics should be "decentralized" and shaped at "various levels" within "networks", include the strategic "involvement of civil society" and the use of "expert advice". The findings of the

Transit Migration project on the political practices and discourse of immigration policy as expressed by the EU within the preliminary rounds on the accession of Turkey, show that the politics of the "Round Table" is *the* incarnation of the politics of governance (see Bahl, Ginal & Hess 2010).

On a discursive level, these new coalitions – as I have described using the example of the Istanbul conference – adapt the discursive positions of human rights activists and feminists to a restrictive border regime. William Walters, a researcher of Europeanization and border management, speaks in this context of the "Birth of the Humanitarian Border" which does not necessarily mean that actual practice becomes more humanitarian (Walters 2010). However, local ethnographic research such as Marc Speer's work on the implementation of the EU border regime in the Ukraine (2010) shows that human rights interventions and activists can in fact challenge law enforcement structures. But the price is often high, as players must accede to the logic of a human rights discourse which, among other things, seems to demand the choice of a policy approach that victimizes the migrant other. Eva Bahl and Marina Ginal come to the same conclusions in their study on the effects of the anti-trafficking discourse on negotiation options and positions on the municipal level. They clearly show the way in which this discourse delegitimizes empowering positions and only an abolitionist, victimizing discourse remains as the legitimate manner of speaking about, or having knowledge about, migrants in sex work (see Bahl, Ginal & Hess 2010).

Thus during the Istanbul conference, all key players spoke of a "victim oriented approach". This is a significant shift in the discourse and moves the focus away from law enforcement and concrete practices of control. Rather, within this discursive shift it seems that all institutions of political control are interested in protecting the victims and posit themselves as biased, almost activist players concerned primarily with the well-being of the women involved. Yet the measures taken in the name of victim protection include stopping and identifying trafficked women, taking them into police custody and interrogating them about their migration routes, placing them at women's shelters for the protection of victims, having them appear as court witnesses, and deporting them back to their home countries. The ICMPD, an organization which has played a key role in furthering this discourse, published interviews with women who had undergone these procedures in a study entitled "Listening to Victims" (Surtees 2007). In this study, the ICMPD – which does not have a reputation for doing pro-immigrant work – cites many women who tell of inappropriate and poor conduct by both the police and NGOs who scared them, threatened them, mocked them, and did not explain their situation to them. Many passages also cite migrant women clearly stating that the measures taken in order to protect them were not what they wanted, and that actions which go by the name of victim protection are actually against their interests. The following passage is one example: "It happened for the first time when I heard that I could not have residence papers and must leave from the centre. I fainted and when I was awakened I started to scream... I did not want to leave the centre; I had no place to go" (ibid.: 110). Many quotes in this section describe the women's distress at and rejection of their repatriation. In this context, the work of NGOs, women's shelters, and the IOM is particularly politically charged, since they support the detained women throughout all procedures up until repatriation. They may try to alleviate the migrants' situation by giving them financial start-up grants or arranging contacts to women's shelters in their home countries, but this is often not what the women themselves want. They want to remain as migrants in the new country.

Anti-Trafficking as the Motor of a Restrictive Border Regime

All in all it can be stated that this package of measures, encoded as victim protection, makes the female migrant body the central target of diverse and connected high-tech practices of knowledge within the migration and border regime, up to and including local NGOs and ending in operative mappings of migration routes such as the so-called i-Map. The i-Map is the brainchild of ICMPD, Frontex, and

Europol. On the surface it shows a digital map that claims to portray current migration routes based on databases (i-Map 2012). The UNODC and other law enforcement agencies continually create data sets and visualizations of this type in the vain hope of being able to make accurate prognoses about migration movements. Victim protection measures objectify the migrant body; they make it penetrable and computable, subject to categorization and selection. More than anything, they limit the migrants' histories to their status as victims. We imagine "victims" as defenceless women, reduced to their corporeality and no longer able to speak for themselves. They must be protected from themselves – in our Transit Migration research we even learned of a women's NGO in Belgrade which locked women in "for their own protection". Migrant sex workers are only interesting for social work organization as victims. Migrants who voluntarily become prostitutes and are then confronted with a situation in which they are subordinated and exploited often have no recourse to support.

Looking at all of this together, we see a convergence between anti-trafficking polices and anti-immigrant policies. As a result, even policies that operate in the name of helping victims in the end act against the interest of women from the European periphery. In sum, the central discursive impact of the anti-trafficking discourse is that it 1) not only legitimizes, but also demands more stringent control of migration to protect possible victims; 2) on a practical level, legitimizes the creation of so-called screening centres which are set up along migration routes in order to filter out "vulnerable" trafficking victims and refugees from the mass of irregular labour migration. As a result, the anti-trafficking discourse furthers a policy of selection, and concomitantly the criminalization and disenfranchisement of most immigrants without papers, who can be categorized neither as trafficking victims nor as refugees. In the end, anti-trafficking policy thus plays a key role in the ascendency of this key biopolitical mechanism of hierarchizing and disciplining migrant passages by means of border management policy (see Mezzadra 2009).[18] Finally, the anti-trafficking discourse 3) legitimizes police practices of detainment and thorough interrogation meant to uncover migration routes and trafficking networks, and ending in numerous processes of knowledge acquisition as exemplified by the i-Map. For this reason, Rutvica Andrijašević comes to the conclusion that "trafficking discourse and anti-trafficking policies sustain and normalise a differential regime of mobility through which the EU hierarchically organises access to its labour market and citizenship" (Andrijašević 2010: 4). Researcher and sex worker activist Jo Doezema therefor asked at a 2002 conference on trafficking at the university of Ghent: "As trafficking is increasingly being used by governments and even by NGOs as an excuse for repressive policies, NGOs are left wondering: where did we go wrong?" (2003: 1).

On the Biopolitical Logic of Feminational Discourses[19]

Against this background, I would like to end with an examination of how it was possible that well-meaning feminist theories and practices – such as those surrounding trafficking in women and forced prostitution – were able to cooperate so easily with restrictive migration and border management policies or rather be coopted by the same without greater friction. I draw on the one hand from the work of the feminist migrant anti-violence activist and theorist Esra Edem, who has conducted an analysis of a similar migration issue – integration policies (Erdem 2009: 190, 192). I also draw from the work of the American queer theorist Jasbir Puar, in particular her book *Terrorist Assemblages: Homonationalism in Queer Times*. Puar observes a similar discursive coalition in the US "war against terror" in which the "terrorist assemblage" integrates discursive positions of the gay and lesbian movement. Puar shows how the normative figure of homosexuality is integrated into a post-liberal, post-colonial construction of the "modern" Occident contrasted with a pre-modern, traditional, and patriarchal Orient. She also speaks of an emerging "homonationalism"[20] which is able to build discursively upon the new-found national unity in the war against terror (see Puar 2007).

Esra Erdem uncovers a similar development in

German integration policy. She describes the way in which gender equality positions have been used in past years in order to legitimize restrictive integration policies.[21] In this case, a feminist anti-violence against women discourse – expressed by German and immigrant women's rights activists such as Alice Schwarzer or Seran Ates as well as by conservative politicians – is used to suddenly impart the equality of women the status of a Western cultural value (Erdem 2009: 189). Erdem asks what it means for the women's movement (and the theory thereof) that it has become a central actor on the terrain of foreigners' rights and that it encourages a discourse and images which place migrant women predominantly in the context of violence, as passive victims who are incapable of action.

Erdem goes on to argue that this feminist-inspired anti-violence policy not only chases after a liberal feminist illusion that jurisdiction and stricter immigration laws could protect women (ibid.: 191), but also that such policies are too reductionist and in the final analysis, racist. They ignore the intersections of other power relations such as policies on immigration and "aliens" or the colonial geographies of the gaze in which this discourse and the speakers' positions are located. Within the context of the debate on integration, as in the context of the US war against terror, the primary topoi, albeit radicalized, are colonial and Orientalist images of the modern Occident and its counterpart, the traditional Orient. From the very beginning of the colonial project, the relation of the sexes, in particular the figure of the subjected wife and the narrative of honour killings, have been used to prove the myth of Western modernity and Eastern (and Southern) traditionalism (see von Braun & Mathes 2007). Chandra Talpade Mohanty (1998) for example has shown that the production of the topos of the oppressed woman of the global South was constitutive for the production of the "emancipated Western woman". Gayatri Chakravorty Spivak argues similarly (1990) when she positions work done by Northern feminists for Southern women within paternalistic mission work. Thus national Western feminist discursive positions have a long tradition of legitimizing both the business of German colonialism and the project of the nation-state, and of putting itself at the service of these projects. Esra Erdem calls those feminist discursive positions which today are inscribed within restrictive debates on integration "racialized gender equality politics" which support the "codification of a racialized hierarchy (...) established by laws on aliens" (Erdem 2009: 191, 195). She speaks further of the "feminist disciplining of the migrant subject" (ibid.: 194), which found legitimatization and a quasi-scientific source of knowledge in, as I shall show in my final section, women's studies and gender migration studies.

The Discourse of Victimization and Feminist Migration Studies

In contrast to the ubiquitous thesis of the invisibility of migrant women, especially in feminist migration studies, in general migration studies show how migrant women receive specific visibility as an object of knowledge and are central to processes of positing migration in cultural and ethnic categories. An unsystematic genealogical look at the history of the analysis of migrant women demonstrates the way in which certain discourses – in particular the topos of women as victims and the discourse of victimization – have a long tradition in feminist migration studies.

Not only Ernest George Ravenstein noted in the 1885 *Journal of the Statistical Society*: "females are more migratory than males" (Ravenstein 1885: 196). In *The Polish Peasant in Europe and America*, a work that is influential in the social sciences to this day, the Chicago sociologists W.I. Thomas and Florian Znaniecki also include the experiences of women immigrants. However, Helma Lutz was able to show that, in contrast to their portraits of male immigration, portrayed as actively breaking out of the past, women are described quite differently in *The Polish Peasant*. As Lutz says: "For women, they write, migration is a calamity" (Lutz 2008). The topos was born of the female migrant as a "victim" dependent upon her family, a topos which – Lutz claims – made an impressive comeback in labour migration research in the 1970s. One of the pioneers of research on women migrants, Mirjana Morokvasic, noted as early as 1984 on the dominant representation of migrant women:

> In important works on migration, the symbolic reference to women as migrants' wives and their stereotypical presentation as wives and mothers has led to a conceptualization of migrant women as followers, dependents, unproductive persons, isolated, illiterate and ignorant. (Morokvasic 1984: 16)

In German research, Umut Erel and Eleonore Kofman have shown that the dominant topoi are the "passive wife and mother" and the "victim of patriarchal honour codes" (see Erel & Kofman 2003). From the very beginning of research on labour migration, these topoi, and the concomitant images of the "defenceless female body" and "women as carrier of culture" played an epistemological role in the general theoretical concept of "migration". These topoi were taken up in processes of cultural and ethnic identification within the social sciences and used to link labour migration with backwardness and patriarchal structures.

This early image of women's migration has a further discursive effect which influences academic and everyday thinking to this day: it implies coercion and dependency and ignores subjective aspects of women's plans for migration – their hopes and desires. The research on women's migration which began in the 1980s, initially meant as a supplement to academic research on migration, helped to continue this ambivalent pictorial history. In particular in the addition of the issues of (forced) prostitution and migration via marriage (see for example Hummel 1993; Schöning-Kalender 1989), this research sector took up the metaphor of the passive victim until biographical studies began to bring the women themselves and their narratives to the centre of study (Karrer & Turtschi 1996).

This victimizing approach was however continually criticized by feminist migrants such as, for example, Sedef Gümen (1996) beginning in the 1980s. Meanwhile, refutation of victimization approaches is standard anti-racist, feminist rhetoric. Nevertheless, this approach, as Helen Schwenken has shown in her dissertation on strategies for the mobilization of domestic workers on an EU level, it is still considered as a successful means of framing political demands. Thus some types of institutionalized feminism still consciously work with the topos of victimization in their political actions, even if the migrants themselves, as Ramona Lenz has shown in her research on Cyprus, need to be convinced of their victim status. One Cypriote women's right activist even uses these very words: "We have to convince them that they are victims" (Lenz 2009). Migrant women themselves also, if not always intentionally, make use of an image of themselves as victims, because they know that the apparatus of victimization is one of their few options within the Western, "humanist" sphere. Paradoxically, sometimes claiming the status of victims and framing themselves as victims is the only way to become a subject and develop a position as a protagonist.

Given the way in which the feminist discourse and practices I have looked at in this essay are almost tailored to fit the racist discourse Philomena Essed has termed "Europism" (1995), and their increasing visibility within and co-optation for racialized policies of regulation, I would like to end by concurring with Esra Erdem's final thoughts. She has identified the recognition of the "struggles of migrants and of feminism" and building upon the same to create a progressive vision for a society open to migration as one of the central challenges for the German women's movement and feminist research. In cultural anthropological research this would mean rethinking the knee-jerk association of migrant women with misery and suffering, because, as we have seen, despite researchers' best intentions these images have a clear function in a hegemonical, restrictive border regime. Rather we should begin anew and ask which knowledge and which images would allow a critical analytical reflection on this policy.

Notes

1 The Budapest Process is a so-called regional consultation process or "informal dialogue" in which mostly eastern and southern European countries – and more recently also Caucasian countries – bring international

organizations and non-government organizations (NGOs) together to convey the logic, practices, and technologies of European migration and border management policies and to train participants in the same (see ICMPD 2012a). Since the beginning of the 2000s, the ICMPD has hosted a further informal dialogue focusing on African and Middle Eastern migration, the Mediterranean Transit Migration Dialogue (see ICMPD 2012c).

2 The ICMPD, founded in 1993 on the initiative of Switzerland and Austria in particular, is today one of the leading consultants for migration policy in Europe. It boasts fourteen member states and employs around 60 people in its Vienna office (see ICMPD 2012b).

3 In the area of women's migration, and occasionally also in the area of undocumented labour migration, the terminology used most is "forced" trafficking in humans; in the area of refugees, there are "smugglers" and "labour brokers", terms that clearly do not imply coercion and trickery (see Karakayali 2008). However, within the public discourse on refugee and asylum policy, investigative practices, technologies, and expert knowledge aimed at reconstructing travel itineraries are also common in dealings with refugees in order to judge applicants' "right to asylum" and whether they are telling the "truth".

4 The term "irregular migration" seems to have gained ascendency in the European political arena as the "politically correct" phrase. However, in research on migration in the cultural and social sciences, a more thoroughgoing process-oriented debate about terminology is taking place which makes it clear that the situations of un(der)documented migrants – that is those without identification documentation and legal status – are in flux. Most common is a continuum of legal and "illegalized" statuses which can take different forms in terms of irregularities in residency and working permits. Migrants themselves deal flexibly and tactically with these statuses (see for example Vasta 2008; Karakayali 2008; Hess 2005).

5 This entrance of anti-trafficking policy into popular culture can be found in other forms of pop culture as well, in particular TV cop shows.

6 To avoid any misunderstandings, I would like to stress that trafficking in human beings and the resultant slave labour and forced prostitution are abominable and must be combated. This is an informal economic sector, often criminal, that is quickly growing around the world. However, legal action against this sector would be quite possible under existing legal frameworks and without migration management policies.

7 According to Reiner Keller, Foucault uses the term "*dispositif*" to refer to "an infrastructural apparatus made up of varying elements" and meant "to serve a particular purpose" (see Keller 2008: 93), whereas Foucault himself defined it as the "system of relations that can be established between these elements" (Foucault 1980: 194). On the other hand Foucault understood the *dispositif* as a "formation which has as its major function at a given historical moment that of responding to an *urgent need*. The apparatus thus has a dominant strategic function" (ibid.: 195, emphasis in the original). These are the meanings which I have ascribed to the *dispositive*/apparatus.

8 It is this discussion of the (susceptibility to) co-optation exhibited by feminist theory and practice as well as the search for a progressive feminist politics of knowledge – leaning on Donna Harraway's postulate of "situated knowledge" – which positions this study in a continued process of feminist query as to how feminist theory and practice today can be articulated in an intersectional manner, critical of power and hierarchies (see Hess, Langreiter & Timm 2011).

9 Members of the research group were Serhat Karakayali, Vassilis Tsianos, Manuela Bojadzijev, Rutvica Andrijašević und Efthimia Panagiotidis.

10 I am indebted to this research project, one element of the research and exhibition project I directed in 2009, Crossing Munich, for many of the ideas in this essay on the negative impact of this discourse even at the municipal level.

11 "It is necessary that the serious criminal offence of trafficking in human beings be addressed not only through individual action by each Member State, but by a comprehensive approach in which the definition of constituent elements of criminal law common to all Member States, including effective, proportionate and dissuasive sanctions, forms an integral part" (preamble, paragraph 7).

12 I call the IOM an "all-around agency" since the IOM is involved in almost all facets of migration policy and practice from voluntary repatriation to public relation campaigns, disaster response, capacity-building measures such as building immigrant detention centres, and restitution payments for former slave labourers (see Georgi 2010).

13 Folmer and Rabe write: "The second report by the UN Office on Drugs and Crime (UNODC) compiles world data on human trafficking from criminal prosecution authorities, but also states that more can be learned from this about the activities of the criminal prosecution authorities than about the real numbers of crimes and victims" (2009: 20).

14 Analogous to the three Cs are the three Ds of men's migration: dirty, dangerous, and dull (see Favell 2009).

15 Alongside border controls outside national borders, there are now also various "borders" which have been drawn within countries as a result of the Schengen

Agreement. For example, train stations and expressways are now considered "border areas" in which border police may control identities at any time. For migrants, this multiplication of borders means they can be confronted with a "border control" at any time.

16 German labour law still has a priority system according to which an open position must be filled first by a "German", second by an "EU foreigner" if no qualified German can be found and third, only if again no one is found, by a so-called third country party.

17 One catalyst was the crises of the national system of asylum in the late 1980s when legal immigration became more difficult, and more and more migrants used asylum as an immigration loophole, "overstretching" the right to asylum, as Sadako Ogata saw it, then director of the UNHCR (see Ogata 1997). Leading functionaries and bureaucrats demanded the Europeanization of migration policy and a shift towards "migration management". The IOM, which pushes global migration management, played a central role in this policy shift (see Ghosh 1997; Hess 2010).

18 Phillip Ratfisch and Stephan Scheel (2010) identified a similar mechanism within the context of asylum policy and practice. In this case too, the rhetoric of protection allows the UNHCR not only to speak *for* refugees, but also allows them to selectively weed out refugees in need of protection from the vast mass of irregular migrants.

19 This conflation of "feminist" and "national" is inspired by Encarnacion Gutierrez Rodriguez's thoughts on Jasbir Puar's ideas about the "biopolitical logic of homonational discourses" in the context of the US war against terror (Rodriguez 2011: 95).

20 In this case, it is the "Muslim man" in particular who is presented as the homophobic, fundamental "other".

21 Whereby here too it is the "Muslim man" who is portrayed as patriarchal and violent.

References

Anderson, Bridget 2009: What is in a name? Immigration Controls and Subjectivities: The Case of Au Pairs and Domestic Worker Visa Holders in the UK. *Subjectivity* 29, 407–424.

Andrijašević, Rutvica 2005: Schöne tote Körper: Gender, Migration und Repräsentation in Kampagnen gegen Menschenhandel. In: www.policy.hu/andrijasevic/IOM.html. Accessed January 15, 2013.

Andrijašević, Rutvica 2009: Sex on the Move: Gender, Subjectivity and Differential Inclusion. *Subjectivity* 29, 389–406.

Andrijašević, Rutvica 2010: *Migration, Agency and Citizenship in Sex Trafficking*. London: Palgrave Macmillan.

Anthias, Floya & Gabriela Lazaridis (eds.) 2000: *Gender and Migration in Southern Europe: Women on the Move*. Oxford & New York: Berg.

Bahl, Eva, Marina Ginal & Bernd Kasparek et al. 2009: Tulbeck 12: Das Münchner Migrationsregime. In: Natalie Bayer, Andrea Engl & Sabine Hess et al. (eds.), *Crossing Munich: Beiträge zur Migration aus Kunst, Wissenschaft und Aktivismus*. Munich: Verlag Silke Schreiber.

Bahl, Eva, Marina Ginal & Sabine Hess 2010: Feministische Kritik am europäischen Grenzregime: Zur Funktionalität des Anti-Trafficking-Diskurses. In: Stefanie Kron, Martha Zapata & Birgit zur Nieden (eds.), *Diasporische Bewegungen im transatlantischen Raum*. Berlin: Verlag Walter Frey.

Birsl, Ursula 2005: *Migration und Migrationspolitik im Prozess der europäischen Integration?* Opladen: Campus Verlag.

Böker, Marion 2004: Die counter-trafficking-Politik der IOM. Eine kritische Sicht aus NGO-Perspektive. In: Forschungsgesellschaft Flucht und Migration (ed.), *Stop IOM! Globale Bewegung gegen Migrationsmanagement*. www.ffm-berlin.de/iomstopdt.pdf. Accessed February 13, 2012.

von Braun, Christina & Bettina Mathes 2007: *Verschleierte Wirklichkeit: Die Frau, der Islam und der Westen*. Berlin: Aufbau Verlag.

Commission of the European Union 1996: Commission communication of 20 November 1996 to the Council and the European Parliament on trafficking in women for the purpose of sexual exploitation. http://europa.eu/legislation_summaries/employment_and_social_policy/equality_between_men_and_women/l33095_en.htm. Accessed May 21, 2012.

Commission of the European Union 1998: Commission communication of 9 December 1998 to the Council and the European Parliament proposing further action in the fight against trafficking in women. http://europa.eu/legislation_summaries/employment_and_social_policy/equality_between_men_and_women/l33096_en.htm. Accessed May 21, 2012.

Commission of the European Union 2000: Decision No 293/2000/EC of the European Parliament and of the Council of 24 January 2000 adopting a programme of Community action (the Daphne programme) (2000 to 2003) on preventive measures to fight violence against children, young persons and women. In: *Official Journal of the European Communities L 34 from February 09, 2000*. http://europa.eu/legislation_summaries/human_rights/fundamental_rights_within_european_union/l33062_en.htm. Accessed May 21, 2012.

Commission of the European Union 2001: White Paper on European Governance. http://eur-lex.europa.eu/LexUriServ/site/en/com/2001/com2001_0428en01.pdf. Accessed May 24, 2012.

Commission of the European Union 2007: Applying the global approach to Migration to the Eastern and South-

Eastern regions neighbouring the European Union, Co(2007)247. http://eur-lex.europa.eu/LexUriServ/LexUriServ.do?uri=CELEX:52007DC0247:EN:NOT. Accessed May 24, 2012.

Council of the European Union 2002: Council Framework Decision of 19 July 2002 on combating trafficking in human beings, 2002/629/JI. In: *Official Journal of the European Communities* L 203/1 from August 1, 2002. http://eur-lex.europa.eu/LexUriServ/LexUriServ.do?uri=OJ:L:2002:203:0001:0004:EN:PDF. Accessed February 13, 2012.

Doezema, Jo 2002: The Ideology of Trafficking. Paper presented at Work Conference "Human Trafficking" on November 15, 2002. www.nswp.org/sites/nswp.org/files/DOEZEMA-IDEOLOGY.pdf. Accessed May 30, 2012.

Düvell, Frank 2002: *Die Globalisierung des Migrationsregimes*. Berlin, Hamburg & Göttingen: Assoziation A.

Erdem, Esra 2009: In der Falle einer Politik des Ressentiments. In: Sabine Hess, Jana Binder & Johannes Moser (eds.), *No integration?!* Bielefeld: Transcript Verlag.

Erel, Umut & Eleonore Kofman 2003: Professional Female Immigration in Post-War Europe: Counteracting an Historical Amnesia. In: Rainer Ohliger, Karen Schönwälder & Triadafilos Triadafilopoulos (eds.), *European Encounters: Migrants, Migration and European Societies since 1945*. Aldershot: Ashgate Publishing Ltd.

Essed, Philomena 1995: Gender, Migration and Cross-Ethnic Coalition Building. In: Helma Lutz, Ann Phoenix & Nira Yuval-Davis (eds.), *Crossfires: Nationalism, Racism and Gender in Europe*. London: Pluto Press.

Favell, Adrian 2009: Immigration, Migration and Free Movement in the Making of Europe. In: Jeffrey T. Checkel & Peter J. Katzenstein (eds.), *European Identity*. Cambridge: Cambridge University Press.

Ferguson, James & Akhil Gupta 2005: Spatializing States: Toward an Ethnography of Neoliberal Governmentality. In: Jonathan Xavier Inda (ed.), *Anthropologies of Modernity*. Malden: Blackwell Publishing.

Folmer, P. & H. Rabe 2009: *Human Trafficking in Germany*. Berlin: German Institute for Human Rights. http://www.institut-fuer-menschenrechte.de/uploads/tx_commerce/study_human_trafficking_in_germany.pdf. Accessed May 23, 2012.

Foucault, Michel 1980: The Confessions of the Flesh. In: Michel Foucault, *Power/Knowledge: Selected Interviews and Other Writings. 1972–1977*. Trans. Colin Gordon. New York: Pantheon Books.

Geiger, Martin & Antoine Pécoud (eds.) 2010: *The Politics of International Migration Management*. London: Palgrave Macmillan.

Georgi, Fabian 2007: *Migrationsmanagement in Europa: Eine kritische Studie am Beispiel des Centers for Migration Policy Development*. Saarbrücken: VDN-Verlag.

Georgi, Fabian 2010: Internationale Organisation für Migration. In: Sabine Hess & Bernd Kasparek (eds.), *Grenzregime: Diskurse, Praktiken, Institutionen in Europa*. Berlin: Association A.

Ghosh, Bimal 1997: Bevölkerungsbewegungen: Die Suche nach einem neuen internationalen Regime. In: Steffen Angenendt (ed.), *Migration und Flucht*. Munich: Oldenbourg Verlag.

Guiraudon, Virginie 2001: De-Nationalising Control: Analysing State Responses to Restraints on Migration Control. In: Virginie Guiraudon & Christian Joppke (eds.), *Controlling a New Migration World*. London: Routledge.

Gümen, Sedef 1996: Die sozialpolitische Konstruktion "kultureller" Differenzen in der bundesdeutschen Frauen- und Migrationsforschung. In: *Beiträge zur feministischen Theorie und Praxis: Ent-fremdung. Migration und Dominanzgesellschaft* 42, 77–90.

Hahn, Kristina 2007: Umstrittene Strategien gegen Menschenhandel: Kontroverse zwischen NGOs bei den Verhandlungen zum UN Protokoll geht weiter. *Femina Politica: Zeitschrift für feministische Politikwissenschaft* 1, 105–109.

Hess, Sabine 2005: *Globalisierte Hausarbeit: Au-Pair als Migrationsstrategie von Frauen aus Osteuropa*. Wiesbaden: VS Verlag für Sozialwissenschaften.

Hess, Sabine 2009: "Man schickt doch nicht eine Ersatzbraut zum Altar": Zur Konfliktualität der neuen Formen des Regierens in und von Europa. In: Gisela Welz & Annalina Lottermann (eds.), *Projekte der Europäisierung: Kulturanthropologische Forschungsperspektiven. Kulturanthropologische Notizen* 78, 181–196.

Hess, Sabine 2010: "We are facilitating states": An Ethnographic Analysis of the ICMPD. In: Martin Geiger & Antoine Pécoud (eds.), *The Politics of International Migration Management*. London: Palgrave Macmillan.

Hess, Sabine 2011: Caught in Mobility: An Ethnographic Analysis of the Context of Knowledge Production on Migration in Southeast Europe. In: Mechthild Baumann & Astrid Lorenz (eds.), Crossing and Controlling Borders – Immigration Policies and their Impact on Migrants' Journeys. Leverkusen: Opladen, pp. 229–248.

Hess, Sabine & Serhat Karakayali 2007: New Governance oder: Die imperiale Kunst des Regierens: Asyldiskurs und Menschenrechtsdispositiv im neuen EU-Migrationsmanagement. In: TRANSIT MIGRATION Forschungsgruppe (ed.), *Turbulente Ränder: Neue Perspektiven auf Migration an den Rändern Europas*. Bielefeld: Transcript Verlag.

Hess, Sabine & Vassilis Tsianos 2007: Europeanizing transnationalism! Provinzializing Europe! Konturen eines neuen Grenzregimes. In: Transit Migration Forschungsgruppe (ed.), *Turbulente Ränder: Neue Perspektiven auf Migration an den Rändern Europas*. Bielefeld: Transcript Verlag.

Hess, Sabine, Serhat Karakayali & Vassilis Tsianos 2009: Transnational Migration: Theory and Method of an Ethnographic Analysis of Border Regimes. In: Sussex Centre for Migration Research. *Working Papers No. 55.* www.sussex.ac.uk/migration/documents/mwp55.pdf. Accessed May 30, 2012.

Hess, Sabine & Bernd Kasparek (eds.) 2010: *Grenzregime: Diskurse, Praktiken, Institutionen in Europe.* Berlin: Association A.

Hess, Sabine, Nicola Langreiter & Elisabeth Timm (eds.) 2011: *Intersektionalität revisited.* Bielefeld: Transcript Verlag.

Hochschild, Arlie Russel 1983: *The Managed Heart: Commercialization of Human Feeling.* Berkeley: University of California Press.

Hummel, Diana 1993: Lohnende Geschäfte: Frauenhandel mit Osteuropäerinnen und der EG-Binnenmarkt. *Beiträge zur feministischen Theorie und Praxis: Europa – einig Vaterland* 34, 61–67.

ICMPD 2012a: Budapest Process. http://www.icmpd.org/Budapest-Process.1528.0.html. Accessed February 12, 2012.

ICMPD 2012b: Mission Statement. www.icmpd.org/ABOUT-US.1513.0.html. Accessed May 31, 2012.

ICMPD 2012c: The Mediterranean Transit Migration Dialogue. www.icmpd.org/MTM.1558.0.html. Accessed May 31, 2012.

i-Map 2012: www.imap-migration.org/index.php?id=471. Accessed June 5, 2012.

Karakayali, Serhat 2008: *Gespenster der Migration.* Bielefeld: Transcript Verlag.

Karrer, Christina, Regula Turtschi & Maritza Le Breton Baumgartner 1996: *Entschieden im Abseits: Frauen in der Migration.* Zurich: Limmat Verlag.

Keller, Reiner 2008: *Michel Foucault.* Konstanz: UVK Verlagsgesellschaft mbH.

Kofman, Eleonore & Rosemary Sales 1998: Migrant Women and Exclusion in Europe. *The European Journal of Women's Studies* 5:3–4, 381–399.

Lahav, Gallya & Virginie Guiraudon 2000: Comparative Perspectives on Border Control: Away from the Border and Outside the State. In: Peter Andreas & Timothy Snyder (eds.), *The Wall around the West: State Borders and Immigration Control in North America and Europe.* New York & Oxford: Rowman & Littlefield.

Lenz, Ramona 2009: "We have to convince them that they are victims". In: Jutta Baccas (ed.), Illegale Migration in Südosteuropa. Unpublished manuscript.

Lindqvist, Beatriz 2007: Migrant Women in Ambiguous Business: Examining Sex Work across National Borders in the Baltic Sea Region. In: Erik Berggren (ed.), *Irregular Migration, Informal Labour and Community: A Challenge for Europe.* Maastricht: Shaker Publishing.

Lutz, Helma 2007: *Vom Weltmarkt in den Privathaushalt.* Opladen: Budrich.

Lutz, Helma 2008: Gender in the Migratory Process. Lecture at the Conference on Theories of Migration and Social Change, St. Ann's College, Oxford, July 1–3, 2008.

Marcus, George E. 1995: Ethnography in/of the World System: The Emergence of Multi-Sited Ethnography. *Annual Review of Anthropology* 24, 95–117.

Mezzadra, Sandro 2009: Bürger und Untertanen: Die postkoloniale Herausforderung der Migration in Europa. In: Sabine Hess & Jana Binder (eds.), *No integration?! Kulturwissenschaftliche Beiträge zu Fragen von Migration und Integration in Europa.* Bielefeld: Transcript Verlag.

Migmap 2006: Governing Migration: A Virtual Cartography of European Migration Policies. Map 1: Actors. www.transit-migration.org/migmap/home_map1.html. Accessed May 24, 2012.

Mohanty, Chandra Talpade 1988: Aus westlicher Sicht: Feministische Theorie und koloniale Diskurse. *Beiträge zur feministischen Theorie und Praxis: Modernisierung der Ungleichheit – weltweit* 23, 149–162.

Morokvasic, Mirjana 1984: "Birds of Passage are also Female". *International Migration Review* 18, 890–910.

MTV 2012: EXIT. http://www.mtv.de/article/2009-02-10/23010643-mtv-exit-when-will-i-feel-love.html. Accessed February 13, 2012.

Ogata, Sadako 1997: Flüchtlinge und Migranten: Möglichkeiten der Steuerung von Wanderungsbewegungen. In: Steffen Angenendt (ed.), *Migration und Flucht.* Munich: Bundeszentrale für politische Bildung, pp. 239–247.

Pro Asyl 2008: Neue Recherchen und Dokumente zur Situation von Schutzsuchenden in Griechenland. http://www.proasyl.de/fileadmin/proasyl/fm_redakteure/Asyl_in_Europa/Griechenland/Neue_Recherchen_Griechenland_Endversion.pdf. Accessed May 31, 2012.

Puar, Jasbir 2007: *Terrorist Assemblages: Homonationalism in Queer Times.* Durham & London: Duke University Press.

Ratfisch, Phillip & Stephan Scheel 2010: Migrationskontrolle durch Flüchtlingsschutz. In: Sabine Hess & Bernd Kasparek (eds.), *Grenzregime: Diskurse, Praktiken, Institutionen in Europa.* Berlin: Association A.

Ravenstein, Ernest George 1885: The Laws of Migration. *Journal of the Statistical Society of London* 48:2, 167–235.

Rodriguez, Encarnacion Gutierrez 2011: Intersektionalität oder: Wie nicht über Rassismus sprechen? In: Sabine Hess, Nicola Langreiter & Elisabeth Timm (eds.), *Intersektionalität revisited.* Bielefeld: Transcript Verlag.

Schöning-Kalender, Claudia 1989: *Frauenhandel in Deutschland.* Bonn: Dietz.

Schwenken, Helen 2006: *Rechtlos aber nicht ohne Stimme.* Bielefeld: Transcript Verlag.

Shore, Cris & Susan Wright 1997: Policy: A New Field of Anthropology. In: Cris Shore & Susan Wright (eds.), *Anthropology of Policy.* London: Routledge.

Speer, Marc 2010: Die Ukraine als migrantisch genutztes Transitland. In: Sabine Hess & Bernd Kasparek (eds.), *Grenzregime: Diskurse, Praktiken, Institutionen in Europa.* Berlin: Association A.

Spivak, Gayatri Chakravorty 1990: *The Post-Colonial Critic:*

Interviews, Strategies, Dialogues. Edited by Sarah Harasym. New York & London: Routledge.

Surtees, Rebecca 2007: Listening to Victims: Experiences of Identification, Return and Assistance in South-Eastern Europe, Vienna: icmpd. www.anti-trafficking.net/251.html?&tx_icmpd_pi2[document]=593&cHash=6688569e46. Accessed May 31, 2012.

Tsianos, Vassilis 2008: Die Karte Europas und die Ströme der Migration. In: *Grundrisse: October 2008*. www.linksnet.de/de/artikel/23757. Accessed May 31, 2012.

Vasta, Ellie 2008: The Paper Market: 'Borrowing' and 'Renting' of Identity Documents. *University of Oxford Centre on Migration, Policy and Society, Working Paper No. 61.* www.compas.ox.ac.uk/fileadmin/files/Publications/working_papers/WP_2008/WP0861%20Ellie%20Vasta.pdf. Accessed May 31, 2012.

UN.GIFT 2007: Joint Conference of the Republic of Turkey, UNODC, Budapest Process and the Organisation of the Black Sea Economic Cooperation (BSEC) on "Trafficking in the Black Sea Region". www.ungift.org/ungift/en/re_turkey_press_release.html. Accessed February 12, 2012.

UNODC 2004: United Nations Convention against Transnational Organized Crime and the Protocols thereto. www.unodc.org/documents/treaties/UNTOC/Publications/TOC%20Convention/TOCebook-e.pdf. Accessed May 23, 2012.

US Department of State 2012: Office to Monitor and Combat Trafficking in Persons. www.state.gov/j/tip/. Accessed May 24, 2012.

Walters, Wiliam 2002: Mapping Schengenland: Denaturalizing the Border. *Environment & Planning: Society & Space* 20:5, 561–580.

Walters, William 2010: Foucault and Frontiers: Notes on the Birth of the Humanitarian Border. In: Ulrich Bröckling, Susanne Krasmann & Thomas Lemke (eds.), *Governmentality: Current Issues and Future Challenges.* London: Routledge.

Sabine Hess is Professor of Cultural Anthropology and European Ethnology at the University of Göttingen. Her most recent book on migration and border-regime research is edited with Bernd Kasparek, *Grenzregime: Diskurse, Praktiken, Institutionen in Europa* (Border Regimes: Discourses, Practices, Institutions in Europe) (2010/2012).
(shess@uni-goettingen.de)

WHO IS AFRAID OF FRANKENSTEIN?
Polish Debate on In-Vitro Fertilization

Magdalena Radkowska-Walkowicz

The in-vitro fertilization (IVF) technology has been in use in Poland for over 20 years, with success and social approval. However, in 2007 a vehement debate on moral, legal, and economic aspects of applying this technology of assisted procreation broke out. This was related to the gaps in Polish legislation lacking the regulations concerning the IVF, especially concerning the coverage by the public health-care system. Moreover, the Catholic voices demanding prohibition of the IVF had been multiplying and intensifying. The article follows this debate, investigates the discursive strategies employed to oppose IVF, and analyses different positions, especially the argumentation of the opponents, and the narratives by those who struggle with infertility.

Keywords: in-vitro fertilization, reproductive rights, the Catholic Church, Poland, Frankenstein

The in-vitro fertilization (IVF) technology has been in use in Poland for over twenty years, with success and social approval. However, at the end of 2007 a vehement debate on moral, legal, and economic aspects of applying this technology of assisted procreation broke out. Then the Minister of Health announced she would launch efforts to finance IVF from the state budget and in that way broke the silence over new reproductive technologies in Poland. This article focuses on the Polish IVF debate. I situate it within a global context, explore its local specificity, and examine its cultural and social parameters and implications. My analysis concentrates on the rhetoric and the discursive strategies used by the main participants as well as the narratives of people struggling with infertility. I am especially interested in reasons for opposing the use of IVF (apart from the most obvious ones, such as accumulating political capital or obeying the Catholic doctrine), mainly because it is the opponents' voices that are best heard in Polish media, imposing the IVF debate's language and thereby shaping the ways of thinking about assisted reproductive technologies (ART). Furthermore, while many works in social analysis critically examine technological optimism, typically drawing on Foucault's critique of modern biopolitics (see e.g., Franklin & Ragoné 1998; for critiques of ART see, e.g., Inhorn & von Balen 2002; Thompson 2002), few anthropological studies have explored voices of disapproval of IVF (e.g., Turney 1998; Throsby 2004: 3–6).

At this point, it needs to be added that to formulate opinions on ART means to engage in political action. This is especially true in the case of Poland, where feminist voices are weak and reproductive rights are both limited and not respected (Graff 2003). Besides, the IVF debate is part of a larger discussion regarding the influence of the Church on policy-making and social life in Poland.

Although Western, especially North-American, socio-cultural anthropology and feminist critique have long explored the challenges posed by reproductive technologies (e.g., Franklin & Ragoné 1998; Ginsburg & Rapp 1995), in Eastern Europe, "the social and cultural meanings and effects of ARTs are heavily understudied" (de Jong & Tkach 2009b: 15; the problem of ART in Europe is explored, e.g., in these works: Bonaccorso 2004, 2009; de Jong & Tkach 2009a; Saetnan, Oudshoorn & Kirejczyk 2000). While one can find works by Polish authors exploring legal and bioethical problems related to IVF, anthropological research on ART practically does not exist in Poland.

In what follows, I offer an anthropological perspective drawing on qualitative methods, primarily discourse analysis. I focus on the largest Polish media: television stations (both public and private), the press (newspapers, weekly and monthly magazines), and the Internet. Drawing from the Internet, I analyse, firstly, journalistic publications, including those published on websites endorsed by the Catholic Church (e.g., opoka.pl, fronda.pl, adonai.pl), and secondly, the biggest Polish Internet forums pertaining to infertility, where infertile women tell their life histories and exchange information about their treatments. The main sites are NaszBocian.pl, affiliated with the Polish Association for Treating Infertility and Supporting Adoption, "Nasz Bocian" ('Our Stork'), and Gazeta.pl, which belongs to the largest group of Polish online services. Both boards are open to the public. I am not taking into account ethnographic observations in infertility clinics or interviews with IVF users. Materials of this kind will be gathered in the second part of my research project.

Historical and Legal Context

Louise Brown, the first "test tube baby", was born in Oldham, Great Britain, in 1978. The procedure was carried out by the doctors of medicine Patrick Steptoe and Robert Edwards, who were awarded the 2010 Nobel Prize in Physiology or Medicine. The first child conceived using this method in Poland was a girl too. She was born on November 12th 1987, owing to the efforts of the team led by Professor Marian Szamatowicz of the Medical University of Białystok. Until October 2012 the child remained anonymous, as is the case with thousands of other children conceived in this way. At that time, after the first Polish IVF,

> The media went crazy. (...) Białystok was deluged with letters. One priest would rail from the pulpit about the inhumane practices of the clinic, which, according to him, were even more harmful than drug addiction and drunkenness, and the women would talk of their dreams in which they were cuddling babies. They were begging, writing that their husbands wanted to leave them, and that their hands were reaching out for other people's infants. (Skibniewska 2009)

It is estimated that around 5 million people worldwide have been born thanks to in-vitro fertilization.[1] In Poland there are currently over 40 clinics, which attain good pregnancy rates on a global comparison. The percentage of IVF children totals approximately 1.5 percent, which is the average for highly developed countries (although in Belgium, Slovenia, Denmark, the Netherlands and Sweden more than 3.0 percent of all babies born were conceived by ART[2]). These are, however, only estimates, for there are no mechanisms of extracorporeal fertilization registration in Poland, and the clinics carrying out these procedures are under no obligation to make the data pertaining to their activities public.

In Poland, ARTs are not regulated by law. Currently, several draft bills have been submitted to the Parliament, ranging from a very restrictive proposal to ban IVF and punish by prison for carrying out IVF to a liberal one holding no limitation on it.

The draft prepared by Jarosław Gowin (the current Minister of Justice) is the most hotly disputed draft among the legislative proposals. It prohibits the destroying and freezing of human embryos, treating them as human beings, to whom the constitutional protection of dignity applies. Therefore, the procedure cannot result in the production of additional embryos. One is only allowed to produce two of them and they both have to be implanted into a woman's body. This method, however, would only be available to married heterosexual couples where the woman is not older than forty years. Moreover, the draft bans the collection of donated eggs and the setting up of sperm banks. Assisted procreation would not be available to couples with genetic diseases or disabilities. Should such a solution be approved, Poland's regulations of this matter would be the most restrictive in Europe (even more so than the extremely restrictive laws adapted in Italy or Germany). A more open project of the ruling party allows for freezing and producing additional embryos and IVF would be available also for single mothers and unmarried couples. However, both draft projects do not provide state funding for the treatment. Nevertheless in October 2012 Prime Minister Donald Tusk declared that reimbursement for IVF will be made available without a change in law, as part of a Health Ministry three-year programme.

Social Acceptance of IVF and the Catholic Church

When mapping out attitudes towards IVF in the main Polish media, one can get the distinct impression that the main actors in the debate are politicians and priests. It is rarely that representatives of feminist circles appear in the press or television – as is also the case in other countries (Saetnan, Oudshoorn & Kirejczyk 2000). But, what may seem more surprising, particularly given the fact that infertility in Europe is strongly medicalized as well (cf. Martin 1987; Unnithan-Kumar 2004), biologists' and physicians' voices too are often ignored in the Polish public debate. The same may be said of the public presence of the infertile couples themselves, who are occasionally quoted in newspaper commentaries, anonymously or under changed names. This way of defining the main actors reduces the discussion to worldview issues and, effectively, the problem of IVF is debated alongside other socially sensitive questions, such as abortion, which is legal in Poland only when the woman's life or health is in danger, when the pregnancy is the result of a rape, or when the fetus is seriously malformed. In fact, IVF is often described as "refined" abortion (about similarity between IVF and abortion debates in Poland see Chełstowska 2011: 104).

Following the Polish debate on IVF one can get the impression that there are about as many opponents as there are supporters of IVF and that the line of division clearly overlaps with their partisan allegiances or even their adherence to the Catholic Church. However, the majority of Poles support IVF, regardless of their attachment to the Church or the party they vote for. According to the Public Opinion Research Centre's (CBOS) report from September 2012, 79 percent of Poles approve of the use of IVF by married couples that cannot have children, and 60 percent in the case of unmarried partners. 41 percent are against the availability of IVF to single women (while 48 percent support it) and 58 percent would allow the creation of additional embryos. Finally, the majority (79 percent) would want the cost of IVF to be at least partially refunded from the state budget (CBOS 2012). These data are similar to those from previous years. In 1995, the acceptance of IVF in the case of heterosexual couples amounted to 73 percent, in 2003 to 64 percent, and in 2005 it was 76 percent. The CBOS report for 2008 – the year the IVF opponents' media campaign was launched – shows a considerable decrease in the support, estimated at 60 percent (CBOS 2008). Nevertheless, and despite the clear and frequent statements issued by the Church firmly opposing the use of IVF, a year later the support was once again high and on the rise.

One may find it worthwhile to consider the origin of such a broad acceptance of extracorporeal fertilization in the country where, according to declarations, the percentage of Catholics may be as high as 90 percent depending on the study (Borowik 2001: 23) and where the second largest party in the Parliament is implicitly endorsed by the majority of Church hierarchs and ordinary priests, who declare their attachment to traditional values, including, of course, Catholic values. Moreover, the Polish Church, while internally divided, speaks unanimously.

One of the reasons that this powerful voice of the Church is not fully taken into account by the Polish society appears to be its moral liberalization in line with European trends. Thus, the Poles' attitudes towards sexual issues (such as premarital sex, non-monogamous relationships or the use of contraception) are far more lax than the official position of the Church would dictate. In other words, one can observe a strong individualization and privatization of religion; although one can hardly talk about an institutional crisis of the Catholic Church, as is the case in Western Europe, many people reinterpret the dogmas and teachings of the Church according to their own point of view.

Despite the strong opposition of the Church, there are about as many Catholics among the people undergoing IVF programmes as in the whole population of Poland. On the forum of the website Gazeta.pl, a girl nicknamed *iwonaczarna* writes:

> you know, it is so strange, because when you leave that place [the doctor's office, where the IVF procedure was carried out] you know that you have been given something that is already working inside of you. It's certainly fighting to stay there, but it is so small and you can't do anything to help him. When I received the two angels [embryos] I prayed for them to somehow manage. Yesterday was Sunday. I went to church and I cried asking Him to let them stay; He already has enough angels. I think it is the only sign that the closer it gets the more strongly you believe in all this. I know the Church speaks badly of this method, but I went there, for the first time in a very long time, so that even my husband was shocked. I hope He will spare us, I pray.

Family, Love and Laboratory

Paradoxically, this strong support of IVF is connected to the Poles' attachment to traditional values, especially to the family as a category organizing social life and hierarchy of values. Although new reproductive techniques have transformed common conceptions of kinship, the main symbols of the ideology of affinity in Euro-American culture have remained constant (Ragoné 2004: 342). It is still the birth of a child that turns a couple into a family, and the reason for the decision to use ART is the strong need to have an offspring. Being a childless couple, as many infertile couples would stress, carries a social stigma. A couple is, therefore, ready to use untraditional methods in order to achieve a traditional result: a family comprising a mum, a dad and at least one child. Although, as many researchers point out (e.g., Laqueur 2000), the development of techniques enabling the birth of a child without a sexual act results in the questioning of the previous concepts of the family, the family itself does not need to be questioned. Rather, IVF gets "normalized, naturalized, and contextualized within the narrowest and most traditional definitions of family" (Franklin & Roberts 2006: 188).

The problem of kinship and the diffusion of the category of the legal, genetic and biological parenthood do not appear in the Polish debate on IVF, including academic discourses. Mainstream media strongly condemn surrogate mothering, which is only discussed in economic-moral categories and almost always critically and sensationally (cf. Radkowska-Walkowicz 2012a). Access to reproductive technologies by gay couples is presented as one example of the kind of degeneration that ART can lead to. The subject of gamete donation or use of sperm banks is also rarely brought up. The debate stops at the level of the IVF procedure itself and the consequences of its use for future embryos.

Thus, the implicit notion of family is never put under discussion. Rather, what underpins the contention are two kinds of sentiments regarding the same ideal of a "full family": on the one hand, the extremely strong cultural need to have it, and, on the other, the fear that IVF would lead to its redefinition. When people who underwent IVF claim it gave them hope for starting a real family, the other side responds by criticizing them for their egoism and disregard for the value of marriage. Indeed, the notion marriage has become one of the rudimentary categories cited by the opponents of ART. Archbishop Henryk Hoser stresses the symbolic meaning of the marital act as "two in one body", and argues:

> It is only in this light that one can notice how very different the marital act is from the reproductive copulation of animals. A child – conceived as a result of a married life – is perceived as something we were given, something of a blessing. In the process of extracorporeal fertilization, however, a child is "made to order" using a particular technique. (Hoser 2009: 4)

Opponents of IVF set marital love against the vial. Marek Czachorowski from the Catholic University of Lublin admits that "objective facts show that in artificial insemination one does not conceive one's own child out of marital love – in an act expressing it – but out of something else, which does not express the specificity of marital love. At the start of our child's life it is not granted love" (Czachorowski 2008). In this rhetoric love is in the family by definition. It can only happen behind closed bedroom doors, where no one will inspect it, control it, or call it a rape.

On December 28, 2008, on the Holy Family Sunday, the Polish Episcopate issued a letter to the faithful, in which it touched upon the issue of IVF (List pasterski... 2008). The Episcopate pointed out that "God and only God is the Master of Life. Children are His gift to us and not a consumption good". Bishop Tadeusz Pieronek explicated it even more pointedly: "Couples who resort to IVF prefer buying a child to adopting it. They do not want an adopted child because they want to have a child that would be their own'. It is precisely the logic of the commodity, not the gift" (Pieronek 2009). The fear of commercialization of births and commodification of the sphere of procreation has accompanied research on IVF from its very beginning (cf. Turney 1998). In modern culture, these two ideas – the child and the commodity – are conflicting. The romantic mythology of childhood precludes pecuniary dealings. The lack of acceptance of IVF may thus be explained by the reluctance to link economic calculation to the concept of the family, which, as Collier, Rosaldo and Yanagisako (1992) argue, was built exactly in opposition to market relations. The Catholic Church perceives the role of the family in a similar way. However, one can also point out that in the European culture marriage was for centuries primarily an economic contract, and it is only due to more contemporary idealization that we perceive it in the romantic-spiritual light.

In Poland, IVF is sometimes viewed as a whim of the rich, a mark of class distinction. The lack of a refund policy together with the high costs of IVF contribute to the perception of ART users in economic categories. Couples who turn to infertility treatment clinics for help are accused of being egoistic, buying themselves a child and of taking a shortcut – such opinions are circulated widely despite the fact that IVF programmes involve long, unpleasant preparations, with little chance of success. The same arguments are put forward regarding people who do not have children – some campaigns aimed at promoting demographic growth have suggested that the lack of offspring results from a simple consumer choice.

Negotiating Oppositions

In their rhetoric, opponents of IVF often refer to oppositions between the commercial and the non-commercial, the public and the private, nature and technology. This kind of argumentation also appears in anthropological texts on reproductive technologies. For example, Franklin notes: "What was once a private act of love, intimacy, and secrecy is now a public act, a commercial transaction, and a professionally managed procedure" (1995: 336). In this very context, too, this way of thinking, especially the opposition between what is private and what is public, becomes problematic. Infertility has been so hard to cope with precisely because it is not a private problem; a child is a kind of social desire, Others' desire.

The private–public opposition is often used by the opponents of IVF – blurring the boundaries between these categories can be a source of fear and resistance. If, as they claim, due to these new technologies reproduction has left the private sphere and become a public issue, it has moved from the bedroom to the doctor's office, one may ask: What is it now that happens in the bedroom? What has taken the place of reproduction? Is it an empty space, waiting to be filled?

The above-mentioned oppositions are negotiated and rejected by users of IVF, but it does not mean that the anthropologist can simply ignore the commercial aspects of ART, which are stressed by many researchers (see Spar 2006; Strathern 1992). The Polish case, as the Italian before 2004 (see Bonaccorso 2004, 2009; Neresini & Bimbi 2000), is peculiar, because there is no legislation regulating the use of assisted conception. As a result, private clinics are the main players on the infertility treatment scene and practically they are neither inspected nor audited. Thus, patients who decided on IVF are largely dependent on the treatment offered by the private sector, which dictates conditions of the IVF treatment programme, manages the information on ART, and shapes the ART language. What is interesting, it is not only the highly medicalized language which consolidated the authority of physicians, but also the "common language" used to empathize with clients (Bonaccorso 2004). However, both patients and opponents do employ scientific rhetoric and refer to medical research. In this case, scientific language is used depending on the purposes of particular users; it is a common property that gets appropriated and negotiated.

Couples undergoing IVF tend to abandon the simple worldview built on oppositions, including that between romantic act in the marital bed and technological act in the Petri-Dash. In their narrations, they stress mutual love and care about the fight for a child. It is often the impossibility of conceiving that causes breaks in relationships. They are also capable of talking about the transfer of embryos in romantic categories. Magdalena Muszyńska, member of the Polish Association for Treating Infertility and Supporting Adoption, "Nasz Bocian", who had IVF, said in the Polish Parliament: "The moment of the transfer of embryos is one of the most beautiful moments in the life of a woman or a couple. It is then, at that moment, that our future, potential children are given to us, so that they could feel at home in my belly for the next 9 months" (2009: 27). Therefore, undergoing IVF procedure is not a transgressive activity. Here, the crossing of the line only serves to enter a safe, well-known path of narration, in line with the reigning models. In order to achieve that, one sacrifices a lot, including one's relationship with the Catholic Church, which for many people is painful.

According to opponents of IVF, all the planned actions aimed at infertility, also those supported by the Church, are only an addition to God's plan. The gift – not a commodity – will come when one does not expect it. IVF, with its fastidiousness, is at variance with the miraculous work of numbers. The whole preparatory protocol, from the puncture to the transfer of the fertilized egg, is described to the patients in detail – it involves strictly dosed portions of appropriate medicines, and a close monitoring of the cycle. A scientific description encapsulates what has, until this point, carried an aura of mystery. The oppositions of control and spontaneity, technology and mystery, or gift and commodity have a long tradition both in common thought and in the scientific worldview. Their roots lie in the old division of nature and culture. It is, however, such technologies as "in vitro" that show that today this opposition has lost its force and, while it is still used as a rhetorical tool, it is not sufficient for the elucidation of a complex social phenomenon. The analysis of Internet message boards relating to infertility demonstrates it well.

There is a tendency on many of them, not only in Polish Internet forums, to describe their participants in reference to their fight against infertility. One can very often find such a description in the signatures of participants of Internet conversations. The list of female participants, who after long efforts finally gave birth to a child, is as follows (www.nasz-bocian.pl):

JULI01 - I ICSI, crio 2 embr. blast. B i <8B (Iw:E-600, P-22, bHCG<1; IIw:P-41), 3 angels [i][i][i] and son Kubuś, DOB 25.05.08

kumkwak - I ICSI 2 blast. B (Iw:E-2605, P-56,

bHCG-2.5; IIw:E-1837, P-72.8, bHCG 27.2; IIIw:E-4295, P-133, bHCG-237; IVw:E-3952, P-122, bHCG 3393) twins! Agatka and Ada, DOB 24.06.08

carmen81 4Y efforts, weak little soldiers, jumping FSH, 2008 1 ICSI, 1 crio - , herbal 3, my natural miracle 16.04 I've seen 2 lines, 19.04 HCG 177, 21.04. HCG 489, 14.05 12mm with a little beating heart

malgosia1978 3x IUI unsuccessful, PCO, I IVF 04.2008 6w-I usg 2 beans, 8w - 1 angel, 11w II angel, I 2009 IVF unsuccessful, waiting for crio since February 2009 herbal 3, beta 20.04.2009 - 4492 MIRACLE!!!!! Allow him to stay

What seems to be an extremely technical language is shot through with elements having very little in common with it. There are angels (referring to a child who died before being born), a miracle, a "12mm with a little beating heart". They neutralize the technical description. The final stage is a diminutive name, a child, a human being. In descriptions that do not end in a name, there is a potential; it legitimizes the actions one takes. These descriptions encapsulate almost everything the given person has gone through in her fight against infertility. In this extremely formalized way, women legitimize their participation in the infertility community and present their biographies of reproductive medical interventions, which have become a significant part of their self-identity narratives. This kind of narrative strategy does not mean that women and their children (potential or real) are reduced to mathematical and medical symbols and dehumanized, or de-individualized. In this case, medical technology gives hope that series of symbols will turn into a child's name (on the use of discursive strategies by couples who have had unsuccessful IVF, see Throsby 2004). Thus, it is not a process of disembodiment, as one could suppose. "Self", defined in this way, becomes indeed a bodily phenomenon – open and ready for technological interventions. IVF does not separate from the body, which is subject to wanton nature or, as one woman wrote on the Internet forum, cruel statistics: a body, which is socially contextualized and controlled. Rather, it allows for the body to become rediscovered, re-experienced and, to some degree, controlled. These women are not passive victims, cultural dupes, as early feminists indicated (see van Balen & Inhorn 2002: 15, Thompson 2002, 2005: 55–75). They actively engage with technology. Thus, medical intervention need not be perceived as oppressive technology or even as "giving nature a helping hand", but it might, instead, be understood as an ally in the unequal fight with nature.

Nevertheless, I agree with Monica Bonaccorso's suggestion:

> Technological newness in the making of babies is used to stress the inefficiency of a body, which is not simply unreproductive, but often unwilling to welcome/receive technology. The emphasis on the bodies of couples is extreme. It is phenomenal the way in which, from being an intervention that helps couples, technologies of procreation turn into interventions to be aided by couples. Technology thus stands, at once, for both aid and its reverse, progression and arrest. (2004: 90)

Many couples treat the IVF procedure as an element in a certain technical puzzle. However, one can also come across quite other sentiments: "After the puncture under a short anaesthetics I was given breakfast and taken care of wonderfully, and the transfer itself was such a mystical experience (my husband was sitting next to me) that it was even more mystical than the last attempts under a duvet, using natural methods" (kolebeczka, forum *Niepłodność* [*Infertility*], Gazeta.pl). Another description shows even more convincingly that the language of technology does not have to be at odds with the language of emotions:

> I have just returned from Szczecin and, 3 days after the puncture, I have two beautiful 10A1 and 6A1 little embryos and one embryo (just for the purpose of competition, so that the good two ones do not get lazy with the division) that will not become 3B1 pregnancy. I cannot look at them enough!!!! Now, I can only wait and hope at least one of them stays with me, which is what I wish you from the bottom of my heart. (luna67, forum *Niepłodność*, Gazeta.pl)

Mystery can thus stealthily enter the laboratory, appear among the vials, on the glass, in the presence of a white-coat-wearing doctor. And the embryos, labelled with letter-numerical code, can be treated as the wished-for, potential children.

On the one hand, infertile women indicate the emancipatory potential of technology and the usefulness of this kind of language in the process of creating women's self-identities and biographies. On the other, one can see the process of normalization of technology. That process is well described in the research literature (de Jong & Tkach 2009a; Franklin & Roberts 2006: 175, 223–224; Thompson 2005; Throsby 2004; Cussins 1998). Thompson (2005) and de Jong (2009) are right linking this process to practices of naturalization, statistification and routinization. It is noticeable in the Polish debate on IVF, too. But one can also observe a reverse practice: describing IVF as the process inconsistent with the nature, biology and social order. The Episcopate is clear about it: "This method is contrary to God's law and human nature" (Komunikat z 352... 2010).

Criminalization of IVF is the common discursive strategy employed in Poland to condemn the use of IVF. For instance, Archbishop Józef Michalik states: "The Killing of an innocent man is a crime and sometimes cruelty and it can never be justified. Both abortion and the elimination of a conceived life in a test-tube is a murder, for a man starts to exists from the moment when two cells: male and female, fuse" (Michalik 2009: 2). The patients of infertility treatment clinics tend to justify their decision by claiming that:

> None of us, people who are infertile, would permit such wickedness as the discarding and destroying of embryos to happen. It is also worth noticing that despite the lack of legal regulations, no one would commit such an evil deed and hurt the embryos. It is true that some of them die, but it happens in nature, too. Does it mean that 99% of women are murderers, and serial ones, at that? (Szczerba 2009: 13)

The well-known argument from the discussion on abortion that claims life already begins at the moment of fertilization is countered by the other party with two kinds of arguments. The first one is connected to the naturalization strategy and points out that when fertilization takes place in a woman's body, many embryos also die even before they nestle in the uterus. The second kind of argumentation underlines that most embryos produced artificially will be given their chance, they will be transferred to the woman's organism, and therefore is not, in fact, based on another definition of the beginning of life than the Catholic definition. Hence, there is no simple opposition between religious and modern (scientific) ideas of the foetal/maternal relation. The Catholic view of the beginning of life encounters the contemporary, modern view, connected with the development of new medical technologies, destabilizing the boundary between mother and foetus. As Susan Squier notes, "the fetus *inside* is increasingly treated as if it were already *outside*, the rightful subject of medical, social and legal intervention" (1999: 102).

Women on Internet forums relating to infertility almost always refer to the frozen embryos as their own potential children that will be implanted into a uterus, or – although one can come across such declarations less frequently – put up for adoption. Although the couples are not indifferent to the fate of the embryos, they realize that only some of them have a chance of becoming a child: "there is no such thing as the groan of abandoned embryos (...) there are no hecatombs, mass murders, and we are talking about a phenomenon where we fight against the SCARCITY, and not the excess. (...) People line up in a queue to adopt those supposedly 'unwanted embryos'" (Krawczak 2010).

It is worthwhile to stress the category of nature which appears frequently in both sides' argumentations and which still turns out to be a powerful factor legitimizing moral decisions and opinions of both parties of the dispute. According to users of reproductive technologies, IVF supports the work of nature that today is imperfect – it is on its behalf that they fend off the effects of civilization, which causes infertility. According to the IVF opponents, it acts against nature and may ultimately lead to the degeneration of our species.

The opposition between nature and culture and, in particular, its interpretational-explanatory powers, still carries considerable weight. It is the modern culture's reference to biology, to the gene as the basis of human identity that makes ART, and especially IVF or surrogate mothering, an increasingly popular way of "acquiring" children by infertile couples as an alternative to adoption. "Our" child means a child who will have our genes (or at least the genes of one of the parents). New reproductive technologies change ideas of kinship, as has been observed by many researchers, and simultaneously reinforce the biological, genetic notion of relatedness (e.g., Ragoné 2004; Edwards et al. 1993). The modern definition of an individual being a bundle of genetic information (cf. Le Breton 2004; Rabinow 1996) serves to legitimize ART methods also in Poland.

Heritage of Frankenstein

Although one of the dividing lines in the Polish debate over IVF is determined by attitudes towards science, it would be false to claim that on one side of the debate there are only supporters of the unrestrained development of science, and its staunch opponents on the other. It is true that the modern compulsion to constantly develop, in the Faustian version, is very often criticized by opponents of IVF. They point to the dangers of constant development, invoking the unambiguous persona of doctor Frankenstein, who paid for the attempt to manipulate the human body and nature with his life and the life of his family. Frankenstein, as a figure embodying the fear of the excessive interference of science and technology in human life is still surprisingly topical. "What is the literary figure of Frankenstein, a creature brought to life against nature, if not a prototype of in vitro?" asked one of the important actors in the Polish political scene, the Catholic bishop, Tadeusz Pieronek (2009).

The fact that a test-tube baby is happy and normal – in contrary to Frankenstein's monster – seems to be the scandal. As Jon Turney (1998) writes, the birth of Louise Brown was so shocking precisely because she was a normal child. The crossing of the boundary between nature and technology, the fact that technology entered the area of reproduction, which until now has been a taboo subject, associated with mystery, evokes fears and creates revenge-seeking monsters (cf. Radkowska-Walkowicz 2012b). And monsters have no families. Artificial lives, in this discourse, should be lonely and miserable. "We are well familiar with the experiences of therapists who observed that children conceived by means of IVF have the features characteristic of people who escaped death" – says Beata Rusiecka, a psychologist. There is, however, no research or accounts of the interested parties to support her words.

> Such a person is racked with intense guilt, asking himself questions like: why do I live, do I have the right to live? Similar experiences are characteristic of people whose siblings were aborted (...) Similarly, children conceived thanks to IVF, because of the fact that in the embryonic stage they were selected by a doctor from among the other children, feel deeply insecure as to their right to live. (...) They give the impression that they are not at all connected to their parents. They are aware that those are their parents, but it seems they do not emotionally experience the ties with them, as if they were incapable of establishing a psychological contact with them and had a deep-seated fear of their parents. The parents, too, have difficulties establishing a warm, spontaneous, spiritual contact with their children. (Rusiecka, *Nasz Dziennik*, cited for: http://adonai.pl/nieplodnosc/?id=90)

Loneliness was the punishment of the monster – and Frankenstein remained lonely. In this rhetoric, also test-tube babies are lonely. The ghost of doctor Frankenstein has been haunting us for almost 200 years and, it seems, it has no intention of stopping. However, science is not criticized as a whole. Today, it becomes – next to nature – a very important legitimizing category, because in modern society, especially, scientific and medical language is able to influence cultural meanings (an ability widely described in anthropological literature, see e.g. chapters by Bonaccorso, Stones and Donner in Unnithan-Kumar [ed.] 2004). Thus, in their argumentation relating to the issues of reproduction, the representatives of the Catholic Church increasingly often cite scientific research and gladly use the language generated by the world of science. Therefore, when they warn us, in line with the Church doctrine, against the use of contraceptives, they refer to research that is supposed to show that hormonal methods are harmful to our health, and the mechanical or chemical ones ineffective. The arguments put forward in the debate over the beginning of life, too, are based on such notions as DNA, the gene, gamete fusion, etc.

In the statement issued by the bioethical conference of the Polish Episcopate one can read:

> One of the frequently advanced views is that an embryo is not a human being. Such opinions have no scientific foundation and are the expression of an ideology that denies human beings their right to life from conception. The truth that our life begins at the moment of conception is not based on religious stipulations, but is a rational stance resulting from the current scientific knowledge. (…) The opinion of the Church is also based on premises of the biological and medical nature. IVF procedures are extremely dangerous to the mother's health (…) A hormone stimulation therapy (…) can lead to a liver function disorder, the development of cancer or venous or arterial thrombosis. (…) Research carried out in the USA and Australia, where the IVF methods have been used longer than in Poland, show that children conceived in an artificial way suffer three times more often from congenital defects, complications and genetic diseases. We cite these arguments to show that the teaching of the Church (…) is corroborated by the results of scientific research. (Oświadczenie Zespołu… 2010)[3]

Thus, the Church frequently refers to medicine. Esther Peperkamp points out this practice in relation to sexual education and "natural family planning" in the Polish Catholic youth movement. She claims that defining the modern body as a secularized body is false, as it "completely ignores the changes that have taken place within Christian traditions themselves" (Peperkamp 2008: 132). Religion has not simply been replaced by modern medicine; rather, the latter "provides the technological means to practice a virtuous life, although it does so with unintended effects, transforming the face of religion and religious authority" (2008: 133).

Gender Biases in IVF Debate

This trend is well exemplified by NaProTechnology (Natural Procreative Technology), the infertility treatment method in accord with the teachings of the Catholic Church and promoted as an alternative to IVF. It was designed 30 years ago by the American physician Thomas W. Hilgers, the founder and director of the *Pope Paul VI Institute* in Omaha, Nebraska. He and his supporters claim that this method is very effective and achieves higher pregnancy rates than IVF. It is, www.naprotechnology.com says, "a new women's health science that monitors and maintains a woman's reproductive and gynecological health". It is, above all, based on the Creighton Model Fertility Care System – the observation of the woman's fertility cycle – conducted by trainers who do not need to have medical education, but it does not exclude medical and surgical treatments (as laparoscopy or surgical removal of endometriosis).

NaProTechnology found extremely favourable conditions in Poland. Today, one can both read and hear about it in important Polish media, including the public ones; the method has also been debated in the Polish Parliament. Both on discussion forums and during other discussions, women who underwent IVF procedures are usually sceptical of NaProTechnology, claiming that it has nothing new to offer apart from the diagnostics focusing mainly on the observation of the fertility cycle each of them underwent during the many years of fighting for a child.

One can notice that it is an entry onto the ground of hard science and an attempt to defeat Western biomedicine by "borrowing" from its achievements, terms, etc. Science is here understood as a common, universal good that has so far not always been put to good use. It needs to be taken from the hands of doctor Frankenstein and show its humanistic (Catholic) character. Implied here is, therefore, a criticism of biomedicine, perceived as harmful to a woman. NaProTechnology could thus seem close to early feminist critiques, which drew attention to patriarchy and technocracy ingrained in biomedicine and to the reduction of the woman's role to that of an object in the game of men's technological fantasies (e.g., Corea 1985; Stanworth 1987).[4] However, when one looks at NaProTechnology more closely, it turns out that it is a proposition that strengthens traditional gender imagery. For example, the motto of one website promoting this method is: "Unleashing the Power in a Woman's Cycle." It draws a direct connection between the vitality of the family and the woman's body. However, statistics pertaining to infertility unequivocally show that today, for at least half of the couples, infertility is related to a problem on the part of the man. Although the advocates of NaProTechnology seem to notice the problem of men's infertility, they claim that the success of infertility treatment still critically depends on the observation of the woman's cycle, or on such surgical procedures as restoration of the patency of the oviducts (thus, still directed at the woman's body). Asked whether NaProTechnology cures men's infertility, Hilgers answers: "If, in line with its indications, we get to know the woman's cycle and determine the fertile period, then, even if the sperm is of low quality, we can increase the probability of impregnation by 35%" (2009: 14). It is, then, the woman that is responsible for the lack of offspring and supposed to create favourable conditions for the child to appear in the domestic hearth. Moreover, the woman is blamed for her infertility. According to the IVF opponents, lack of offspring is a result of the use of hormonal contraception, early age of sexual initiation and delay in starting a family, and even wearing short skirts. In short: the modern woman conducts herself badly and the punishment for this sin is childlessness.

As van Balen and Inhorn note: "women worldwide appear to bear the major burden of infertility, in terms of blame for the reproductive failing; personal anxiety, frustration, grief, and fear; marital duress, dissolution, and abandonment; social stigma and community ostracism" (2002: 7). Being a mother, now or in the future, is a strong element of the self-identity narrative of the vast majority of women not only in Euro-American culture; when infertility disrupts the plot, women very often feel helpless and confused (Kirkman 2008: 243; on male stigma related to infertility, see Becker 2000: 44–49; Thompson 2005: 128).

What seems to be disturbing for the opponents of IVF is the man's participation in infertility diagnosis. In the Catholic weekly magazine *Niedziela* (with circulation about 150,000) one reads: "In order to obtain the man's genetic material, the act of masturbation is necessary. This should be enough to discard this method of reproduction" (Konik-Korn 2008: 25). Reading this kind of statement one can get the impression that the old bête-noire of the moralists resurfaces once again. Indeed, the authors of NaProTechnology.com argue that the standard medical evaluation of a man's infertility is "dehumanizing and humiliating", because men are "placed in a washroom with pornographic literature and asked to masturbate, [while] (…) the seminal fluid can be collected with an act of intercourse, at home, in a way which is not contraceptive". By masturbating in a clinic a man not only enters the path of sin, but also degrades himself as a man. Androcentric sensitivity cannot stand the way the material for IVF is obtained. What should stay inside the body flows out of it and is then given to a laboratory technician for analysis. Maybe masculinity, unlike femininity in this rhetoric, is not to be the subject of discussion and generally should not be evaluated catalogued, and verified?

Today, it is typically still women that are blamed for the inability to conceive. The persistent stereotype of a strong man with strong sperm (often referred to as "soldiers" or "the army") makes many Polish men reluctant to undergo tests. Infertility treatment remains the domain of women. It is they who are the participants of discussion forums on infertility (where they often complain about their partners' lack of commitment), seek solutions to the problem, and encourage their husbands and partners to have semen analyses. On the one hand, therefore, infertility treatment illustrates traditional family relations, where the woman is responsible for reproduction and supposed to create domestic hearth. On the other hand, in-vitro fertilization constitutes a space of women's activity and agency. The fact that IVF procedures are not refunded and the idea of a partial or total ban of IVF may thus be perceived as denying women a possibility to be rational, moral actors, who make their own decisions concerning reproduction (on women's agency in the context of reproductive technologies see Unnithan-Kumar 2004).

Urszula Dudziak from the Catholic University of Lublin asks: "Can a woman be truly happy, when she is treated as a stud mare?" (2008). "What right does the laboratory technician-inseminator have to be given the privilege that should be her husband's in the context of the act of a complete union?", asks psychologist Maria Klepacka-Środoń(2008). Maciej Barczentewicz, gynaecologist and president of the Foundation of John Paul II Institute for Marital Infertility Treatment, adds: "A technician replaces the marriage and God in giving life" (2008). May it be that what is so outraging here is the fact that a technician takes the man's right to the woman? When opponents of IVF claim that it deprives women of their dignity and causes them to be treated as stud mares, and when they write about the pain and serious threats to health (such as overstimulation), they make women the victims of the bad, androcentric biomedicine, oppressive to the female body. The example of Poland proves wrong the view that sees women simply as victims of technology. Today, women fight for their right to have access to state-of-the-art medical technologies, which, among other things, allow them to avoid suffering. Presenting women as victims of evil technology, or using the language of the pro-life movement and the "civilization of death" is also a way of depriving them of a chance to voice their opinion. Voices of infertile couples are rarely heard in the Polish traditional media. Somebody always speaks on their behalf. The victims are no longer the important social actors and have no right to a rational voice.

However, we may also note that power is already ingrained in the very compulsion to be a mother, which drives a woman to surrender to technology. It is not the woman's choice, but rather a restriction, a means to subjugate her; it has risen to the point of absurd. For the very desire to be a mother can be perceived as a desire of the current discourses producing norms of motherhood which bind women to their identity as mothers and offer specific and ever more technologically perfect methods of dealing with the problem of infertility, at once restricting the ground for new ways of defining themselves outside of motherhood (cf. Sawicki 1999; on feminist studies on ART see McNeil 2007, especially part II). Franklin and Roberts note: "The possibility that conception can be achieved through IVF (...) produces *a new form of social responsibility* as well as new choices" (2006: 189). Moreover, a result of this process is "an intensification of women's investment in procreation, realized in the regimented orientation and surveillance of her body for this purpose" (McNeil 2007: 86). In this context, Jane Sawicki writes about "new norms of health and responsibility in motherhood" (1991: 84) and McNeil designate it as "an extension of maternal responsibility" (2007: 87).

Conclusion

Discussions on IVF, as Turney (1998) rightly indicates, started before the birth of Louise Brown. One might suppose that after all arguments both in favour and against IVF have been advanced, IVF will be silently accepted as just another technology that appeared in our lives and, similarly to what happened to many other achievements in medicine, it will become invisible. However, debates which time and again break out with different strength in different countries, along with the powerful voice of the Catholic Church on this matter, show that this issue is neither straightforward nor closed. Poland, where one can watch the IVF debate go on, is not an exception. Such discussions take place in other countries as well and they very often include similar argumentations. At the same time, we deal with their local peculiarities visible, for instance, in different legal solutions adopted in particular countries: from very liberal in Great Britain, Israel or the Scandinavian countries, to restrictive ones in Germany, Italy, Austria or several US states. As I am writing these words it is still difficult to predict the fate of the Polish bioethical act. The Polish debate is similar to the one that took place in Italy, a fact related to the specific legal situation in both countries and their Catholic character. On the other hand, as Bonaccorso states, the Catholic framework "cannot be taken too much for granted" (2009: 1), and it seems reasonable to assume that in Poland religious beliefs do not have a determining influence on the negotiation and legitimization of decisions regarding medical intervention. Nevertheless, the Catholic Church does have a prominent role in politics and society and is influential in constructing the meanings assigned to reproduction. It seems that the Church is interested in sex, family and reproduction more than in other aspects of human life and that, de facto, it is interested in controlling women. Above all, this control occurs by means of language (see Graff 2001, 2003). The question is, can its discursive power and privileged position in the public debate change the popular attitude towards IVF?

The Catholic Church is undoubtedly the main actor in IVF debate in Polish mainstream media (the representatives of other Churches are not asked to take a stance on the issue, and their opinion is less radical). At the same time, however, public acceptance of reproductive technologies is very high. The voices of scientists or doctors are, in fact, scarce – although they have much influence on the infertile couples' decisions and ways of thinking about the treatment. People who decided to use IVF, rarely asked about their opinion by the mainstream media, discuss their views on Internet forums. But Internet, as Jill Allison (2011) argues convincingly in the context of the Irish IVF debate, rather than creating public discourse, reproduces silence and isolation.

Seemingly, Polish debate on IVF is marked by an oppositional way of thinking: on the one hand scientific, modern, and technical, and on the other religious, moral, and emotional. But these oppositions are negotiated both by the users of the reproductive technology and its opponents. They transcend simple binarism, typical for the language of ART that – as Bonaccorso points out – "always incorporates one thought and its opposite" (2004: 90). Moreover, all participants of the Polish debate use all kinds of argumentation: medical, ideological, ethical, and emotional. Thus, the language of the representatives of the Catholic Church is medicalized, while the language of scientists or physicians is full of emotional references, and women expressing themselves on Internet forums very often demonstrate expert knowledge.

What is interesting about the Polish debate on IVF is the strongly medicalized language of the Catholic activists. Moreover, the Catholic view is often close to the modern, scientific one. Simultaneously, the language of the debate remains full of moral and religious references. Thus, in churches, people pray for "IVF victims" and Jarosław Gowin, who endorses the restrictive draft of the bioethical act, claims that he can "almost hear the scream of despair of those tens of thousands of frozen embryos, feel their distress" (2009).

But it is not only frozen embryos that scream in this debate – one may point out the outcry of Catholic activists about genocide allegedly going on in IVF laboratories. It seems, however, that, more than the screams, it is silences and concealments that are crucial in the IVF discourse.

> The silence about infertility is "heard" as a resounding confirmation of fertility as the norm. Maintaining silence means that infertility is rarely mobilized to challenge the naturalization of gendered social expectations and heteronormative values. Silence obscures the fact that fertility is not universal and makes virtually impossible any dialectic move toward a denaturalization of fertility and motherhood. (Allison 2011: 6)

These silences are mostly connected with the social stigma associated with infertility and the hegemonic norms of motherhood. However, the silence is not only a part of private experience. Polish feminists remain silent about negative sides of ART and its reductive foundationalism (Rapp 2001), Polish gays do not talk about their reproductive rights and Polish Catholic activists ignore male infertility and the contemporary need to have a genetic offspring. Fertility clinics also resort to a kind of silence, as they are afraid of changes in the reproductive law. Lurking in the background is the issue of excessive interference of science in the contingency of the birth of a human being and, consequently, the possible dangers to the development of the human species. There is also a scarcity of arguments, shown so well in Andrew Niccol's film *Gattaca* (1997) – arguments related to genoism and the new social stratifications that may be awaiting us. The Polish debate on IVF focuses on the question of beginnings of life and the analysis of this problem in connection with the fierce debate on the admissibility of abortion. The two IVF discourses one may discern in Polish media portray IVF in opposite terms: one sees it as a technological nightmare and the heritage of Frankenstein, the other as a miraculous remedy for infertile couples.[5] Central to this discussion, however, are issues like family, tradition, and marriage – which all the main actors define similarly. Meanwhile, other questions, such as access to reproductive technologies by gay or lesbian couples, are not discussed at all.

Silence and concealment are the discursive strategies. Actors use them along with other strategies, like normalization and naturalization of ART; denormalization, de-naturalization, and criminalization of IVF; vilification of IVF users; monsterization of IVF children; victimization of infertile women; and medicalization of language.

What is at stake in this discursive play? First of all: women's position in the Polish society, especially within the family. And second: the role of the Catholic Church in Poland, its discursive power and the influence on the government, parliament, law and the choices of ordinary people.

Notes

1 According to ESHRE, the European Society of Human Reproduction and Embryology, http://www.eshre.eu/ESHRE/English/Guidelines-Legal/ART-fact-sheet/page.aspx/1061. Accessed August 20, 2012.

2 Ibid.

3 However, as e.g. Barbara Dolińska convincingly argues in the *Nauka* magazine, many arguments deployed by the Polish opponents of IVF are based on unreliable research, the cited data can be broadly interpreted or quote research without providing any references. It especially applies to the controversial issue of the health of children born by means of IVF (2009: 96).

4 More recent feminist critiques are less condemnatory and radical, but they, too, pay attention to the deeply gendered nature of reproductive technologies; see Inhorn & van Balen (2002: 15).

5 That, one should add, is not a Polish peculiarity; see Throsby (2004: 2).

References

Allison, J. 2011: Conceiving Silence: Infertility as Discursive Contradiction in Ireland. *Medical Anthropology Quarterly* 25:1, 1–21.

van Balen F. & M.C. Inhorn 2002: Introduction. Interpreting Infertility: A View from the Social Sciences. In: M.C. Inhorn & F. van Balen (eds.), *Infertility around the Globe: New Thinking on Childlessness, Gender, and Reproductive Technologies*. Berkeley, Los Angeles & London: University of California Press.

Barczentewicz, M. 2008: Niepłodność – dziecko dobrobytu. *Nasz Dziennik* 19, January 23. www.naszdziennik.pl/bpl_index.php?typ=my&dat=20080123&id=my21.txt. Accessed August 5, 2010.

Becker, G. 2000: *The Elusive Embryo: How Women and Men Approach New Reproductive Technologies*. Berkeley, Los Angeles & London: University of California Press.

Bonaccorso, M.F. 2004: Programmes of Gamete Donation: Strategies in (Private) Clinics of Assisted Conception. In: M. Unnithan-Kumar (ed.), *Reproductive Agency, Medicine and the State: Cultural Transformations in Childbearing*. New York & Oxford: Berghahn Books.

Bonaccorso, M.F. 2009: *Conceiving Kinship: Assisted Conception, Procreation and Family in Southern Europe*. New York & Oxford: Berghahn Books.

Borowik, I. 2001: Pluralizm jako cecha przemian religijnych w kontekście transformacji w Polsce. In: T. Doktór & I. Borowik (eds.), *Pluralizm religijny i moralny w Polsce*. Kraków: Nomos.

CBOS 2008: Opinions about Acceptability of In Vitro Fertilization. Research Report. January.

CBOS 2012: Postawy wobec stosowania zapłodnienia in vitro. Research Report. September.

Chełstowska, A. 2011: Stigmatisation and Commercialisation of Abortion Services in Poland: Turning Sin into Gold. *Reproductive Health Matters* 19, 37.

Collier, J.F., M.Z. Rosaldo & S.J. Yanagisako 1992: Is there a Family? New Anthropological Views. In: B. Thorne & M. Yalom (eds.), *Rethinking the Family: Some Feminist Ques-*

tions. Boston: Northeastern University Press.

Corea, G. 1985: *The Mother Machine: Reproductive Technologies from Artificial Insemination to Artificial Wombs*. New York: Harper & Row.

Cussins, Ch. 1998: Producing Reproduction: Techniques of Normalization and Naturalization in Infertility Clinics. In: S. Franklin & H. Ragoné (eds.), *Reproducing Reproduction: Kinship, Power and Technological Innovation*. Philadelphia: University of Pennsylvania Press.

Czachorowski, M. 2008: Metoda zła moralnie, bo nie szanuje człowieczeństwa. Z Markiem Czachorowskim rozmawia Justyna Wiszniewska. *Nasz Dziennik* 19, January 23. http://adonai.pl/nieplodnosc/?id=56. Accessed August 20, 2010.

Dolińska, B. 2009: Uczciwość i wiarygodność nauki – odpowiedzialność za słowa w walce o dopuszczalność in vitro. *Nauka* 4, 87–101.

Dudziak, U. 2008: Bezdroża In vitro. *Nasz Dziennik (dodatek Rodzina)*, January 23. http://www.szansaspotkania.net/index.php?page=10055. Accessed August 20, 2010.

Edwards, J., S. Franklin, E. Hirsch, F. Price & M. Strathern 1993: *Technologies of Procreation: Kinship in the Age of Assisted Conception*. Manchester: Manchester University Press.

Franklin, S. 1995: Postmodern Procreation: A Cultural Account of Assisted Reproduction. In: F.D. Ginsburg & R. Rapp (eds.), *Conceiving the New World Order: The Global Politics of Reproduction*. Berkeley: University of California Press.

Franklin, S. & H. Ragoné (eds.) 1998: *Reproducing Reproduction: Kinship, Power, and Technological Innovation*. Philadelphia: University of Pennsylvania Press.

Franklin, S. & S. Roberts 2006: *Born and Made: An Ethnography of Preimplantation Genetic Diagnosis*. Princeton: Princeton University Press.

Ginsburg, F.D. & R. Rapp (eds.) 1995: *Conceiving the New World Order: The Global Politics of Reproduction*. Berkeley: University of California Press.

Gowin, J. 2009: Aborcja zarodka to zabicie dziecka: Z Jarosławem Gowinem rozmawia Paulina Nowosielska-Kucharska. February 3. http://ekai.pl/wydarzenia/wywiad/x17960/polska-aborcja-zarodka-to-zabicie-dziecka. Accessed August 20, 2010.

Graff, A. 2001: *Swiat bez kobiet*. Warszawa: WAB.

Graff, A. 2003: Lost Between The Waves? The Paradoxes of Feminist Chronology and Activism in Contemporary Poland. *Journal of International Women's Studies* 4:2, 1–30.

Hilgers, T. 2009: Alternatywa istnieje: Z Thomasem Hilgersem rozmawiają Joanna Bątkiewicz-Brożek i Maciej Müller. *Kościół o metodzie in vitro: Bioetyka katolicka (bezpłatny dodatek)*, December 13, 14–15.

Hoser, H. 2009: Cywilizacyjna debata: O najważniejszych problemach bioetycznych z ks. abp. Henrykiem Hoserem rozmawia Marcin Przeciszewski. *Kościół o metodzie in vitro: Bioetyka katolicka (bezpłatny dodatek)*, December 13, 3–5.

Inhorn, M.C. & F. van Balen (eds.) 2002: *Infertility around the Globe: New Thinking on Childlessness, Gender, and Reproductive Technologies*. Berkeley, Los Angeles & London: University of California Press.

de Jong, W. 2009: Reproductive Technologies and the Concept of Normalisation. In: W. de Jong & O. Tkach (eds.), *Making Bodies, Persons and Families: Normalising Reproductive Technologies in Russia, Switzerland and Germany*. Berlin, Hamburg & Münster: LIT Verlag.

de Jong, W. & O. Tkach (eds.) 2009a: *Making Bodies, Persons and Families: Normalising Reproductive Technologies in Russia, Switzerland and Germany*. Berlin, Hamburg & Münster: LIT Verlag.

de Jong, W. & O. Tkach 2009b: Researching Reproductive Technologies in East and West. In: W. de Jong & O. Tkach (eds.), *Making Bodies, Persons and Families: Normalising Reproductive Technologies in Russia, Switzerland and Germany*. Berlin, Hamburg & Münster: LIT Verlag.

Kirkman, M. 2008: Being a "Real" Mum: Motherhood through Donated Eggs and Embryos. *Women's Studies International Forum* 31, 241–248.

Klepacka-Środoń, M. 2008: 40 lat "Humanae vitae". O ludzki kształt prokreacji: Z Marią Klepacką-Środoń rozmawia Małgorzata Jędrzejczyk. *Nasz Dziennik* 174, July 26–27. http://www.naszdziennik.pl/bpl_index.php?dat=20080726&typ=ro&id=ro13.txt. Accessed August 20, 2010.

Komunikat z 352 posiedzenia plenarnego Konferencji Episkopatu Polski, 2010. June 20, 2010. www.duszpasterstworodzin.gniezno.opoka.org.pl/go.php/pl/varia/2010/czerwiec/komunikat_z_352_zebrania.html. Accessed August 20, 2010.

Konik-Korn, M. 2008: Grzechy in vitro. *Niedziela* 2, 25.

Krawczak, A. 2010: List do redaktora naczelnego dziennika "Rzeczpospolita". www.nasz-bocian.pl/node/15804. Accessed August 20, 2010.

Laqueur, T.W. 2000: "From Generation to Generation": Imagining Connectedness in the Age of Reproductive Technologies. In: P.E. Brodwin (ed.), *Biotechnology and Culture: Bodies, Anxieties, Ethics*. Bloomington: Indiana University Press.

Le Breton, D. 2004: Genetic Fundamentalism or the Cult of the Gene. *Body & Society* 10:4, 1–20.

List pasterski Episkopatu Polski na Niedzielę Świętej Rodziny 2008, December 28. http://ekai.pl/wydarzenia/temat_dnia/x17191/biskupi-do-polskich-rodzin-nie-bojmy-sie-adoptowac-dzieci/?print=1. Accessed August 20, 2010.

Martin, E. 1987: *The Woman in the Body: A Cultural Analysis of Reproduction*. Milton Keynes: Open University Press.

McNeil, M. 2007: *Feminist Cultural Studies of Science and Technology*. London: Routledge.

Michalik, J. 2009: Egzamin z dekalogu. *Kościół o metodzie in vitro: Bioetyka katolicka (bezpłatny dodatek)*, December 13, 2.

Muszyńska, M. 2009: Zapłodnienie in vitro – szansa na godne

rodzicielstwo. *Wysłuchanie Obywatelskie*, February 23. www.federa.org.pl/Informacje/Wysluchaniezapis02.2009.pdf. Accessed August 20, 2010.

Neresini F. & F. Bimbi 2000: The Lack and the "Need" of Regulation for Assisted Fertilization: The Italian Case. In: A.R. Saetnan, N. Oudshoorn & M. Kirejczyk (eds.), *Bodies of Technology: Women's Involvement with Reproductive Medicine*. Ohio: Ohio State University Press.

Oświadczenie Zespołu Ekspertów KEP ds. Bioetycznych ws. in vitro 2010. March 24. http://www.piotrskarga.pl/ps,5005,2,0,1,I,informacje.html. Accessed August 20, 2010.

Peperkamp, E. 2008: The Fertile Body and Cross-Fertilization of Disciplinary Regimes. Technologies of Self in a Polish Catholic Youth Movement. In: N. Dyck (ed.), *Exploring Regimes of Discipline*. New York & Oxford: Berghahn Books.

Pieronek, T. 2009: Pierwowzorem in vitro jest Frankenstein. Z biskupem Tadeuszem Pieronkiem rozmawia Wojciech Harpula. http://wiadomosci.onet.pl/1527301,240,1,1,pierwowzorem_in_vitro_jest_frankenstein,kioskart.html. January 16. Accessed August 20, 2010.

Rabinow, P. 1996: *Essays in the Anthropology of Reason*. Princeton: Princeton University Press.

Radkowska-Walkowicz, M. 2012a: Aaaby wynająć brzuch: Antropologiczne konteksty macierzyństwa zastępczego. In: R.E. Hryciuk & E. Karolczuk (eds.), *Pozegnanie z Matka-Polka?* Warsaw: Warsaw University Press.

Radkowska-Walkowicz, M. 2012b: The Creation of "Monsters": The Discourse of Opposition to In Vitro Fertilization in Poland. *Reproductive Health Matters* 20, 40.

Ragoné, H. 2004: Surrogate Motherhood and American Kinship. In: R. Parkin & L. Stone (eds.), *Kinship and Family: An Anthropological Reader*. Oxford: Blackwell Publishing Ltd.

Rapp, R. 2001: Gender, Body, Biomedicine: How some Feminist Concerns Dragged Reproduction to the Center of Social Theory. *Medical Anthropology Quarterly* 15:4, 466–477.

Rusiecka, B. 2010: http://adonai.pl/nieplodnosc/?id=90. Accessed August 20, 2010.

Saetnan, A., N. Oudshoorn & M. Kirejczyk (eds.) 2000: *Bodies of Technology: Women's Involvement in Reproductive Medicine*. Ohio: Ohio University Press.

Sawicki, J. 1991: *Disciplining Foucault: Feminism, Power, and the Body*. New York & London: Routledge.

Sawicki, J. 1999: Discipling Mothers: Feminism and the New Reproductive Technologies. In: J. Price & M. Shildrick (eds.), *Feminist Theory and the Body: A Reader*. New York: Routledge.

Skibniewska, A. 2009: Szczęcie z in vitro. *Przeglad* 24. http://przeglad-tygodnik.pl/index.php?site=artykul&id=15296. Accessed August 20, 2010.

Spar, D.L. 2006: *The Baby Business: How Money, Science, and Politics Drive the Commerce of Conception*. Boston, Massachusetts: Harvard Business School Press.

Squier, S.M. 1999: Negotiating Boundaries: From Assisted Reproduction to Assisted Replication. In: E.A. Kaplan & S.M. Squier (eds.), *Playing Dolly: Technocultural Formations, Fantasies, and Fictions of Assisted Reproduction*. New Brunswick, New Jersey & London: Rutgers University Press.

Stanworth, M. 1987: *Reproductive Technologies: Gender, Motherhood and Medicine*. Minneapolis: University of Minnesota Press.

Strathern, M. 1992: *Reproducing the Future: Essays on Anthropology, Kinship and the New Reproductive Technologies*. Manchester: Manchester University Press.

Szczerba, B. 2009: Zapłodnienie in vitro – szansa na godne rodzicielstwo. *Wysłuchanie Obywatelskie*, February 23. www.federa.org.pl/Informacje/Wysluchaniezapis02.2009.pdf. Accessed August 20, 2010.

Thompson, Ch. 2002: Fertile Ground: Feminist Theorize Infertility. In: M.C. Inhorn & F. van Balen (eds.), *Infertility around the Globe: New Thinking on Childlessness, Gender, and Reproductive Technologies*. Berkeley, Los Angeles & London: University of California Press.

Thompson, Ch. 2005: *Making Parents: The Ontological Choreography of Reproductive Technologies*. Cambridge: The MIT Press.

Throsby, K. 2004: *When IVF Fails: Feminism, Infertility and Negotiation of Normality*. London: Palgrave.

Turney, J. 1998: *Frankenstein's Footsteps*. New Haven & London: Yale University Press.

Unnithan-Kumar, M. 2004: Introduction: Reproductive Agency, Medicine and the State. In: *Reproductive Agency, Medicine and the State: Cultural Transformations in Childbearing*. New York & Oxford: Berghahn Books.

Unnithan-Kumar, M. (ed.) 2004: *Reproductive Agency, Medicine and the State: Cultural Transformations in Childbearing*. New York & Oxford: Berghahn Books.

Magdalena Radkowska-Walkowicz is Assistant Professor at the Institute of Ethnology and Cultural Anthropology, University of Warsaw, Poland. Her research interests are anthropology of the body, new reproductive technologies, gender, and anthropology of literature. In 2008 her book *Od Golema do Terminatora: Wizerunki sztucznego człowieka w kulturze* (From Golem to Terminator: Images of the Artificial Man in the Culture) was published (Warsaw: Wydawnictwa Uniwersytetu Warszawskiego).
(m.radkowska-walkowicz@uw.edu.pl)

COMMENTS

KAROL'S KINGDOM

Marie Sandberg

"(...) We are like the Great Britain guys. We have our cup of tea together," Karol explains, after his wife and one of his two sons back home in Poland have ended their daily talk on Skype. We are sitting in Karol's room, which he shares with his colleague from the construction site placed nearby, just outside a middle-size town about one hour drive from Copenhagen, Denmark. The room forms part of a dormitory and is approximately 12 square metres, has two single beds, a toilet with shower, a fridge and access to a pretty worn-out, shared kitchen. Together with his colleague he pays 450 euro rent, and importantly this includes free Internet access. Still placed at the computer, after the Skype call has finished, I am trying not to look at the 44-inch flat-screen TV that decorates the wall. The Polish *Tvn* channel is broadcasting a show on breast enlargements, so the living pictures are rather eye-catching. Karol has invited us and obligingly he tells us about how he ended up here in Denmark as a foreman for a small team of Polish workers on a building project run by a Danish entrepreneur. Here he earns approximately twice as much as he could in Poland. Karol works 46 hours Monday till Saturday for three weeks and then he returns to his family in Poland during the fourth week. "Everything we need for our living is here. For existing. (...) It's my kingdom," Karol states.

While sitting there in Karol's room, I cannot help pondering why Karol chooses this way of life. What does it take to break up from the well-known routines at home in order to live in a small, shared room in a dormitory without having the family around? What I learned from Karol is that it takes more than one wo/man's choice to make a migratory practice a reality. Rather, a whole range of heterogeneous entities, settings and devices are involved. As they are assembled in various ways they take an active part in rendering a migratory practice such as Karol's both possible and desirable. Close allies are, for example, the specific means of transportation used when moving back and forth across the border; the social networks and networks of communication; the institutional as well as private actors facilitating labour migration across borders, such as recruiters and housing or estate agents; the specific regulations and tax allowances making working abroad even more financially attractive; the special agreements between employers, migrant workers, and the Danish trade union, which enables the pooling of working hours, not to mention the role of the family members, and their acceptance and active partaking in the migratory venture.

In order to grasp the character and various rationales of migratory movements it is necessary to put a human face on migration processes as suggested by Favell (2008, 2009). However, in doing so, it is also decisive to go beyond a frame of explanation that focuses solely on various acts of choice (cf. van der Velde & van Naerssen 2011). Overall, this special issue of *Ethnologia Europaea* on "Imagined Families in Mobile Worlds" is taking important steps towards a broader conceptualization of practice than one of rational choice-making. Further, in scrutinizing the emergence of new models of familiarity beyond the domestic unit in transnational space the articles avoid focusing on mobile individuals alone.

Outline

In this commentary I discuss how ethnology can contribute to the interdisciplinary field of international migration studies. Such a contribution, I suggest, can take the form of historically informed, materiality-oriented ethnographies which provide a basis for further examining the interrelatedness between migratory regimes and everyday life practices. Using examples from a current research project on Polish working migrants in Copenhagen,[1] I will offer a few reflections on the conceptual understanding of migratory practices. I propose a broad comprehension of such practices that can be seen as complex matters of feasibility as opposed to a rather reductionist question of choice. I am inspired by Maja Povrzanović Frykman's call for a "shift of ethnographic focus towards people's *practices* in connection with migration" (2008: 17, original emphasis) arguing that "only ethnographic methods can capture what migrants actually do – in the places of their everyday life, in the places they keep returning to and on the journeys between them" (ibid.). Further, I point out how the authors of this special issue raise important questions and provide new knowledge by paying analytical attention to practices of migration; their historicity and materiality/technology. I therefore, firstly, direct my attention towards migration studies and the need for including practice approaches in the rethinking of the so-called "mobility turn". Secondly, I look at the interrelatedness between migration and historicity, and thirdly, I pick up on the role of materiality and technology as co-constructors of migration practices. In conclusion I discuss how the scrutinization of interfaces between migratory regimes and migration practices can both add new insights to the interdisciplinary field of migration studies and develop new questions for future ethnological inquiry.

Migration Studies and the Mobility Turn

The growing fields of interdisciplinary migration studies, mobility studies and globalization studies often depict a world that has become more mobile than ever before. However, in a Eurobarometer survey conducted by the Dublin-based European Foundation for the *Improvement of Working and Living Conditions* (of the EU) in 2005, data indicate that "EU-citizens who had ever lived in another EU member state amounted to 4% of the population" (Favell, Recchi & Kuhn et al. 2011: 21). Worldwide the numbers are surprisingly similar: only 3% of the world's population is living outside the country where they were born (United Nations 2009). These data together with results from similar surveys compel van der Velde and van Naerssen to state that, rather than mobility, "immobility is still the rule" (2011: 219). Such a statement is thought-provoking in an era that is frequently characterized as "an era of mobility" and in a space often referred to as a "borderless Europe" (cf. Andersen & Sandberg 2012). The question is, has the highly praised free mobility across the EU internal borders remained much more a "political dreamscape" (Löfgren 2008) than a reality of everyday life in Europe?

Migration and Practice

However, as recent discussions within migration and mobility studies have shown, the question of increased mobility needs to be rethought (Canzler, Kaufmann & Kesselring 2008; Favell 2009; Larsen, Urry & Axhausen 2006; Sheller & Urry 2006; Urry 2008). To state that either you are a migrant on the move or a stationary resident simply makes no sense. For example, not all East–West migrants of Europe seem to stay on a permanent basis in their country of destination. As shown by Pijpers (2007), it is very seldom that East-West labour migration is uni-directional, which means that it is inaccurate to characterize the 2004 EU accession countries exclusively as *e*migration countries. In several Eastern European countries the numbers of *return* migrants and *transit* migrants are growing. Within recent years a classical emigration country like Poland receives labour migrants from Ukraine, Belarus and other countries of the former Soviet Union which makes notions such as "chain migration" relevant to apply (ibid.). This development of new concepts for migration processes confirms the need to critically evaluate the analytical potential of thinking in commonsensical dichotomies such as mobility vs. immobility, "the movers" vs. "the stayers", the "sedentary" vs. the "nomads", a point that was also made by the transnational approach migration studies already in the early 1990s (Glick Schiller, Basch & Blanc-Szanton 1992; Düvell 2009). Various flows of migration take place in an "extensive system of mobilities" across and beyond EU borders which make dichotomies together with divisions of home/host or sending/receiving countries rather useless (Favell, Recchi & Kuhn et al. 2011: 22). We should therefore not forget the many different ways migration is enacted and made possible in practice (cf. Povrzanović Frykman 2008). When migration practices are put under empirical scrutiny, it is very unlikely that we will discover practices of either mobility or settlement. On the contrary, we might find complex *patterns* of mobility/immobility even within the same migratory practice.

Therefore I find this special issue on imagined families stimulating. In her article "Grounding the Family: Locality and its Discontents in Popular Genealogy" Elisabeth Timm convincingly argues for a relational complementarity between mobility and immobility. When analysing the role of locality in the use of parish registers in Austrian popular genealogy it becomes clear that "'settledness' is not a given, and that 'migration' is not its Other". Rather, "mobility and immobility can only be adequately understood as relational complements" (Timm, this issue, p. 39). Through three Austrian cases Timm illustrates the active role played by genealogies in the ideological forming of families. Further, Timm shows how a production of "settledness" has been tightly knitted together historically with the idea of family kinship as linked to territory (together with house, estate and property). This examination over time of the constant production and reproduction of associating kinship and "settledness" *within* a territory is thought-provoking and adds new insights to the mobility turn within migration studies (cf. Rolshoven 2007).

Migration and Historicity

Apart from the rethinking of the division between mobility and immobility a second point of discussion within migration studies is the need for greater awareness of historical migration processes (cf. Favell 2008, 2009; Düvell 2009). It is often forgotten that waves of intra-European as well as extra-European working migrations took place also before the First World War (cf. Kolstrup 2010). Until the First World War Europe experienced a period of free movement of labour where passports and other kinds of entry documents were not even required (Wimmer & Glick Schiller 2002). To display such historical continuities in recent labour migration movements of Europe is hence crucial.

I would like to emphasize the article by Karen Körber entitled "So Far and yet so Near: Present-Day Transnational Families". Her historical comparison between labour migration within transnational families in Austria and Germany during the 1960s and 1990s respectively provides a fine illustration of how migratory movements have been facilitated and regulated differently by national authorities as well as EU legislation over time. In contrast to the present-day East–West migration of Europe, the labour migration of the 1960s was based on labour recruitment agreements between Western European countries (such as Germany) and South and Eastern European countries such as Italy, Greece, Turkey and the former Yugoslavia. These "guest worker" agreements secured among other things work permits and the legal status of the migrants' residential status in the country of destination. Due to special restrictive requirements introduced in most of the "old" EU member states the present-day East–West labour migration differs from the "guest worker" agreements of the 1960s. After the EU accessions of 2004 the "old" EU member states (with the exceptions of Sweden, Ireland and the U.K.) introduced special – and temporary – agreements regulating, among other things, the numbers of labour migrants and the issuing of work permits for the "new" EU member states (cf. Pijpers 2006, 2007). Consequently, as according to Körber, this type of regulation "limits in principle the right of people from Eastern Europe to move and reside freely and abolished the right to settle – with few exceptions – almost entirely" (Körber, this issue, p. 19). Comparing such differences in legal conditions and special agreements among EU member states can shed new light on our understanding of current migratory movements as well as of those in the past.

The Materiality and Technology of Migration Practices

A third point of discussion, where I think ethnological approaches can contribute to international migration studies, is related to the attention towards materiality and technology of migration practices. In order to know cross-border practices better, we need to explore how these practices are attached to and receive backup from specific but heterogeneous assemblages of other actors and entities. We must therefore consider not only the practices and their variable differences but also take the settings, materials and devices that enable migratory movements into account. I would like to draw on the piece by Körber again, because she clearly shows how communication technologies are active allies in the production of family at and across a distance.

Positioning herself within the transnational research approach to family studies, Körber focuses not only on mobile actors, but also on family members that are "staying behind", "at home". The focus is chosen in order to analyse the nurturing of the social and symbolic family member relations that are indeed challenged by the migration process. With this analytical strategy Körber emphasizes the practices, strategies and negotiations through which family life is created across time and space instead of conceptualizing the family as a community consisting of individual units.

That there are intimate and intricate links between the use of new communication technologies and the specific production of familiarity is clearly illustrated in the case of Ingrida Einars presented by Körber. Einars is a woman from Kaunas, Lithuania, who labour migrated to Germany in 2004 leaving her teenage daughter at home with the grandparents. Körber shows how the initially troubled and conflict-ridden communication between the teenage daughter and her mother becomes improved through the use of emails instead of Skype/webcam. Without the camera the typewritten contact provides a relieving space for communication that works well for the teenage daughter who dyes her hair and pierces her skin also without her mother's approval. Likewise the communication becomes more relaxed for the mother who can momentarily focus on what the daughter writes, rather than her appearance. Hence, a virtual closeness is maintained between mother and daughter across borders. Körber concretizes the paradox pointed at by the editors in the Introduction to this special issue, namely that

> despite geographical distance and the experience of dispersal, the very social group whose core elements include spatial proximity and direct community is capable of sustaining the family virtually as its principal point of orientation and reference. As such, it is proving both resistant and creative in the face of the new demands of globalized societies. (Körber & Merkel, this issue, p. 5)

From Matter of Choice to Matters of Feasibility

So far I have argued that the strength of ethnological approaches to international migration studies in particular lies in the depicting of patterns of mobility/immobility when analysed in practice, as well as in the incorporation of historicity and materiality/technology of migration processes. I would now like to return to the before mentioned focus on the migrant and the migratory process as a simple matter of choice. Following the argument of van der Velde and van Naerssen (2011) we need to broaden the explanatory figure usually called "the decision-making process" of migratory movements. Overall this special issue contributes to such broadening because it focuses on the family as an important co-actor in migration processes (cf. Kolstrup 2010). However, the article by Sabine Hess entitled "How Gendered is the European Migration Regime? A Feminist Analysis of the Anti-Trafficking Apparatus" calls in particular for a further discussion on the concept of choice. This contribution deals with the effects and implications of border regulations and migration policies within the area of trafficking.

Situating herself as a researcher *in medias res* among counter-trafficking NGO's, policy makers, women's rights movements, and feminist research agendas, Hess compellingly shows how anti-trafficking policies in fact contribute to a victimization or de-subjectification of migrant women. For example when official European immigration policies only grant residence permits as a result of marriage, heteronormative ideals of gender interdependencies and differences are reproduced, according to Hess. Appallingly such regulations resemble the mechanisms of the trafficking migration industry when trafficked women get caught in exploitative nets of (male) dealers and middle-men which yet again contribute to the reproduction of a gendered dependency pattern.

However, as a further point Hess shows that migrating women cannot be depicted as victims only. Her ethnographic analyses of everyday life migration patterns indicate that the destiny of these women in question cannot be judged solely as either initiated by force or as volunteered by choice. For these women, it is not a question of either/or, but rather a matter of both/and. Voluntary migration and migration by force cannot be divided into two neat categories. Rather, "voluntary actions and direct and structural violence intersect in contradictory manners and are judged and negotiated in myriad ways, both in migrants' interpretations and in their actions" (Hess, this issue, p. 56). This article therefore both constitutes a counter narrative to singularizing discourses of migrating women-as-victims as well as exemplifies how migratory movements cannot be reduced to a rational choice. It confirms the capability of ethnographic analyses of everyday life migration patterns to depict the various and often ambivalent strategies and negotiations among in this case migrant women.

Linking Migratory Regimes and Migratory Practices

Introducing the articles within this special issue, the guest editors emphasize that "by interlocking ethnographic and discourse-analytical methods and combining them with gender theory, they share a focus on the technologies, genealogies, policies, and regulations that participate crucially in the construction of family, gender, and bodies" (Körber & Merkel, this issue, p. 6). No doubt these contributions give important insights into concrete experiencing and shaping of migration processes in practice. As a final point of discussion I would like to address two questions: How are such practices constituted? How are practices related to, involved in and presupposed by other practices? Indeed, as I have already argued here, practices do not unfold in a vacuum; they are made feasible by other practices, settings, materials, and devices. Within this special issue a common point of departure for a number of the authors seems to be the concept of *regimes*, such as the "European border regime", "European immigration regime", "security regimes" or regimes of free mobility across borders. Yet further questions arise, such as what constitutes one regime as compared to others? Where do the analyses of various regimes and their impact leave the migrants crossing the borders? Are migrants passive products *of* the regimes or how can regimes be resisted? Leaving the concept of "regime" to some extent untouched makes it easy to fall into an explanatory trap: either the analyses provide evidence of how migrants are subjected to various regimes or they seek to stress the agency of mobility across borders (cf. Favell, Recchi & Kuhn et al. 2011). The contributions show the potential of the concept of "regime", but I see an important future challenge in discussing more thoroughly what the notion of regimes entails and what it does to our understanding of the connections between practices of different kinds.

The Kingdom

As is evident from this collection of *Ethnologia Europaea* contributions, there are several practices and entities involved in past and current migratory movements across intra-European borders.

It is certainly not a one-man show to migrate. Family members who are staying at home take active part in decision-making processes and render the practices of mobility/immobility possible. The case of Karol has illustrated the importance of the support from his wife and sons who contribute to rendering "Karol's kingdom" feasible and desirable. The daily "five-o-clock tea" on Skype forms a particular assemblage of entities, devices and settings that seems to be in accordance with Karol's idea of what a good family relation is. It is only in collaboration with a(nother) specific but heterogeneous assemblage of allies that Karol manages to remain attractive to the Danish job market by fitting in perfectly with the ideal migrant "flexi-worker" that is hard working, flexible, and mobile (Pijpers 2007). Finally, the historical fact that there have been working migrants before him, such as Polish rural workers of the nineteenth and early twentieth century, also might influence his possibility to succeed. To explore patterns of mobility/immobility practiced over time thus constitutes an important task for further ethnological scrutiny (cf. Kolstrup 2010; Nellemann 1981). By paying attention to the historicity, materiality, and technology it becomes possible to depict the different ways Karol's migratory practice of mobility/immobility correspond to his idea of the "good life".

As I have argued here, there is a general need for greater empirical and historical awareness within the interdisciplinary field of migration studies in order to break out from reductionist explanation models of rational choice and to avoid that questions of mobility and immobility are turned into misleading terms of either-or. The need for empirically rich depictions of everyday life mobility and migration patters calls for further ethnographic studies similar to those of the special issue at hand.

Note

1 The example derives from an ongoing research project on Polish working migrants in the area of Copenhagen, Denmark, conducted by Associate Professor Niels Jul Nielsen and Assistant Professor Marie Sandberg, at the Ethnology Section, the Saxo Institute, University of Copenhagen (2011-).

References

Andersen, Dorte J. & Marie Sandberg 2012: Introduction. In: Dorte J. Andersen, Martin Klatt & Marie Sandberg (eds.), *The Border Multiple: The Practicing of Borders between Public Policy and Everyday Life in Europe.* Aldershot: Ashgate Border Regions Series.

Canzler, Weert, Vincent Kaufmann & S. Kesselring 2008: Tracing Mobilities – An Introduction. In: Weert Canzler, Vincent Kaufmann & Sven Kesselring (eds.), *Tracing Mobilities: Contributions from the Cosmobilities Network.* Abingdon, Oxdon, GBR: Ashgate Publishing Group, pp. 11–17.

Düvell, Franck 2009: Migration, Minorities and Marginality: New Directions in Europe Migration Research. In: Chris Rumford (ed.), *The SAGE Handbook of European Studies.* London: SAGE Publications Ltd., pp. 329–346.

Favell, Adrian 2008: The New Face of East–West Migration in Europe. *Journal of Ethnic Migration Studies* 34:5, 701–716.

Favell, Adrian 2009: Immigration, Migration, and Free Movement in the Making of Europe. In: Jeffrey T. Checkel & Peter J. Katzenstein (eds.), *European Identity.* Cambridge: Cambridge University Press, pp. 167–189.

Favell, Adrian, Ettore Recchi & Theresa Kuhn et al. 2011: The Europeanisation of Everyday Life: Cross-Border Practices and Transnational Identifications among EU and Third-Country Citizens. State of the Art Report. Eucross Working Papers no. 1. http://www.eucross.eu/cms/index.php?option=com_docman&task=cat_view&gid=7&Itemid=157. Accessed August 31, 2012.

Glick Schiller, Nina, Linda Basch & Cristina Blanc-Szanton 992: Transnationalism: A New Analytical Framework for Understanding Migration. In: Nina Glick Schiller, Linda Basch & Cristina Blanc-Szanton (eds.), *Towards a Transnational Perspective on Migration, Race, Class, Ethnicity, and Nationalism Reconsidered.* New York, N.Y.: New York Academy of Sciences Annals of the New York Academy of Sciences.

Kolstrup, Søren 2010: *Polske stemmer: Polske indvandringsbølger 1892–2008.* Copenhagen: Frydenlund.

Larsen, Jonas, John Axhausen & John Urry 2006: Mobilities. In: Jonas Larsen, John Axhausen & John Urry (eds.): *Mobilities, Networks, Geographies.* Aldershot: Ashgate Publishing Group, pp. 47–62.

Löfgren, Orvar 2008: Regionauts: The Transformation of Cross-Border Regions in Scandinavia. *European Urban and Regional Studies* 15:3, 195–209.

Nellemann, George 1981: *Polske landarbejdere i Danmark og deres efterkommere: Et studie af landarbejderindvandringen 1893–1929 og indvandringens integration i det danske samfund i to generationer.* Copenhagen: Nationalmuseets Forlag.

Pijpers, Roos 2006: 'Help! The Poles are Coming': Narrating a Contemporary Moral Panic. *Geografiska Annaler*, 88B:1, 91–103.

Pijpers, Roos 2007: *Between Fear of Masses and Freedom of Movement: Migrant Flexiwork in the Enlarged European Union.* Doctoral thesis, Nijmegen School of Management, Radboud University Nijmegen, The Netherlands.

Povrzanović Frykman, Maja 2008: Beyond Culture and

Identity: Places, Practices, Experiences. *Ethnologia Europaea* 38:1, 13–22.

Rolshoven, Johanna 2007: The Temptations of the Provisional. Multilocality as a Way of Life. *Ethnologia Europaea* 37:1–2, 17–25.

Sheller, Mimi & John Urry 2006: The New Mobilities Paradigm. *Environment and Planning A*, 206–226.

United Nations Department of Economic and Social Affairs 2009: Population Division 1. *International Migration Report 2009.*

Urry, John 2008: Moving on the Mobility Turn. In: Weert Canzler, Vincent Kaufmann & Sven Kesselring (eds.), *Tracing Mobilities: Towards a Cosmopolitan Perspective in Mobility Research.* Aldershot: Ashgate.

van der Velde, Martin & Ton van Naerssen 2011: People, Borders, Trajectories: An Approach to Cross-Border Mobility and Immobility in and to the European Union. *Area* 43:2, 218–224.

Wimmer, Andreas & Nina Glick Schiller 2002: Methodological Nationalism and beyond: Nation-State Building, Migration and the Social Sciences. *Global Networks* 2:4, 301–334.

Marie Sandberg, Ph.D., is Assistant Professor of Ethnology at the University of Copenhagen. Her research focuses on the rethinking of European integration processes, border practices and experiences in everyday life, labour migration within the EU and the reordering of borders in Europe – past and present. Among her recent publications is the book *The Border Multiple: The Practicing of Borders between Public Policy and Everyday Life in Re-Scaling Europe* (edited together with Dorte J. Andersen & Martin Klatt, 2012, Ashgate Border Regions Series).
(sandberg@hum.ku.dk)

FROM ACCOMPANYING FAMILY MEMBER TO ACTIVE SUBJECT
Critical Perspectives on Transnational Migration

Beatriz Lindqvist

Today, a growing number of people spend their lives beyond the borders of nation states. They create homes, families and identities that are not easily understood if one adheres to the concept of "true belonging" as meaning solidly anchored to one territory, one culture and one language. Even in the era of globalization, however, this concept retains its force. It is, after all, still the nation state, and only the nation state, that guarantees individuals' fundamental rights and grants them their true home, their proper place. Refugees are still viewed as exceptional, for they lack the basic protection which only the native country can give (see Bauman 1998). Thus, despite modern global mobility, the nation state's legal regulations, border controls and migration policies are still of pre-eminent importance. During periods of rapid social change, the nation, accordingly, often becomes a socially, culturally and politically charged subject within a symbolic battle over how to define so-called normal relations and healthy family ties. The breakthrough of industrialism and urbanization and the modernization of the European welfare states meant new ways of conceptualizing and organizing marriage, parenthood and family life (see Frykman & Löfgren 1987). Today, the family is again the focus of social debates conducted in the light of growing international migration, the transformation of the welfare state, assisted fertilization of childless couples and the emergence of same-sex parents in "rainbow" families.

International research on ethnic relations and international migration has shown how many migrants' everyday life takes place in several places simultaneously. Personal relations and family economy, life goals and identities are formed by social interrelations that reach across national borders – sometimes beyond continents. Transnational contacts and family ties link together geographically disperse worlds. In many cases, they create a virtual homeland consisting of several different places. Marita Eastmond and Lisa Åkesson (2007) have shown that global families are shaped by interplay between migrants' lives, as lived in different local contexts, and the global communities of which they form a part. Munzoul Assal's 2003 study of Somali and Sudanese living in Norway discusses how these engage in an intense social exchange with relatives and friends outside Norway's borders. This exchange is, moreover, not confined to people in the migrants' country of origin; it reaches out to several other parts of the world, as well. Assal argues that one must position these groups' views on home, family and belonging against this wide, mobile horizon. He also calls attention to the number and variety of everyday actions and communication forms that together create a home that lies beyond the narrow logic of the nation state. Family and kin, here, is not something one simply is or has. One *creates* family in the everyday practices of sending money to relatives, celebrating holidays together, participating in ethnic associations, joining Facebook groups and chatting with relatives who can partake of family pictures. The same findings emerge in Anna Lindley's study of Somali refugees in Great Britain (2010). She shows that refugees' money-transfers to relatives in other countries involve more than sending resources from afar. They are also a means of providing moral support, of exchanging information of how it is to live and work in different countries and on the opportunities and difficulties encountered in one's everyday life.

Family and kinship are formed in many different ways, going far beyond the community (if any) constituted by members of a biological group. Social, cultural and emotional ties are essential to communities that extend over time and space. In this edition of *Ethnologia Europaea*, ethnographers use case studies of migrants' own experience and perspectives to illuminate these processes. The authors show how close family relations are created despite geographical distance, in studies of how people handle the complex and sometimes contradictory demands that a transnational life entails. This special issue's broad spectrum of empirical studies ties together two highly topical theoretical debates. The first is concerned with transnational migration, the second with family and gender. The case studies are diverse and imaginative, ranging from assisted fertilization through sex work to nuns' and migrants' accounts of their lives. Körbel and Merkel's thoughtful and well-structured introductory text shows how the different texts are linked in a dialogue "crosswise" over a number of empirical fields, in the cross-roads, of the major research themes of transnational migration, family and gender.

The growing corpus of international literature on transnational networks paints, in broad brushstrokes, a dark picture of a strongly polarized world in which a privileged cosmopolitan elite and faceless global market forces rapidly cross all and any borders, while an ever-growing mass of refugees and paperless migrants risk their lives to circumvent national border controls, only to end up at the mercy of human smugglers in the West. This somber picture has replaced earlier visions of globalization's international brotherhood with dystopian images of global exploitation, trafficking and increasing marginalization. Such dichotomizing images are, of course, problematic. They tend to be mutually self-enforcing, depending, as they do, on the same type of binary logic. The articles in this volume are, therefore, a welcome contribution to the discussion. They approach transnational processes from below, from the point-of-view of individual experiences. This gives new visibility to the complexity and ambivalences in different forms of transnational imagined families.

Earlier migration research often took as its point of departure the processes that brought migrants to a new country. Equally often, the unquestioned norm was to focus on a male subject – the adult male migrant, sometimes accompanied by wife and children, encountering opportunities and difficulties in the new country. The inquiry was, finally, framed in terms of how people who were torn loose from their "natural" context adapted to the receiving country. The studies in this issue provide a different, and innovative, type of analysis.

A common point of departure in the articles is Nina Glick Schiller's discussion of the concept of a "transnational social field". Glick Schiller shows how immigrants can construct ties to two or more nation states. This allows appreciation of how immigrants *concurrently* partake in the daily life of their country of origin, with all the political, social and emotional implications that entails, *and* in the everyday life of their new country, participating in the daily communities created at home, among friends and acquaintances, and at the workplace. An important point emphasized by the articles in this issue is that this type of simultaneous multi-national daily life applies not only to migrants who have changed countries, but also to those of their relatives and friends who have stayed in the country of origin – that is, have not physically crossed nation-state borders. In 2008, Lewitt and Glick Schiller distinguished between "transnational ways of belonging" and "transnational ways of being" (2008: 189). Belonging, they argue, is based on ideas of kinship ties, roots, origin and ethnicity. No matter where in the world a person lives, it is assumed that she or he is a member of a group united by a common past and a "community of fate". This belonging is unaffected by the person's movement across national borders. Ways of being, on the other hand, signify the ways in which a person can exist and interact over borders, without necessarily saying anything about where that person feels at home or about his or her self-identification. Notions of belonging address the ways in which people use remembrance, nostalgia, narratives and artifacts to reach out to other places, often in other countries – whether they live as migrants or are among those staying behind in their native locality.

Helma Lutz has provided a detailed discussion of the theoretical and methodological implications of an intersectional approach to migration (Lutz, Herrera Vivar & Supik 2011). In the same vein, ethnologist Maja Povrzanović Frykman (2011), in her current research project The Transnational Life of Objects: Material Practices of Migrants (financed by the Swedish Research Council), discusses a closely related way of viewing transnationalism. She sees it as a ribbon or flow of people, ideas and things over national state borders. Lewitt and Glick Schiller develop the point of analytical distinctions between the concepts of being and belonging as follows:

> If individuals engage in social relations and practices that cross borders as a regular feature of everyday life, then they exhibit a transnational way of being. When people explicitly recognize this and highlight the transnational elements of who they are, then they are also expressing a transnational way of belonging. Clearly, these two experiences do not always go hand in hand. (2008: 189–190)

A Transnational Service Sector

Every year thousands of women leave their countries of origin to work in richer countries, finding employment within the domestic sector as servants, child minders or personal assistants for elderly and sick in well-to-do families (Lindio-McGovern & Wallimann 2009; Parreñas 2001; Yeates 2009). A large proportion of these women migrate legally, their visa, tickets, contracts and work permits provided by employment agencies. A still larger proportion, hoping to penetrate EU borders, put their trust in illegal contractors (Agustin 2007). In many cases, the home countries' governments encourage this emigration: The money that the women send home is of great importance to the country's monetary reserves. Most of the women involved are between 18 and 40 years of age; they have varying educational backgrounds. Many leave children behind in the care of grandparents or other relatives. The primary reason for these women's migration is low family income – too low to cover the family's most basic needs. Often, the woman's subsequent earnings, sent home from abroad, serves to improve the family's long-term economy, through (for instance) making it possible to start a small business in the home town. These prospects encourage many women to leave their homes and countries of origin, traveling, sometimes, to nations in other continents (Ehrenreich & Handschild 2003).

My own research on women from the Baltic States working in the Scandinavian sex industry shows that their employment within economic sectors regarded as socially low-value and morally dubious can be given a different meaning when viewed in terms of earnings earmarked for a particular use. Women so employed can retain their feeling of self-worth by placing their personal sacrifices within a discourse of respectability – the respectability of taking responsibility for one's family. Fulfilling their duty as the family's breadwinner is defined as the highest virtue. Accordingly, migrant sex-workers may position themselves as responsible and respectable rather than as victims – the position given them in main-stream Swedish discourses – or as the "dirty whores" of their home-countries' discourse.

The fact that private services involving bodily contact and touch are sold by migrants from the southern parts of the globe and Eastern Europe to West Europeans and Americans maintains an ethnic segmentation of work. This confirms and strengthens the social division between a national "us" and a foreign "them", as well as a division between different sorts of women (Lindqvist 2007, 2008). It cements an essentialist understanding of well-paid productive work as the purview of well-qualified, independent, self-conscious and reflexive women from the Western world. Reproductive work joins other forms of lowly-esteemed work as the natural occupation of under-qualified, low-earning and unreflexive foreign women (Mohanty 2003). According to several studies, the increasingly global market economy has, when conjoined with the feminization of poverty, transformed reproductive work into a transnational economic sector that operates, in large part, unseen (see Ehrenreich & Handschild 2003; Parreñas 2001).

This gives us the context for understanding the young women who arrive in European countries to work, in periods, either on their way to other countries or as a temporary solution to the problem of earning a living. Intimacy, bodily contact and care are important pillars in this mobile employment market, a market which transforms those involved into senders and receivers. The services that are sold are almost all connected to the traditional duties of women – care of small children, care for the sick, cleaning houses, washing and ironing clothes, providing men with sexual satisfaction. While many Western women and men pay for care, domestic and sexual services, the transnational migrant, in her turn, often depends on someone in her country of origin for the domestic care of her own family. The sisters or aged parents who may be taking care of the children she has left behind are, in turn, supported by her long-distance earnings. In different ways, Hess's article on sex-workers affected by Europe's increasingly restrictive migration policies, and Hüwelmeier's on German nuns in North America, exemplify the fruitfulness of discussions on "the international division of labor" (Sassen 1983), "the ethnic division of reproductive labor" (Parreñas 2001) as well as feminist theory's abrogation of the binary opposition between productive and reproductive work, particularly when used within a longer historical perspective.

Looking at both those who Migrate and those who Stay at Home

When focus is redirected to the interplay between the migrants' life in Europe and the transnational family relations in both their country of origin and in the other countries of which they have become part, it also becomes possible for the scholar to go beyond the "nationalistic ideology" that otherwise easily leads to the analytical dichotomies of "at home, and abroad", "local and global", and the like (Amelina 2012).

Geographically separate worlds become interconnected; the narratives that tie together persons and events across national, linguistic and generational borders become the basis for experiences where the "home land" often consists of several different places (see Eastmond & Åkesson 2007). The combined use of ethnographic and discourse-analytic methods and different theoretical perspectives interrogates the relationship between local integration and transnational networks. It is only by focusing on everyday life that one can study the role that kinship plays in transnational migration, allowing people to maintain a close community over time and at great distances. Only this, further, allows an understanding of how this is achieved in everyday practice. In this volume, ethnographic and experiential approaches provide important insights into the significance of these communities for their members. It becomes clear that migration is not a one-way process, destined for the terminus of integration within the frames of a nation state. Even after family relations are detached from their local context, they will often continue to organize relationships, senses of belonging, and material welfare. Narratives concerning who one is, as well as what it is that unites the family, including each family member's rights and duties, are maintained, adjusted and renegotiated in a process that includes both continuity and change. Family ties can thus be strengthened or weakened as they are invested with (partly) new meanings and emphasis.

Family and migration have been studied in many ways. But, regardless of focus – whether on monastic orders' symbolic mothers and daughters, the sex worker and her parents and children, or migrants' genealogies – there exist commonly shared practices which, in varying degrees, link together spatially scattered family members. These may be the exchange of economic and material resources with relatives who have remained in the country of origin, or the social care of children and old parents who were left behind, or the emotional support that can contribute to the family members' feeling of being valued simply for who they are. Today's adaptable and inexpensive means of communication can promote close contacts around everyday concerns and decisions. Different conditions for relatives in different places can also create tensions. An unequal division of power and resources and inevitable conflicts of interest necessitate constant renegotiation of roles and expectations across transnational space. Often, family ties that have worn thin over time can be picked up again, in a different context, later in life, or even by the next generation. An important insight provided by this broad empirical spectrum is that engagement with relatives on the other side of the globe does *not* conflict with the migrant's integration into the society of the receiving country. The relation between different places and generations is complex, and migrants take on different positions in the transnational space. These vary between and within families, and during an individual's life. They cannot be explained, in any simple way, by one-sided references to class, generation or gender. Especially Karen Körber's article shows the advantages of using narrative analyses of stories of migration to understand generation-specific constructions of family and of belonging in transnational spaces. It becomes clear that an intersectional analysis which includes the interaction of different power dimensions is more productive, even if it is significantly more difficult to carry out in practice.

The articles bring up many important questions concerning women, migration and transnational processes. Here, for once, the adult male has ended up in the margins. This raises new questions on the shifts in power made possible by women's mobility. Other questions can be asked about the children that migrant mothers often leave behind. Has their mothers' migration and employment abroad had any direct effects on the children's living conditions? How is the money that the mother sends back spent – on education, on bettering living space, and/or consumption, and if so, of what and by whom? Körber's and Hess's articles call attention to the invisible work that is an undercurrent integral to today's welfare economy. The move away from migration studies' traditional focus on the immigrant male and his accompanying family allows us to see new patterns and strategies. Hopefully, this critical approach to transnational processes, international migration and gender will open up for more studies in which not only adults but children, those who migrate and those who are left behind, will both be seen and heard.

References

Agustín, Laura María 2007: *Sex at the Margins: Migration, Labour Markets and the Rescue Industry*. London: Zed.

Amelina, Anna (ed.) 2012: *Beyond Methodological Nationalism: Research Methodologies for Cross-Border Studies*. New York: Routledge.

Armine Ishkanian, Armine 2002: Mobile Motherhood: Armenian Women's Labor Migration in the Post-Soviet Period. *Diaspora: A Journal of Transnational Studies* 11:3, Winter 2002, 383–415.

Assal, Munzoul A.M. 2003: *Beyond Labelling: Somalis and Sudanese in Norway and the Challenge of Homemaking*. Diss. Bergen: Univ.

Bauman, Zygmunt 1998: *Globalization: The Human Consequences*. London: Polity.

Eastmond, Marita & Lisa Åkesson (ed.) 2007: *Globala familjer: transnationell migration och släktskap*. Hedemora: Gidlund.

Ehrenreich, Barbara & Arlie Russell Handschild (eds.) 2003: *Global Woman: Nannies, Maids, and Sex Workers in the New Economy*. 1st ed. New York: Metropolitan Books.

Frykman, Jonas & Orvar Löfgren 1987: *Culture Builders: A Historical Anthropology of Middle-Class Life*. New Brunswick: Rutgers Univ. Press.

Lewitt, Peggy & Nina Glick Schiller 2008: Conceptualizing Simultaneity: A Transnational Social Field Perspective on Society. In: Alejandro Portes & Josh DeWind (eds.), *Rethinking Migration: New Theoretical and Empirical Perspectives*. New York: Berghahn Books, pp. 181–218.

Lindio-McGovern, Ligaya & Isidor Wallimann (eds.) 2009: *Globalization and Third World Women: Exploitation, Coping and Resistance*. Farnham: Ashgate Pub.

Lindley, Anna 2010: *The Early Morning Phone Call: Somali*

refugees' Remittances. New York: Berghahn Books.

Lindqvist, Beatriz 2007: Migrant Women in Ambiguous Business: Examining Sex Work across National Borders in the Baltic Region. In: Erik Berggren (ed.), *Irregular Migration, Informal Labour and Community: A Challenge for Europe*. Maastricht: Shaker, pp. 255–266.

Lindqvist, Beatriz 2008: Östersjöns Bangkok? En transnationell sexmarknad. In: Beatriz Lindqvist & Mats Lindqvist, *När kunden är kung: Effekter av en transnationell economi*. 1st ed. Umeå: Boréa.

Lutz, Helma, Maria Teresa Herrera Vivar & Linda Supik (eds.) 2011: *Framing Intersectionality: Debates on a Multi-Faceted Concept in Gender Studies*. Farnham: Ashgate.

Mohanty, Chandra Talpade 2003: *Feminism without Borders: Decolonizing Theory, Practicing Solidarity*. Durham: Duke Univ. Press.

Parreñas, Rhacel Salazar 2001: *Servants of Globalization: Women, Migration, and Domestic Work*. Stanford, Calif.: Stanford University Press.

Povrzanović Frykman, Maja 2011: The Transnational Life of Objects: Material Practices of Migrants' Being and Belonging. Vetenskapsrådet. http://forskning.mah.se/id/immafr.

Rosenthal, Gabriele & Artur Bogner (eds.) 2009: *Ethnicity, Belonging and Biography: Ethnographical and Biographical Perspectives*. Berlin: Lit.

Sassen, Saskia 1983: Labor Migration and the New Industrial Division of Labor. In: June C. Nash & María Patricia Fernández-Kelly (eds.), *Women, Men, and the International Division of Labor*. Albany: State Univ. of New York Press.

Yeates, Nicola 2009: *Globalizing Care Economies and Migrant Workers: Explorations in Global Care Chains*. Houndmills, Basingstoke, Hampshire & New York: Palgrave Macmillan.

Beatriz Lindqvist is Associate Professor of European Ethnology at Södertörn University, Sweden. She has published in the fields of migration, female ageing, diversity and education, and the commodification of sex in the Baltic Sea region. Her latest publication was edited together with Peter Strandbrink and Håkan Forsberg (2011): *Tvära möten: om utbildning och kritiskt lärande* (Södertörn Studies in Education) – a book on education and critical learning. Her current research focuses on activists in post-communist Lithuania.
(beatriz.lindqvist@sh.se)

IMMIGRATION – AND SECRETS

Karin Lützen

Despite this issue's title, *Imagined Families,* I did not see the famous quote by John Gillis: "We all have two families, one that we live *with* and another we live *by.* We would like the two to be the same, but they are not" (Gillis 1996: xv). To me, this sentence seems to say all there is to be said about our relationsship to families, in reality and in dream, and it has been an underlying theme in much of my own research.

All the articles in this issue look at "imagined families in mobile worlds", in which especially transnational families are the focus of research. It ties in well with my latest book from 2009: *Mors hemmelighed* (Mother's Secret: On the Track of a Jewish Immigrant History) and I will now explore some of my themes and discuss them in context with the articles in this issue.

My mother was French, born in Paris in 1923 and came to Denmark after the war to marry my Danish father. You could say that she thus founded a transnational family, since her parents stayed in France and she had to keep in touch with them, not through phone calls but through weekly letters. My grandmother died a year after my mother's wedding, so I never met her, but I knew her father, my "grandpère". My mother had no siblings, nor did we ever hear about any aunts or uncles or cousins. It seemed like my mother and her parents had appeared out of nowhere without any roots or kinship. This was a sharp contrast to my father who had a big family and whose mother's family had lived in our town for generations. On my paternal side of the family we were strongly rooted in Danish soil and we knew the history of the family.

Both my mother and grandfather were very proud of being French and I early on learned how brilliant France was: the language, the food, the climate, the culture – in short, that everything was better in France than in Denmark. As a very secular person my mother stressed the advantage of the separation of Church and State. Though she lived in Denmark and also seemed to like it, her cultural antenna was tuned in to France.

In 2004, six years after my mother's death, I started doing genealogical research. It suddenly occurred to me that I knew nothing about her parents nor her grandparents, and I had no clue as to where in France they were born. Imagine my surprise when I found out that her parents were not born in France at all but in Romania. It turned out that they were immigrants, and just had imagined themselves to be French. Even greater was my shock when I discovered that they were Jewish. My great-grandparents had fled Romania in 1899 to avoid the very bad conditions for Jews. The last surprise was to discover that my grandparents had lots of siblings and that my mother therefore had had many uncles, aunts and cousins. My mother was not without relatives as I had always believed. On the contrary, she had a whole world of kin.

Through more genealogical research, I managed to find some still living relatives. I asked them to tell me the story of my mother's family and help me solve the mystery of why they had been kept a secret. They said they had lost contact with my mother and her father after her marriage in Denmark, and since it was right after the war, when so many Jewish families were uprooted they did not really wonder about it.

I learned about the tragic histories of several families on both my grandmothers' and grandfathers' side during the Second World War. Several members of the family had been deported to Auschwitz, and not all had returned. My grandfather lost his younger brother, who perished in the concentration camp together with his wife and two small children: my mothers' uncle, aunt, and cousins. I wondered if it was this tragedy that had made my mother and grandfather bury their family history and never whisper a word about kin – and certainly never mention being Jewish.

But it was not as simple as that. Though my mother never lied about her background she created a past as she would have liked it to be, emphasizing parts of it and being silent about other parts. One can't say that she made up her family since she never talked about her kin, only about her parents. But she and they imagined themselves to be their own ideal of a secular, French, intellectual, middle-class family when in reality they came from a Jewish immigrant working-class family.

My mothers' cousin told me that in the interwar years my mother and her parents had been part of the big Yiddish-speaking Jewish Eastern European immigrant community in Paris. They had been members of Jewish mutual aid societies, my great-grandparents were buried in the Jewish plot in the cemetery, they had all attended the Jewish holidays and my grandparents were married in a synagogue – after their civil marriage, as is the law in France. But my grandparents had stood out as something special among all their relatives. Everybody worked in the garment industry as tailors or seamstresses, which is typical for the Eastern European immigrants not only in France but also in England, the United States and Scandinavia.

Like immigrants from other countries such as the ones studied by Körber in this issue they had close networks and helped each other to jobs. But unlike the usual working migrants, these Eastern European Jews were refugees who had fled a country that treated them badly. It was not just one family who left but their relatives, including grandparent, aunts, uncles, and newborns. This means that there was nobody left "back there" to keep in touch with and it also means that these refugees were eager to embrace their new country as their homeland.

My great-grandfather had a little workshop at home and employed some garment workers. My grandfather had been trained as a tailor. But, as my mothers' cousin said, my grandfather had ambitions. He wanted to climb the social ladder, he wanted to get out of the narrowness of immigrant society with all its social control and enter the French middle class. And he managed. After his marriage to my grandmother – who was of course also a child of Romanian Jewish immigrants who were in the garment industry – he got a job as a salesman. He continued in the same trade, since it was fabric he was selling but at least he was no longer confined to a small workshop where they gossiped in Yiddish all day long. My mother's cousin also said that he was always elegantly dressed, spoke correct French, had refined manners and looked down upon his more shabby relatives with their deplorable accents.

My purpose in telling this – and in publishing the story in my book – is to show that my mother and her parents created an image of themselves as they wanted to be. They are in a way an imagined family, though they did not imagine their relatives to be something else. They knew all too well the family they, in Gillis' sense, lived *with*, but they created themselves anew. They are a splendid example of how modernity allows you to untie yourself from kin and to construct the life of your dreams.

I have no idea what the emotional costs of that liberation must have been and I am sure it was not without pain and solitude, but they must have found that their new life was worth it. Being Jewish was a burden, and during the war it was of course dangerous if people knew you were Jewish. I am sure my grandparents and my mother survived because they managed to pass themselves off as secular and French. But for them, being Jewish also meant being immigrant and working class and therefore they had to discard that part of their history.

In the introduction to this issue the authors write

about tracing "the special significance accorded to 'memories and narratives' in diasporically dispersed families, as ways of enabling a shared understanding of family in circumstances of separation" (Körber & Merkel, this issue, p. 7). In my family's case their "memories and narratives" certainly take on a special meaning since the memories are very carefully selected and the narratives are created so that they fit in with a self-created new life.

In my book I place the little history of my family in the context of the bigger history of Eastern European Jewish immigrants. I write more generally about the garment industry, mutual aid societies, traditions and daily life, application for French nationality and the painful story of how France has coped with the wartime Vichy government. I have also looked closely at my own interest in doing this genealogical research that I apparently have in common with many other people. Of course in my case there has been the discovery of this big secret which in itself has changed the genealogical research into a detective story.

But I – who have always subscribed to a constructionist view of the world, who believe that we have feet and not roots, who praise a modernity that makes it possible for us to get rid of our histories and to create our own lives – nonetheless became very sentimental every time I got in touch with a still living relative. And even if that relative had never met my mother or was as remotely related to me as for instance my grandmothers' mothers' younger brothers' youngest son, we felt an instant connection as soon as we met and still keep in touch as if we had been close relatives all our lives. Why have even I succumbed to the idea that you have something in common with distant kin? I still do not have the answer. I can only say that I am not just a clear-headed scholar but also a sentimental, ordinary person.

I do manage, however, to see the irony in genealogy as such. Genealogy attributes blood related kin enormous importance, even if we have never met them. There is also the self deception in believing that we are the direct descendants of our forefathers and foremothers, forgetting that we have to share them with several other relatives: We all have two parents, four grandparents, eight great-grandparents, sixteen great-great-grandparents and so on. If we go back ten generations, to around the year 1700, we theoretically will have about two thousand direct ancestors. If we go back twenty generations it will be as much as about two million. So which one to choose as the ancestor we see ourselves as direct descendants of? By writing this book I have paid great attention to my four Jewish great-grandparents who emigrated from Romania to France. But they ought not be more important to me than my Danish great-grandparents, some of whom immigrated from Schleswig to the Faroe Islands to Greenland and then to Denmark. There seems to be a lot of mobility in my family.

Through genealogy we highlight blood related kin but downplay the importance other people have played in our lives. My mother and her parents created narratives where relatives had been written out of history and "families of choice" had been given great importance. Though my mother never mentioned her family beyond parents, she very often spoke of her friends from school with whom she formed lifelong friendships. She also fondly recalled neighbors she named aunt and uncle, whom she and her parents had chosen as their relatives. In that respect this story is not only about "transnational families" but also about "imagined families in mobile worlds" just like the theme of this issue.

References

Gillis, J. 1996: *A World of their own Making: Myth, Ritual, and the Quest for Family Values*. New York: Basic Books.

Lützen, K. 2009: *Mors hemmelighed: På sporet af en jødisk indvandrerhistorie*. Copenhagen: Gyldendal.

Karin Lützen, Ph.D., is a senior lecturer in history at Roskilde University. She has written books and articles on so diverse subjects as the history of homosexuality, the city, benevolence, and social reform. Her latest book is about Eastern European Jewish Immigration and she is now working on a history of silver manufacturing in Denmark 1880–1980. (lutz@ruc.dk)

THE MATERIALITY OF THE IMAGINED FAMILY

Laura Stark

The volume *Imagined Families* draws welcome attention to recent developments in transnational families and their use of technologies. When Ulla Vuorela used the term "imagined families" in 2002, she was describing the different ways in which transnationally dispersed family networks with deep historical roots in the colonial period are perceived by kin group members themselves. In the present volume, the term "imagined" is intended more broadly to encompass how agencies, institutions and groups perceive the new possibilities offered to families by technology and mobility. The volume focuses on the discourses, images and political interests through which understandings of migration, mobility and family are socially constructed and reified. Its authors have drawn attention to important dimensions of these topics such as individual experience and motives, as well as ethical and emotional dilemmas. The point that all families and kinship relations are to some extent imagined is well taken, but as the authors point out, in many cases these most recent exercises in "imagining" the family do not necessarily result in innovation in new family forms and ideals. Although new technologies and new political alliances are sometimes utilized to disrupt older assumptions of the family as rooted or fixed in a geographic place, as in Timm's article, they are often used to shore up and protect conservative notions of the family: for instance the family as incomplete without biological children, as engaged in close daily interaction, or as characterized by a gendered division of labour in migration contexts, in which men are expected to migrate as wage labourers, but women are expected to adopt a passive role as the accompanying spouse.[1] Families may use new technologies and mobilities to expand their opportunities, but in some cases they do it simply to ensure the family's survival. It may be useful to see the family *itself* as a material "survival strategy" for individuals in societies where other social institutions and groupings offer little concrete support. Even in Europe, the current youth unemployment rate of over 20 percent highlights the continuing importance of the family as a survival net. It is to be hoped that this volume will generate new interest in how the family is currently understood and organized in the context of current challenges facing European societies.

As mentioned above, in each of the articles of this theme issue, the authors have chosen to critically examine the discursive dimensions of the transnational and/or technologically-assisted family and to bring attention to the nature and source of the rhetoric surrounding controversial family issues. In a volume of limited space, this is a worthy and justified aim. At the same time, however, it has meant that the material causes and consequences of these discourses remain under-problematized: we are given few insights into how individual agency is impacted by the nature of IVF technologies, or by the opportunities and limitations of mobile telephony and Skype, by economic conditions in Eastern Europe, or by the nature of prostitution in different contexts. We receive little sense of how familial ties, which have been of concern to the Catholic Church in Hüwelmeier's and Radkowska-Walkowicz's articles, historically have played a role in the Church's political aims, in other words in the expansion of its power through international networks of young migrating nuns, or as a bulwark against the intrusion into private lives of science and technology, which represent the main challenges to the Church's authority today. Moreover, if understood as a discursive creation alone, the mobile family becomes a difficult category for historical analysis. Without an account linking the discursive to the material, an adequate conceptualization of change is not possible.

For this reason, in my commentary I would like to take up the thematic thread of materiality which is only implicitly present in the articles in this theme issue. By materiality, I mean the physical and economic aspects of family organization and mobility, in other words livelihoods, resources and labour (other material aspects which I do not address are the body, disability, sexuality, health and illness). As an adherent of practice theory, I do not consider the material level of analysis to be logically prior to the level of social discourse, and it is important to refrain from essentializing such seemingly material facts as human reproduction or the global economy, which we experience primarily through rhetorical constructs. Particularly in the man-made environments in which most of us live today, material conditions do not reproduce themselves but are rooted in human practice.

I became interested in the issue of families and material resources when researching the first public discussion on Finnish rural women's rights, which took place in newspapers in the early 1860s (Stark 2011). This discussion in the press centered on so-called "home thievery", a common practice in which rural farm women covertly sold the products of the farm household (chiefly butter and grain) behind the farm master's back. With the proceeds of the sale, these farm wives and daughters then secretly bought consumer goods which were important in maintaining their social status as distinctive from lower-class servant women and laborers' wives. Although most who wrote to the press on this topic were educated social reformers and farm masters, several young farm women also discussed home thievery in their letters to the press. From the 64 letters published in Finnish-language newspapers on the topic between 1849 and 1901, it became clear to me that the issue of home thievery, while couched in moral terms as an evil, a vice and a "sickness", was recognized by many male and female writers to be rooted in the problems of unequal inheritance. Farm masters who wanted to save money needed their adult children to work on the farm without pay rather than work for other farms as paid servants (at which point the father would have had to hire servants from the outside to replace his children). The incentive intended to keep elder sons working on their birth farm was the promise of later inheriting the farm as a whole, but no such formal incentives were provided for daughters. Although farm daughters were legally entitled to receive half of the inheritance that their brothers received, in eastern Finland they often received nothing more than a few basic dowry goods when they married. Male writers from a wide range of backgrounds argued that without equal inheritance, women would never be motivated to work for the common good of the farm but would instead pilfer from the farm's storehouses to accumulate the goods they felt were rightfully theirs. Farm masters were reported as having traditionally turned a blind eye to the whole practice, yet in the early 1860s they began to speak out in condemnation of it. I concluded that home thievery had earlier been a tacit incentive to keep daughters laboring on the farm, one which did not undermine the public authority of the farm master as long as it remained hidden. However, when retail trade became legal in the countryside in 1859, consumer goods came within reach of even those family members who had little opportunity to travel to distant markets. Since farm women sold pilfered goods secretly to the new rural shops through intermediaries, the practice of home thievery after 1859 quickly became expensive for farm masters, as "gallons of grain and pounds of butter began to slip away to the shops".[2] Home thievery went from being a hidden incentive to a visible embarrassment for farm masters when farm women's wearing of the latest fabrics and high consumption of expensive coffee made it clear to others in the community that the family patriarch was unable to control the actions of his household members.

Although to explain human motives solely in rational economic terms would be reductionist and counterproductive, I was intrigued in my research by how a micro-level examination of material organization and resource distribution opened up new insights into the linkages between economic motives and cultural discourses on gender and family. Applied to the late modern family, a materialist perspective could, for example, explain why family members separate in the first place, why some members migrate while others stay behind, why some persons invest time and energy maintaining transnational family ties while others do not, or which specific family forms attract the greatest investment from their members. This question may be more easily answered for past societies, in which inheritance and socio-symbolic capital (honor and social prestige) were channeled to individuals primarily through roles occupied within the family. But are the present-day functions of the family so different? Inheritance, for instance, continues to be a highly pertinent issue for many Europeans, even for those who have left their birth communities, as anthropologist Nancy Konvalinka (2009, in press) suggests in her study of *embodied inheritance*. Konvalinka argues that persons can be shaped, by themselves and others, to maximize the use of the capital they inherit, when, for example, diplomats' children become diplomats or farmers' children become farmers. In the area of Spain she examines, economic conditions are pushing rural men to embody both their own and their sisters' inheritances. Daughters inherit land and thus control some of the land farmed by their brothers. A new implicit contract between brothers and sisters has recently appeared, however, in which brothers work hard on the farm to pay for their sisters' education, enabling their sisters to be more mobile than rural women used to be. As sisters become successful, move out of the rural context and marry non-farmers, they abstain from both using and selling the land they own, and brothers continue to use this land as if it were theirs.

While attention should be paid to the material and economic *causes* of family mobility or the family's use of new technologies, the material *consequences* of these practices should also be examined, and here there can be no *a priori* assumption that families and their strategies are characterized by solidarity and cohesion. In the 1980s and 1990s, anthropologists and socio-economists[3] undertook a theoretical re-examination of the political and material factors underlying the family as an economic unit and began to peer into the "black box" of the household, in order to deconstruct the unitary socio-economic model of the family which had prevailed from the late 1950s to the late 1980s.[4] Previously, the question of what went on *inside* the family and household with regard to work and resource allocation had been overlooked, and if resource allocation had been considered at all, it was assumed that resources and family members' tasks were rationally allocated by a benevolent household head seeking to maximize household utility for the common good. Later critiques defined the family and farm household instead as a locus of political struggle involving competing interests, negotiations over resources, and even conflict. Peering "inside" the family and household to perceive the internal conflicts therein would be a first step to understanding whether we can speak of "family" as a unitary concept in, for example, the issue of IVF in Poland: do wives and husbands view the concepts of childlessness, family, and reproductive rights in the same light? A non-unitary, material view of the household is also important for understanding the issue of female migration. Do we know, for instance, all the intrahousehold factors that push women to migrate? How are other family members affected materially by the migration of wives and mothers? Which relatives can make claims on female emigrant labourers' remittances and resources?

Material perspectives on the family may be even more pertinent for so-called developing countries. Economic restructuring and the withdrawal of the state from social and economic intervention, the explosive growth of the informal economy, and the influx of cheaply-made goods to low-income countries are resulting in severe unemployment and deprivation of basic needs. They are also contributing to a phenomenon which has been called "the feminization of obligation" within low-income countries, in which women must increasingly take on the primary burden for the survival of the family and dependent children, while men are becoming more likely to desert their families, withhold earnings from them or take the earnings of wives to fund self-oriented consumption (Chant 2006, 2008). Another consequence of relative income and labour structure differences among societies is the rise of global care chains (Hochschild 2000), in which, typically, a Filipina woman who migrates to work as a nanny in a high-income country uses her wages to employ someone to care for her children in Manila, who may in turn have her children cared for by another woman in the rural Philippines, who may depend on her older daughter to care for the younger siblings.

Families may in some sense be "imagined", but they have also always been mechanisms of resource distribution and the transmission of wealth. In many ways they also serve as structures which oversee the organization of labor. Families must always find ways to survive materially from day to day, which often means competing with other family groups. New forms of family arise when resources and livelihood opportunities themselves become redistributed in new ways in time and space (i.e. livelihood opportunities become seasonal or only available after lengthy training or education, or certain types of work become centered in particular geographical locations). These considerations give rise to questions such as: How do changes in the resources available to families lead to different re-imaginings of the family? How do new discourses surrounding the family affect the ways in which families manage their assets and strategize for continued survival?

Notes

1 See also Madianou and Miller's 2011 article in which they argue that for Filipina emigrant mothers, the immediacy of communication offered by mobile telephony has served to reinforce traditional notions of the mother as domestic caretaker who must continue to invest time and emotion in her children from a distance.

2 Oct. 19, 1888. *Karjalatar* no. 83, "Joensuusta. Maataloudellisetolotläänissämme".

3 E.g., Collier & Rosaldo (1981); Hartmann (1981); Sen (1983); Delphy (1984); Yanagisako & Collier (1987); Guyer & Peters (1987); Phillips (1989); Hart (1992, 1995); Moore (1992); Kabeer (1994); Agarwal (1997); Kandiyoti (1998).

4 E.g., Chayanov (1966). The unitary model of the household was made popular by the work of Gary Becker (1965, 1974, 1981).

References

Agarwal, Bina 1997: Bargaining and Gender Relations: Within and Beyond the Household. *Feminist Economics* 3:1, 1–51.

Becker, Gary 1965: A Theory of the Allocation of Time. *Economic Journal* 299:75, 493–517.

Becker, Gary 1974: A Theory of Marriage: Part II. *Journal of Political Economy* 82:2, 11–26.

Becker, Gary 1981: *A Treatise on the Family*. Cambridge, Mass.: Harvard University Press.

Chant, Sylvia 2006: Re-thinking the "Feminization of Poverty" in Relation to Aggregate Gender Indices. *Journal of Human Development* 7:2, 201–220.

Chant, Sylvia 2008: Beyond Incomes: A New Take on the Feminisation of Poverty. In: *Poverty in Focus: Gender Inequality*. International Poverty Center, www.undp-povertycentre.org.

Chayanov, Aleksandr 1966: *The Theory of Peasant Economy*. Edited by Daniel Thorner, Basile Kerblay & R.E.F. Smith. Homewood, IL: Richard Irwin.

Collier, Jane & Michelle Rosaldo 1981: Politics and Gender in Simple Societies. In: Sherry Ortner & Harriet Whitehead (eds.), *Sexual Meanings: The Cultural Construction of Gender and Sexuality*. Cambridge: Cambridge University Press.

Delphy, Christine 1984: *Close to Home: A Materialist Analysis of Women's Oppression*. London: Hutchinson.

Guyer, Jane & Pauline Peters 1987: Conceptualizing the Household: Issues of Theory and Policy in Africa. *Development and Change* 18:2, 197–214.

Hart, Gillian 1992: Household Production Reconsidered: Production, Patronage and Gender Politics in Rural Malaysia. *Rural Development* 20:6, 809–823.

Hart, Gillian 1995: Gender and Household Dynamics: Recent Theories and their Implications. In: M.G. Quibria (ed.), *Critical Issues in Asian Development*. Hong Kong: Oxford University Press.

Hartmann, Heidi 1981: The Family as the Locus of Gender, Class, and Political Struggle: The Example of Housework. *Signs* 6:3, 366–394.

Hochschild, Arlie 2000: Global Care Chains and Emotional Surplus Value. In: Will Hutton, & Anthony Giddens (eds.), *On The Edge: Living with Global Capitalism*. London: Jonathan Cape.

Kabeer, Naila 1994: *Reversed Realities: Gender Hierarchies in Development Thought*. London: Verso.

Kandiyoti, Denise 1998: Gender, Power and Contestation: "Rethinking Bargaining with Patriarchy". In: Cecile Jackson & Ruth Pearson (eds.), *Feminist Visions of Development: Gender Analysis and Policy*. London & New York: Routledge.

Konvalinka, Nancy 2009: When Equal-Part Inheritance is not Equivalent: Gender and the Value of Land in a Spanish Village. In: P. Olsson & H. Ruotsala (eds.), *Gendered Rural Spaces*. Helsinki: Finnish Literature Society.

Konvalinka, Nancy In press: *Gender, Work and Property*. Frankfurt: Campus Verlag.

Madianou, Mirca & Daniel Miller 2011: Mobile Phone Parenting: Reconfiguring Relationships between Filipina Migrant Mothers and their Left-behind Children. *New Media & Society* 13:3, 457–470.

Moore, Henrietta 1992: Households and Gender Relations: The Modelling of the Economy. In: S. Ortiz & S. Lees (eds.), *Understanding Economic Process*. New York: University Press of America.

Phillips, Lynn 1989: Gender Dynamics and Rural Household Strategies. *Canadian Review of Sociology and Anthropology* 26:2, 294–310.

Sen, Amartya 1983: Economics and the Family. *Asian Development Review* 1:2, 599–634.

Stark, Laura 2011: *The Limits of Patriarchy: How Female Networks of Pilfering and Gossip Sparked the First Debates on Rural Gender Rights in the 19th-Century Finnish-Language Press*. Helsinki: Finnish Literature Society.

Vuorela, Ulla 2002: Transnational Families: Imagined and Real Communities. In: D.F. Bryceson & U. Vuorela (eds.), *The Transnational Family: New European Frontiers and Global Networks*. Oxford: Berg.

Yanagisako, Sylvia Junko & Jane Fishburne Collier 1987: Toward a Unified Analysis of Gender and Kinship. In: Jane Fishburne Collier & Sylvia Junko Yanagisako (eds.), *Gender and Kinship: Essays Toward a Unified Analysis*. Stanford: Stanford University Press.

Laura Stark is currently Professor of Ethnology at the University of Jyväskylä, Finland. Her research interests include modernization processes in nineteenth-century Finland, gender relations in Finnish agrarian society, nineteenth-century concepts of body and self in rural Finland, as well as magic, witchcraft and folk religion. She is the author of *The Limits of Patriarchy: How Female Networks of Pilfering and Gossip Sparked the First Debates on Rural Gender Rights in the 19th-Century Finnish-Language Press* (2011, Finnish Literature Society).
(laura.stark@jyu.fi)

Springer Theses

Recognizing Outstanding Ph.D. Research

Aims and Scope

The series "Springer Theses" brings together a selection of the very best Ph.D. theses from around the world and across the physical sciences. Nominated and endorsed by two recognized specialists, each published volume has been selected for its scientific excellence and the high impact of its contents for the pertinent field of research. For greater accessibility to non-specialists, the published versions include an extended introduction, as well as a foreword by the student's supervisor explaining the special relevance of the work for the field. As a whole, the series will provide a valuable resource both for newcomers to the research fields described, and for other scientists seeking detailed background information on special questions. Finally, it provides an accredited documentation of the valuable contributions made by today's younger generation of scientists.

Theses are accepted into the series by invited nomination only and must fulfill all of the following criteria

- They must be written in good English.
- The topic should fall within the confines of Chemistry, Physics, Earth Sciences, Engineering and related interdisciplinary fields such as Materials, Nanoscience, Chemical Engineering, Complex Systems and Biophysics.
- The work reported in the thesis must represent a significant scientific advance.
- If the thesis includes previously published material, permission to reproduce this must be gained from the respective copyright holder.
- They must have been examined and passed during the 12 months prior to nomination.
- Each thesis should include a foreword by the supervisor outlining the significance of its content.
- The theses should have a clearly defined structure including an introduction accessible to scientists not expert in that particular field.

More information about this series at http://www.springer.com/series/8790

Jens Karschau

Mathematical Modelling of Chromosome Replication and Replicative Stress

Doctoral Thesis accepted by
the University of Aberdeen, UK

Author
Dr. Jens Karschau
Biological Physics Division
Max Planck Institute for the Physics of Complex Systems
Dresden
Germany

Supervisor
Dr. Alessandro de Moura
Department of Physics
University of Aberdeen
Aberdeen
UK

ISSN 2190-5053 ISSN 2190-5061 (electronic)
ISBN 978-3-319-36282-3 ISBN 978-3-319-08861-7 (eBook)
DOI 10.1007/978-3-319-08861-7

Springer Cham Heidelberg New York Dordrecht London

Softcover reprint of the hardcover 1st edition 2015

Printed on acid-free paper

Springer is part of Springer Science+Business Media (www.springer.com)

Supervisor's Foreword

DNA replication is arguably the most crucial process in living cells. It is the mechanism by which organisms pass their genetic information from one generation to the next, and life on Earth would be unthinkable without it. Recent revolutionary advances in experimental techniques in molecular biology allow the dynamics of chromosome replication of whole genomes to be investigated with unprecedented accuracy, resolution and detail. This extraordinary wealth of data makes it possible to use quantitative and predictive mathematical models to investigate this crucial biological process. In fact, many of the recent advances in the field come from multidisciplinary approaches involving applications of modelling to address important biological questions.

This thesis makes important contributions to this line of research. In particular, it addresses two key questions in the area of DNA replication: what evolutionary forces drive the positioning of replication origins in the chromosome; and how the spatial organisation of replication factories observed in many organisms is achieved. These questions lie at the heart of much of cutting-edge research in the field, and the application of mathematical modelling described in the thesis yielded new insights as well as new predictions.

The first part of this work deals with the fundamental problem that locations on the DNA have to bind with proteins first to become an origin of replication. However this process is the result of a series of stochastic events, and hence the probability of a particular location to act as an origin of replication during a particular round of cell cycle varies; and so does the distance from one eventually active origin to its nearest neighbour. Some locations have a very high protein-binding affinity and activate in nearly every cell cycle; some others are less prone to do so. Many of the previous models on DNA replication however have taken origin loci and their activation probability as an input parameter, and neglected the question whether loci positions have been chosen in a manner that depends on the likelihood of their activation. A naive assumption would be to equally distribute origins along a chromosome to give cells minimum replication; then every pair of forks that emerges to either side from an origin travels the same distance until it coalesces with another. Here, a mathematical model of replication timing that encompasses both parameters—origin position as well as origin activation probability—shows that however sparsely spread groups of origins achieve minimum replication time, if their activation probability is low in contrast to an equally spread out origin distribution. This monograph shows the importance of origin grouping in nature using a genetic algorithm (that mimics evolution by giving benefit to those individuals with least required time to replicate their genome, i.e. those with optimal origin locations). The result particularly relates to an example of yeast, where origin locations and activation probabilities are known; where Jens shows that low probability origins are predominantly found grouped together. He also adds two further examples to the discussion of origin grouping. One is with regard to early frog embryos, where there is seen variation in the actual time of origin activation, and the other concerns organisms with multiple origins on a circular chromosome, which show little grouping behaviour in nature.

The second part culminates in an intuitive explanation for the formation of replication factories: they result from random encounters of distal replication forks that are seen to localise together in an energetically preferred state. Conversely, there is no requirement for an active transport and controlling mechanism to bring them together, and random association can become achieved simply by means of diffusion. The herein developed mathematical model takes a set of experimentally measured association probabilities of neighbouring replication forks in yeast. These forks have a maximal possible separation from another, which is given by the length of the piece of DNA that connects them. A fit of the model to data shows that their probability of association decays as a function of their distance from another as well as their binding energy. This model then extrapolates well to the replication factory size distribution of an entire yeast cell, which experimental collaborators also have measured in vivo. Conclusively, this makes the process described in this thesis a classic example for developing a physical model of a biological process that not only produces a fit using known data, but is also able to correctly produce new predictions.

This work is the result of real cross-disciplinary collaborations between biologists and physicists, and as a result its findings represent advances in both physics/applied mathematics and molecular biology. This kind of intrinsically multidisciplinary research is becoming more and more necessary in the rapidly evolving field of molecular biology, and this work is a fine example of that.

Aberdeen, May 2014 Dr. Alessandro de Moura

Abstract

DNA replication is a common feature of life, and proper genome synthesis is crucial for error-free cell division to occur. Failure in this can be lethal for an entire generation of cells, or even give rise to cancer. Replication starting points (origins) play an important role for proper DNA synthesis. It is their distance from one to another that determines the replication fork travel time, and thus the time required until synthesis completion. Much of previous theoretical work on how DNA replication can be faithful neglected how these origins take their place and how replication time is affected when origins fail to activate. It is however crucial that origin loci are chosen so that too large gaps between them are avoided; otherwise the time until completion of chromosome replication becomes much longer than is allowed by the cell cycle.

We address this lack of knowledge here using mathematical modelling to describe swift progression through the cell cycle and efficient manners of copying the DNA. On one hand, the DNA synthesis rate is fixed, and thus the time for replicating DNA between origins should be too. On the other hand, origin activation is stochastic which might cause delays in replication completion times. It is therefore a balancing act to spread out origins in a certain manner to compensate for variations in activation. We show both analytically and through numerical simulations that there exist two regimes for origins, either positioned together in groups spaced far away from the next, or as equally scattered single origins depending on the uncertainty when activation occurs. We apply the model to known origin locations in yeast and show that grouping is a means of organisation driven by evolutionary pressure. The model is able to reproduce origin distributions of early frog embryos which are thought to be random, and shows contrarily that grouping must occur in order to swiftly complete replication. The model also holds when considering a circular DNA topology as for instance archaeal genomes have, as well as if applied to the whole replication profiling data of yeast.

We also introduce a model to account for the interaction of replication forks with each other which leads to their assembly into *replication factories*. For simplicity, cartoons often depict DNA replication on a straight one-dimensional line. In fact we deal with a polymer that is packed and modified on different levels yielding higher order structures of organisation. DNA replication also appears to be spatially organised within the cellular nucleus. Active replication forks are experimentally observed to organise in clusters of *replication factories*. We initially investigate these by describing the process with a bead-on-a-string model. The initial model represents two active pairs of replication forks connected by DNA. We show using Boltzmann-statistics that their assembly into a factory is stochastic and matches experimental association probabilities. The model then extends to describe properties of experimental distributions such as fork numbers per cluster during the DNA synthesis phase for genome wide yeast replication data. Our in silico distribution of forks per factory matches in vivo data well; which suggests that active forks encounter each other randomly for an association into replication factories.

Acknowledgments

I would first like to thank my supervisor Alessandro de Moura. I feel very grateful to him for offering me his guidance, training and support to create and develop my own ideas. I would also like to thank my co-supervisor Julian Blow for his support, and thank him for his time, patience and constructive criticism during our discussions on how to model DNA replication. Most of all I am indebted to both of my supervisors and the Scottish Universities Life Science Alliance for giving me the chance to work on a fascinating project. It allowed me to establish further collaborations and I would like to thank all my collaborators for their experimental contribution to this thesis, particularly Peter Gillespie, Conrad Nieduszynski, Nazan Saner, Renata Retkute and Tomo Tanaka.

I would also like to acknowledge the rest of the Physics group at Aberdeen for their helpful and stimulating discussions, my office-mates Luca Ciandrini and Kelly Iarosz, my flat-mates Christopher Brackley and Nicolas Rubido-Obrer, my house-mates Tina and Aaron Schiavone, and not to forget all my other friends Michael Budnitzki, Thomas Burghagen, Stuart Campbell, Lucas Fernandes, Fiona Harden, Stefan Heldt, Martin Klauke, Thomas Pfau, Elahe Radmaneshfar, James Reid, Markus Rehberg, Julia Safier, Marcillio dosSantos, Ulli Seeger...

Finally I would like to thank my parents and my sister, as well as everyone I forgot to mention here and who have offered me support and encouragement during my Ph.D. studies.

Contents

List of Publications

I list here publications that have arisen from this work.

J. Karschau, J. J. Blow, A. P. S. de Moura Optimal placement of origins for DNA replication. *Physical Review Letters*, 108(5):058101 (2012).

N. Saner, J. Karschau, T. Natsume, M. Gierlinski, R. Retkute, M. Hawkins, C. A. Nieduszynski, J. J. Blow, A. P. S. de Moura, T. Tanaka Stochastic association of neighboring replicons creates replication factories in budding yeast. *Journal of Cell Biology*, 202(7):1001–1012 (2013).

A further publication, other than those described herein, is.

J. Karschau, C. de Almeida, M. C. Richard, S. Miller, I. R. Booth, C. Grebogi, A. P. S. de Moura A matter of life or death: modeling DNA damage and repair in bacteria. *Biophysical Journal*, 100(4):814–821 (2013).

Chapter 1
Introduction

To accomplish their numerous tasks cells must create and control an internal (spatial and temporal) order of processes by properly organising their resources. One of these processes—arguably the most crucial process of all—is DNA replication whose mechanisms appear to rely on random events. At first, this seems counter-intuitive as one would expect tremendous fluctuations in the time it takes cells to duplicate, but this is not the case: most cells have a well-timed cell cycle, and this is necessary if they are to have consistent growth rate and generation times. DNA acts as the blueprint of the entire protein machinery and cellular architecture, and its integrity when passed on from mother to daughter cells is therefore of particular importance. Diseases are a common consequence of replication failure, which can lead to embryonic death, cell apoptosis, or abnormal cell growth. This has the potential to imbalance tissue growth leading to malignant tumour growth—making replication failure one of the most common causes of cancer. In order to understand how such failure arises it is necessary to first comprehend how robust (precisely timed) DNA replication occurs under normal and healthy circumstances. Although the structure of the DNA has been known for over 50 years we still lack complete understanding of all facets of DNA replication. The aim of the work presented in this thesis is to address the lack of knowledge in this area using mathematical modelling, and to ultimately further our fight against diseases such as cancer.

1.1 The Cell Cycle

DNA replication occurs inside the nucleus of eukaryotic cells. Unlike bacteria, that do not have compartmental structures like the cellular nucleus and that can have concurrent rounds of DNA replication, DNA replication in eukaryotes is subject to a strict timing regime. This is the cell cycle, and it sets the time line of events in the life of a cell. Figure 1.1a depicts a typical cell cycle as we find it in most animal, human and yeast cells. It contains 4 phases, one of these is the mitosis phase (M-phase) where cells divide and produce offspring. Two further phases of the cell cycle are

J. Karschau, *Mathematical Modelling of Chromosome Replication and Replicative Stress*, Springer Theses, DOI 10.1007/978-3-319-08861-7_1

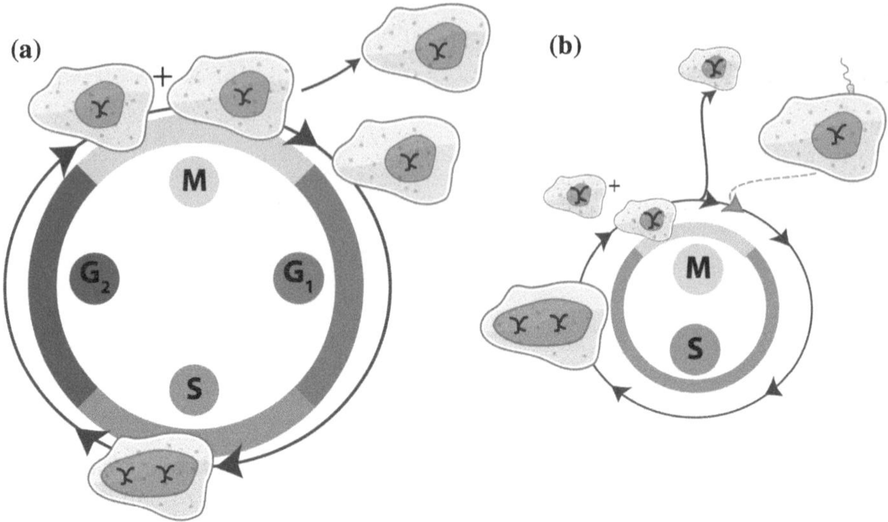

Fig. 1.1 The eukaryotic cell cycle. **a** The cell cycle of most eukaryotic organisms such as *Saccharomyces cerevisiae* contains four phases. Cell division occurs during M-phase, origin licensing during G_1-phase, DNA synthesis during S-phase, and cells grow and prepare for division in G_2-phase. **b** Early *Xenopus laevis* embryos have an abbreviated cell cycle which only consists of M-phase (during which the cells divide and origin licensing follows), and S-phase (during which the DNA is copied). Once fertilised, zygotes—eggs fused with spermii—begin replicating and dividing for 12 rounds each lasting 25 min. During this time cells only double their genome and then divide without going through G_1- and G_2-phase

G_1 and G_2 phase which are also often called gap phases as they sit in between the DNA synthesis phase (S-phase) and M-phase. Their role during the cell cycle is to either prepare the cell for DNA replication (G_1-phase) or to give the cell time to grow and prepare for division into two daughter cells (G_2-phase). The transition from one phase to another is regulated by biochemical agents called cyclines and cycline dependent kinases [1] which govern the timing of events in a cell. Their levels can be biochemically measured which can hint which cell cycle phase is currently active at a particular point during an observation of cells. There is an ever-growing body of also theoretical works that try to model cell cycle events using for example signalling networks or sets of ordinary differential equations. We invite the interested reader to explore the work by Radmaneshfar [2] for further information on modelling cell cycle as well as the consequences of stresses when exerted on a cell—particularly for the case of varying osmotic pressure.

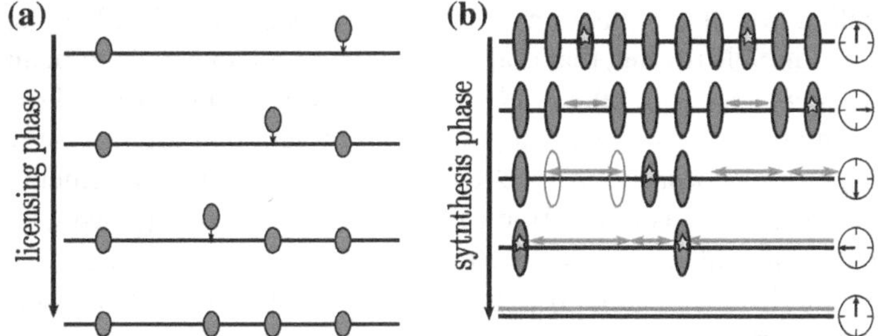

Fig. 1.2 DNA replication consists of two separate phases. **a** During the licensing phase origin-forming proteins bind to the DNA (*orange ovals*). **b** During the later synthesis phase, these origins become activated (indicated by *star*). From an activated origin replication forks emerge from either side of it (*blue arrows*) synthesising the DNA. Origins which have yet to become activated become unlicensed once DNA in this region has been replicated (*hollow ovals*). Their activation is then impossible

1.2 General Principles of the DNA Replication Process

Several mechanisms, the complexity of which is not yet fully understood, work to ensure that the DNA is properly copied—in its entirety—prior to cell division. A temporal separation of processes avoids multiple copies of DNA: the loading of inactive proteins onto potential replication initiation sites (*origins*) occurs only during a distinct phase of the cell cycle before actual origin activation [3, 4] (cf. Fig. 1.2a). The activation of licensed origins occurs in another phase when bidirectional forks emerge from origins (Fig. 1.2a). Depending on the organism the timing of these two phases can differ. For example, the yeast *Saccharomyces cerevisiae* has a cell cycle consisting of four phases (Fig. 1.1a), only two of which have relevance for DNA replication (G_1 and S-phase); it takes about 90 min to complete one round of the cell cycle. In contrast, early *Xenopus laevis* frog embryos have a shorter cell cycle consisting only of those DNA replication relevant phases (as shown in Fig. 1.1b), and completion of their cycle is within 25 min.

The first stage of DNA replication is often referred to as *licensing* (Fig. 1.2a); this is where various proteins bind to the DNA at the origin sites. Depending on the organism, licensing can be at random or sequence specific DNA positions [5], and although the licensing components are known to assemble into the *pre replication complex* (preRC), details of the interaction amongst the components is not yet fully understood. The current model suggests that proteins find their licensing binding site via diffusion, i.e. it is a stochastic process. Recently, it has also been shown that the choice of licensed origin sites in higher organisms varies from tissue to tissue or from one embryonal stage of development to another [6–8]. Another study suggests that changes to several limiting factors could lead to a prolonging of the replication time [9]; this also fits with another model where the cell cycle slows down during the mid-blastula transition in embryonal development [10]. Despite these advances, that work does not explain how the positions of the cohort of origins are chosen, and crucially how this results in a consistent timing for replication.

It is puzzling how this collection of stochastic processes in DNA replication can still yield reproducible timing, that is aligned with the cell cycle. Specifically, origins in *Xenopus laevis* appear to take random places and it is currently unknown how a random placement can give reliable replication completion times; this is the so called *random completion* or *random gap* problem [5, 11]. Besides the placement of origins, dynamic processes such as replication fork progression or stall (pausing due, e.g. to DNA damage) have also been shown to impact replication timing. For example, fork movement also plays some role in replication timing such as consequences of asymmetries in forks progressing either in a $3' \rightarrow 5'$ or $5' \rightarrow 3'$ direction [12], as well as does the DNA sequence appear to shape genomic positions which eventually leads to preferred origin locations, i.e. so termed timing domains [12–14].

Specifically, proper origin spacing is necessary because after licensing there is no further opportunity to lay out more origins once DNA synthesis begins. If origin sites are too far apart, replication fails and genomic information is lost because cells would divide before all DNA has been copied. Origin activation itself is also a stochastic process. So not only must the origins be sufficiently closely located, one needs them to be sufficiently closely loaded in the right ratio—active to inactive ones—without protein and energy resources being wasted. It has been suggested that particular higher order DNA modifications, for example DNA methylation (epigenetic factors) or histone modifications can hinder licensing and are sources of timing variation [15, 16].

1.3 Aims of This Thesis

The purpose of the work presented here is to resolve current questions surrounding the effects of noise in DNA replication. This will aid in solving problems such as the *random completion problem* and how replication forks interact inside the nucleus. This thesis elucidates three key elements centred around these problems using physical modelling. Specifically, these chief questions here are:

1. Why are origins located where they are? We consider *Saccharomyces cerevisiae*, where origin locations are encoded in the sequence and ask what are the optimal origin positions given noisy conditions during origin licensing and origin activation.
2. How should origins in *Xenopus laevis* be positioned to give minimum replication time?
3. Is there an interaction between replication forks? How do they interact with each other inside the cellular nucleus?

Answering these questions will further our understanding of the DNA replication process as a whole. Within the bigger picture this will help to identify particular targets within the DNA replication mechanisms which can be used to attack or avoid cancer.

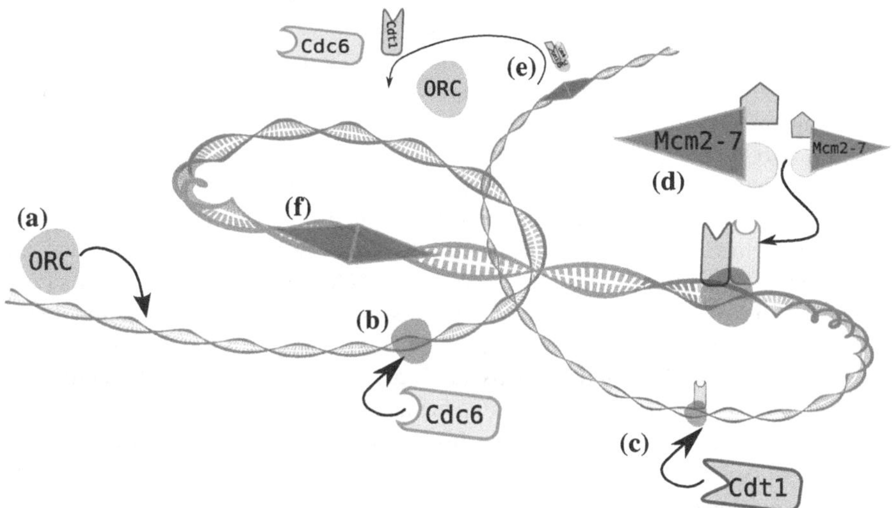

Fig. 1.3 Schematic representation of the steps involved in origin licensing. Not yet bound proteins are marked by their names, DNA-bound proteins are only marked with their symbols. **a** ORC binds to DNA which then recruits Cdc6 (**b**) and Cdt1 (**c**). These reactions are reversible. **d** In the final step, Mcm2-7 irreversibly binds as a double-hexamer. **e** This releases the previously bound components ORC, Cdc6 and Cdt1. Mcm2-7 remains irreversibly bound to DNA and forms the pre-replicative complex (preRC) in (**f**). This one can become active during S-phase as an origin of replication

1.4 Origin Licensing

As mentioned above, prior to the synthesis of DNA, replication starting points (*origins of replication*) are established at certain genomic locations (*origin loci*). This process is named origin licensing, and the fact that it is temporally separated from the DNA synthesis process means that DNA which has already been replicated does not become re-replicated.

Licensing consists of a sequential docking of proteins onto origin loci. The components have been found to be involved in a four-step mechanism as shown in Fig. 1.3. First a protein called the origin-recognition complex (ORC) binds to DNA (Fig. 1.3a). This is followed by the binding of two further scaffolding proteins called Cdc6 and Cdt1 that bind sequentially as depicted in Fig. 1.3b and c. Finally, the minichromosome maintenance complex (Mcm) consisting of several individual Mcm2-7 proteins is recruited to form the so-called *pre-replication complex* (preRC) (Fig. 1.3d), and triggers the release of ORC, Cdc6 and Cdt1 (Fig. 1.3e). However at this stage the preRC is still inactive and it shall remain inactive until the licensing phase is completed. Recent studies have shown that Mcm2-7 binds in the form of a pairwise hexamer (pMcm) [17, 18], i.e. there are always two Mcm2-7 complexes bound back-to-back with DNA [19] as shown in Fig. 1.3e and f. This suggests that Mcm2-7 is a driving force in processing the DNA during synthesis, and in fact it was shown that

Mcm2-7 acts as a helicase which unwinds the DNA [20–23], allowing the polymerase to access and copy it. So Mcm2-7 has an integral role in the replication machinery.

The way in which origin loci—those not yet licensed sites—are chosen differs depending on the organism or the tissue being studied. In this work we mainly focus on two systems, namely the yeast *Saccharomyces cerevisiae*, and the early embryos of the frog *Xenopus laevis*. It is well accepted that the yeast has signatures of specific origin loci encoded into its genomic sequence which ORC recognises. These have been termed *Autonomously Replicating Sequences* (ARS) [24, 25], and are distributed in distinctive 11 basepairs (bp) long DNA sequence specific motifs [26]. In contrast, in *Xenopus laevis* such clear and distinctive loci for ORC-binding do not exist, and ORC can bind anywhere on the chromosome [27, 28]. Both organisms, *Saccharomyces cerevisiae* and *Xenopus laevis* are good model systems for helping us to understand the organisation of licensing in man. Having these two model organisms allows us to study each mode of licensing—random locations and specific origin location—in isolation. Organisation of licensing in man does not seem as clear as in either *Saccharomyces cerevisiae* or *Xenopus laevis*. For example, a study finds that there are human genomic regions with sequence specific origin loci (as is the case for *Saccharomyces cerevisiae*) and there are also DNA segments in which there are no clear origin loci, and licensing appears to occur randomly (as is in the early *Xenopus laevis* embryo) [27]. Another investigation by Besnard et al. [29] showed that there exist a consensus guanine sequence (G-quadruplexes) which acts as a signature for origins of replication in man. G-quadruplexes consist of four guanine bases that become stacked in a way so that they form higher order structures amongst them. Yet more recently unpublished data by the Arneodo group suggests that epigenetic factors and histone-binding proteins such as H2A variants open up regions along the chromosome where origins can form (*personal communication with Alain Arneodo*). The inter-play of the accessibility of DNA with licensing has also been suggested previously in studies of DNA sequences which showed a jump in the ratio of its guanine and cytosine bases amongst leading and lagging strand DNA [30], which can act as DNA break point or as sites where origins of replication are established.

Origin licensing ends with a down-regulation of further assembly of proteins at origins [31]. The current model suggests that a degradation of the licensing factors in the cell nucleus can achieve this [32–34]; a further route to down-regulation is through blocking of the scaffolding proteins, i.e. the intermediate proteins which recruit the Mcm2-7 to form licensed origins. For example the protein Geminin blocks licensing by binding to Cdt1 preventing it from binding with an ORC-Cdc6 complex on the DNA, and ultimately inhibiting the recruitment of Mcm2-7 [35].

1.5 Origin Firing During DNA Synthesis

Once licensing completes, the cell cycle progresses to its next phase, where origin activation and the replication of DNA occurs. It is therefore called the synthesis or S-phase. The origins which were licensed during the previous phase lie *dormant*

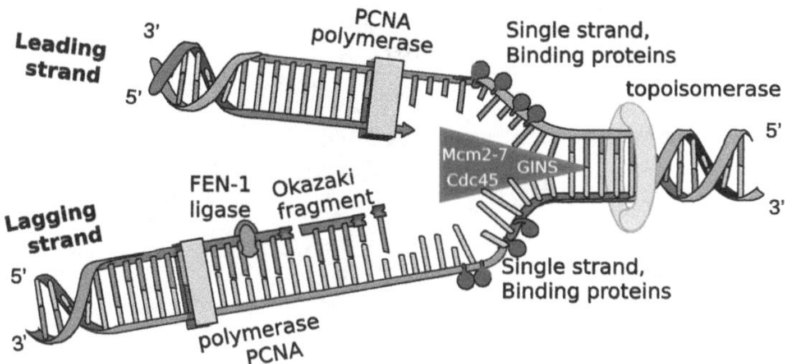

Fig. 1.4 The main components of a replication fork are a topoisomerase, a helicase (Mcm2-7), a polymerase (pol δ/ϵ), as well as further accessory proteins, e.g. Cdc45 and the GINS complex. Polymerase can only act in the $3' \to 5'$ direction. Thus it works continously in that direction on the leading strand, but forms *Okazaki* fragments on the lagging strand, which then require ligation and maturation through the ligase and FEN-1 proteins. This image is an adaption of [39]

(inactive) for some period of time until they become activated. Activation requires the binding of further proteins until the full replication machinery has assembled. In replication terminology one refers to this machinery as replication forks; they operate bi-directionally, meaning that forks emerge from either side of the origin with its machinery at their head, as shown in Fig. 1.4. The figure also shows that the polymerase (the DNA-copying element of the fork) only acts in one direction, namely in the $5'$ to $3'$ direction. So when replication forks progress, one strand, the *leading strand*, is copied continuously as the forks move in $3' \to 5'$ direction; the other is synthesised discontinuously, i.e. polymerases replicate a section of DNA in the $3' \to 5'$ direction, and then jumps back in the $5' \to 3'$ direction to replicate the next section. Such discontinuity creates intermediate fragments on the lagging strand called Okazaki fragments which require post-processing (*maturation*) to join them together (*ligate*) to form one continuous DNA strand.

The protein machinery of a replication fork consists of the following main components [36]:

- a helicase that unwinds and opens up the DNA, i.e. Mcm2-7,
- a polymerase which copies template DNA, e.g. a polymerase on the leading and another on the lagging strand.
- accessory proteins such as processivity factors that clamp polymerase tightly and prevents it from dissociating, i.e. PCNA,
- nucleases such as FEN-1 that cleave and prepares DNA for later Okazaki fragment ligation,
- further proteins for example DNA ligase I which joins Okazaki fragments or topoisomerase that unlinks parental strands,
- initiator proteins which are involved in the activation of the replication machinery and its progression [19, 37, 38]: Cdc45 and the GINS proteins.

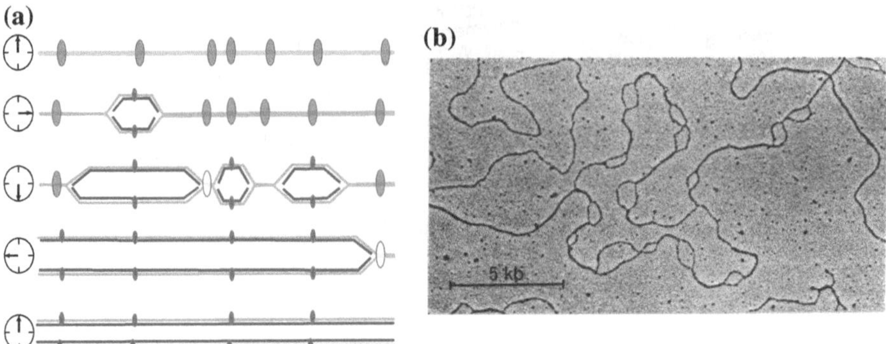

Fig. 1.5 Replication bubbles. **a** Replication starts from origins of replication shown as *oval shapes* (*top figure*). Once an origin activates replication bubbles form which carry newly synthesised DNA inside of them shown in *red*. The active origins sites are marked as *small blue circles* on either replicated DNA strand, not yet activated origins loose their ability to activate once a replication fork moves across them (*hollow ovals*). Replication finishes when forks reach the end of a chromosome or coalesce with another fork which originated elsewhere. **b** Electron micrograph image of replication bubbles in *Drosophila melanogaster*. This image was acquired from Fig. 2 from the original paper by Kriegstein and Hogness [41] who gave their kind permission to reprint it

As the protein machinery of a fork moves along the DNA, it leaves duplicated DNA in its wake, resulting in *replication bubbles*, as shown in Fig. 1.5. Replication forks flank the bubbles at either side, and a bubble carries newly synthesised DNA inside it. By comparing bubbles to linear DNA, i.e. not yet replicated DNA, one can infer the position of an origin of replication. Assuming furthermore at a constant speed this should be the midpoint of bubble. What can be gleaned from the study of replication bubbles is whether an origin was activated early or later during S-phase. For example, a large bubble suggests that forks have had longer to move further away from an origin at its centre, compared to a smaller replication bubble where replication might have only just started. However such information can also be ambiguous, because a large bubble could also be the result of the merging of two smaller bubbles. One way of visualising newly synthesised DNA uses two differently labelled nucleotides in the cellular growth medium. Their addition at different times to the medium during replication highlights some of the dynamics during replication [40]. For instance two differently labelled nucleotides can be added one at a time during replication. This will result in patterns on the DNA where those replicated from one labelled nucleotide will have one particular colour. This then aids in the identification of origin positions similar to studying the length of a replication bubble. The method also allows to distinguish between an early or late origin depending on the colour-coding of a replicated DNA stretch.

Localising origins of replication, as well as forks, is also possible using sequencing techniques (e.g. oligonucleotide microarrays [42], ChIP-chip sequencing [43], deep sequencing [44]) to examine DNA extracted from the cell during different times of the S-phase. These approaches use a set of known DNA snippets that hybridise

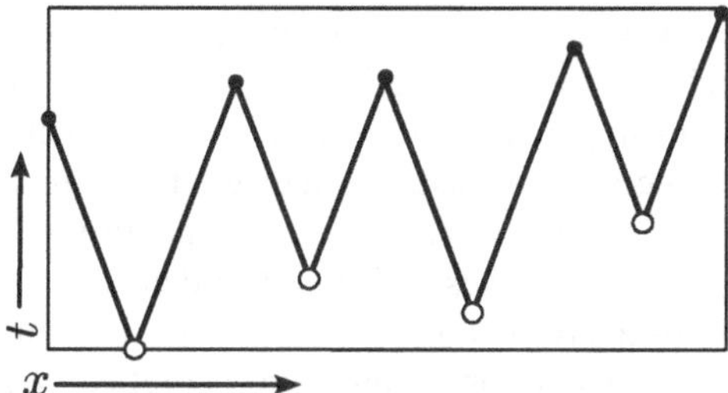

Fig. 1.6 A schematic representation of a replication timing profile is shown for the case of four origins (*hollow circles*). We assume this is how forks move if we observe a single cell. Origins are located at different positions x along the a chromosome. Origins activate at different times t and their forks progress from either side of the origin (*solid line*), until they encounter another fork or reach the end of the chromosome. Termination points are shown as *filled circles*

(are matched) with the sample DNA. Quantifying the extent of matches then relates back to the known DNA segment sequence and the marker at the time the sample was taken. For example, the study by Raghuraman et al. [42] labels replicated DNA with heavy isotopes. Doing this they can then sort replicated from unreplicated DNA and identify the corresponding known DNA sequence belonging to it. Sekedat et al. [43] make use of a different marker and they mark key proteins on the DNA during replication. They label a fork component (the GINS complex), and sort the DNA pieces that bound to it. They then determine the corresponding DNA sequence where the GINS complex sits and therefore location of replication forks over time. Samples taken at different times during DNA replication resolve fork movement spatially as well as temporally. The data produces *replication timing profiles* and these space-time plots reveal which origins activate when, when do forks merge, as well as which piece of DNA was replicated at which point in time during S-phase. A sketch of such a timing profile is shown in Fig. 1.6 for the case of four origins activating at different times when we observe this in a single cell.

When replication forks move along the DNA they might encounter a dormant origin, as is shown in the second last sequence of Fig. 1.5 (see also Fig. 1.2b). Since a dormant origin is inactive, it then becomes passively replicated [45] meaning that it loses its ability to act as a replication starting point. From there, replication then continues normally along the remaining stretch of DNA. Whenever a replication fork collides head-on with another fork, replication terminates at this point and the open ends of newly replicated DNA become ligated. Replication also terminates if a fork reaches the end of a chromosome. A replication fork might also stall, as a result of, for example, damaged DNA sites; in this case dormant origins play an important role. Their presence allows replication to restart from outside a stalled region, and they contribute not only to keep replication going, they also contribute in a manner to keep replication on-time [46]. Activating dormant origins helps to repartition not yet replicated DNA into smaller pieces which will reduce the overall replication completion time—the time the last segment of DNA takes to be fully replicated.

One particular drawback of most experimental procedures is that measurements usually observe a population average of cells (or origins). For example, experiments are normally carried out using synchronised cell cultures, so the onset of replication can be timed. However there is stochasticity in origin licensing and activation which then averages out some aspects of origins, e.g. probability of becoming licensed, the exact activation time. This makes it difficult to detect origins which have little probability to activate in a given round of cell cycle. For this single cell data is required and hard to come by, so one requires a theoretical approach as well as in silico models for a complete resolution of all facets of origins during licensing and during their activation in S-phase.

1.6 Replication Timing, Origin Positioning, and the Random Completion Problem

Replication timing and the timing of cellular division are strongly interlinked since cells would lose genomic information if they divided prior to the completion of replication. Previous research in the *Xenopus laevis* early embryo system showed that after fertilisation egg cells double at a constant speed for the first twelve rounds [10]. The time between divisions is ~25 min which is comparably short to a 24 hour-long division cycle of most differentiated, somatic cells. However the genomic content of both cell types is the same, i.e. an information content of $6.2 \cdot 10^9$ bp (about the same magnitude as for humans).

There are several points that form a conundrum of how such rapid doubling within 25 min can be achieved in the early frog embryo system. The speed at which replication forks process the DNA in eukaryotes is apparently fixed at about 1 kbp/min with its exact value depending on the specific organism, e.g. 1.5 kbp/min in *Saccharomyces cerevisiae* [42, 43] and 0.5–0.6 kbp/min in *Xenopus laevis* [47]. As a consequence of *Xenopus laevis* early embryos undergoing cellular division within 25 min, the distance from one origin to the next must be no larger than ~20 kbp to achieve this. However DNA saturates at approximately one Mcm2-7 per 1.5 to 3 kbp [19, 48] which means that there are about 200,000 origins from which replication starts in every cell cycle. Keeping in mind that in *Xenopus laevis* embryos origins can assemble at any given DNA sequence, then a random distribution of origin sites of this extent juxtaposed with the possibility to lay them out along $6.2 \cdot 10^9$ bp results in a high probability of having at least one gap >20 kbp [5, 11][1]; which would prolong S-phase and retard the cell cycle. However experiments show that this is not the case, moreover origins appear to have a bias towards a regular spacing with one

[1] The maximal gap allowed to complete replication on time is given by $20\,\text{min}/(2 \cdot 0.5\,\text{kb/min}) = 20\,\text{kbp}$. This is if we consider that all origins activate at the same time under the conditions of two forks replicating each at 0.5 kb/min for a period of 20 min.

origin every 5–15 kbp [11]. This conundrum has therefore been termed the *random completion problem* and also *random gap problem* which to-date has not been fully resolved [49, 50].

1.7 Mathematical Modelling of DNA Replication

Within the school of mathematical modelling of DNA replication there are two views on the importance of licensing-defined origin sites [50]. Whether or not to include licensing in a modelling approach is of special importance to resolve the aforementioned *random completion problem.*

In the first view, origins can literally form anywhere, and modelling of the replication process depends only on an initiation function. It governs the amount of origins that activate at a particular time in not yet replicated DNA regions [51, 52], and it thus acts as a rate of origin activation over time. The essence of this approach is a one-dimensional nucleation and growth model which holds a long-history and myriad applications [53] in the statistical physics realms known as the *Kolmogorov-Johnson-Mehl-Avrami* (KJMA) model [54]. The KJMA model considers random nucleation events along a one-dimensional line whose rate of nucleation depends on the particulars of the initiation function. From each nucleation point the line undergoes a transition (e.g. from unreplicated to replicated) at some speed to either side from it. The elegance of the KJMA model is its direct provision for analogy to the replication mechanism: nucleation points are origins of replication, transformation of DNA acts as changing DNA from an unreplicated to a replicated state [54] (cf. also Fig. 1.2b). However this approach falls short of biological details; it mainly addresses the question of how cells are able to replicate their genome in a short time lacking the relationship between the stochasticity of the location of origin *and* their activation times [13, 51, 54, 55]. The KJMA model of DNA replication works only properly (works out the *random completion problem*) if the initiation rate increases towards the end of S-phase [56–58]. However an increasing initiation rate requires an arbitrary amount of origins to be licensed which lacks the known biological model of *Xenopus laevis* embryos. In other words the KJMA model always requires the potential presence of a licensed origin at every arbitrary position to allow for random initiation. However there is only a finite amount of origins loaded during licensing [59], and once licensing completes the origin positions are fixed. The KJMA model is therefore incomplete and lacks a full explanation for a solution to the *random completion problem* from a licensing point of view.

Despite this shortcoming of explaining the origin positions, applying the pioneering KJMA model to *Saccharomyces cerevisiae* replication profiles yields insight into the likelihood of their known location to act as an origin [60]. One can hence use this model to extract the probability of an origin locus to contribute in a particular round of the cell cycle, i.e. its *efficiency* [13]. There exist also several other modelling approaches to extract information by also taking into account several cell cycle progression regulators [61, 62].

The second view of modelling DNA replication, considers two ingredients for a possible model. It divides the entire process into two separate phases as are in biology—licensing and activation—because an origin can only activate if it was previously licensed. For example Moura et al. developed a model in such a way, and as a result they require extra parameters [63] compared to the KJMA model. In their scenario, an origin locus has a probability to actually become licensed or not. It is therefore considered to have certain *competence* to activate later for DNA synthesis. During S-phase the licensed origin has a further probability attached to it to become activated over time. The authors achieve this by introducing a time-dependent activation distribution [64, 65] which is defined by mean activation time and standard deviation per origin. Such model can then be fitted to *Saccharomyces cerevisiae* experimental replication timing profile data to extract these relevant parameters as well as describing an origins' overall efficiency as was in the aforementioned KJMA modelling approach. There have also been further approaches [66, 67] which consider such separation of phases for DNA replication as well as linking them to players of the cell cycle for a holistic model of a population of yeast cells. As modelling separated into licensing and origin activation results in a more realistic approach, we will investigate in Chap. 2 what the best origin positions are; whether those give minimum replication time according to their parameters. We then reverse engineer the optimal origin positions by simulating an evolutionary process and find that origins take positions so that replication completes quickly.

1.8 The Spatio-Temporal Organisation of Replication Forks

A typical eukaryotic chromosome has a length of $2 \cdot 10^8$ bp and it is contained within the nucleus of a typical eukaryotic cell. It would be about 6 cm [68] long, if it were fully stretched out. So this is much longer than the actually size of a cell or even its nucleus where chromosomes are located. DNA must thus be packaged and compacted to fit into the cellular nucleus, and it is known that this occurs at different scales [1], for example DNA is wound around histones forming chromatin, chromatin condenses further to form chromosomes. Chromatin as well as chromatin organisation occur in three spatial dimensions which has been of long-standing interest by experimental and theoretical groups alike and is also of particular interest in polymer science (as reviewed in [69]). It is hypothesised that chromatin organisation also plays a role in the activation or down-regulation of a particular gene by compacting the DNA sequence of a protein and shielding it from transcription factors that try to bind with it [1]. DNA is thus much more active than the usually projected picture which only sees it as a sole means to encode for information.

When DNA condenses particular genomic regions come into contact with another which, if they were stretched out linearly in 1D would be otherwise far away from each other. For example, Duan et al. [70] suggested that packaging DNA inside the nucleus creates higher order structures that organise into regions inside the nucleus. They further suggest that localisation organises the DNA into structures which aid

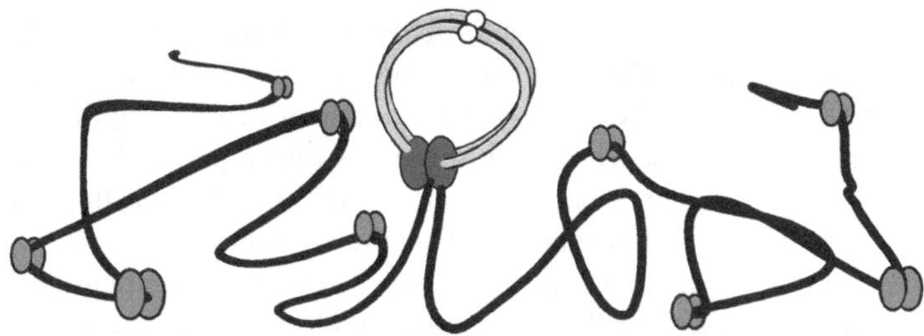

Fig. 1.7 A replisome pair. Active replication forks (*blue ovals*) synthesise unreplicated DNA (*black line*) by pulling it through them from one side and ejecting the newly synthesised DNA (*yellow*) on the other. In doing this sister replisomes, i.e. the active replication forks, move away from their origin of replication (*white circle*), but always stay attached with each other. Not yet activated origins which are shown as two *green ovals* to represent DNA-bound Mcm2-7 double hexamers waiting to become activated

in accessing a particular gene or help during replication. Boulos et al. also suggested such functional dependency of intra- and inter-chromosomal interaction during their network analysis of human chromatin regions which have potential to play a role in DNA replication. Previous to these theoretical works there has also been convincing experimental evidence for a spatial organisation of DNA during replication (and mRNA transcription) into compartment-like structures that have no physical boundaries; these observations are termed *replication factories* [71]. It is currently unresolved how these structures form and stay together despite no clear compartment wall. Work by Cisse et al. [72] suggests their formation to be more dynamic, and assembly and disassembly transiently occur with an average life-time of 5 s of equivalent structure called *transcription factories*, i.e. where DNA is copied into messenger RNA. Data we use for our analysis of replication factories in Chap. 3 also displays dynamic rates of close localisation and dislocation of unreplicated DNA regions with each other, however once DNA becomes replicated movement of these regions becomes constrained (see also [73]) that we interpret as a strong interaction between nearby replicating DNA regions. A possible difference in the organisation of replication and transcription is that transcription only acts on one DNA strand whereas during DNA replication both strands become duplicated simultaneously which might require a stronger force to keep the replication machinery associated.

The models of replication kinetics which are discussed in the previous Sect. 1.7 considered DNA replication to happen spatially in only one dimension: replication forks move away to either side from an origin. Experiments however suggest that in a three dimensional space of a nucleus replication forks nucleated from one origin stay bound together as *sister replisomes* [74–76]. Sister replisomes are sketched in Fig. 1.7. They spool unreplicated DNA from one side and then spool out replicated DNA to the other. The replisome pairs stay associated for the course of replication of a DNA segment, but more importantly they were also shown to group together with other replisomes eventually forming *replication factories* [75, 77, 78]—regions with a high fork content. A proposed function for factories is that there is a high pool of essential proteins required for DNA synthesis localised around them [79]. This can aid to, for example, activate dormant origins under replicative stress such as DNA damage [80–82], and when there is a large amount of origins required to activate quickly. To-date, it is not clear what keeps these factories together, however previous modelling shows that an energy barrier must be overcome to bear the entropic cost from forming DNA loops to have factory structures [83–85].

We address this lack of knowledge in Chap. 3. Using Boltzmann statistics and numerical simulations we show that replisomes randomly associate with each other on a chromosome. We establish a model for two sister replisomes to pair and then extend our model to account for replisomes associating on a genome-wide scale. This model is firmly grounded at the core biological question and supplements experimental data of the probability of observing associations in vivo in *Saccharomyces cerevisiae* cells.

References

1. B. Alberts, D. Bray, J. Lewis, M. Raff, K. Roberts, J.D. Watson, *Molecular Biology of the Cell* (Garland Publishing, New York, 1994)
2. E. Radmaneshfar, *Mathematical Modelling of the Cell Cycle Stress Response* (Springer International Publishing, Switzerland, 2014). doi:10.1007/978-3-319-00744-1
3. H. Nishitani, Z. Lygerou, Control of DNA replication licensing in a cell cycle. Genes Cells **7**(6), 523–534 (2002)
4. A.C. Porter, Preventing DNA over-replication: a Cdk perspective. Cell Div. **3**, 3 (2008). doi:10.1186/1747-1028-3-3
5. O. Hyrien, K. Marheineke, A. Goldar, Paradoxes of eukaryotic DNA replication: MCM proteins and the random completion problem. Bioessays **25**(2), 116–125 (2003). doi:10.1002/bies.10208
6. J. Nordman, T.L. Orr-Weaver, Regulation of DNA replication during development. Development **139**(3), 455–464 (2012). doi:10.1242/dev.061838
7. M. Méchali, K. Yoshida, P. Coulombe, P. Pasero, Genetic and epigenetic determinants of DNA replication origins, position and activation. Curr. Opin. Genet. Dev. **23**(2), 124–131 (2013). doi:10.1016/j.gde.2013.02.010
8. O. Hyrien, C. Maric, M. Méchali, Transition in specification of embryonic metazoan DNA replication origins. Science **270**(5238), 994–997 (1995)
9. C. Collart, G.E. Allen, C.R. Bradshaw, J.C. Smith, P. Zegerman, Titration of four replication factors is essential for the xenopus laevis midblastula transition. Science **341**(6148), 893–896 (2013). doi:10.1126/science.1241530
10. M. Kirschner, J. Newport, J. Gerhart, The timing of early developmental events in Xenopus. Trends Genet. **1**, 41–47 (1985). doi:10.1016/0168-9525(85)90021-6
11. J.J. Blow, Control of chromosomal DNA replication in the early Xenopus embryo. EMBO J. **20**(13), 3293–3297 (2001). doi:10.1093/emboj/20.13.3293
12. A. Arneodo, C. Vaillant, B. Audit, F. Argoul, Y. D'Aubenton-Carafa, C. Thermes, Multi-scale coding of genomic information: from DNA sequence to genome structure and function. Phys. Rep. **498**(2–3), 45–188 (2011). doi:10.1016/j.physrep.2010.10.001
13. A. Baker, B. Audit, S.C.-H. Yang, J. Bechhoefer, A. Arneodo, Inferring where and when replication initiates from genome-wide replication timing data. Phys. Rev. Lett. **108**(26), 268101 (2012). doi:10.1103/PhysRevLett.108.268101

14. T.J. Newman, M.A. Mamun, C.A. Nieduszynski, J.J. Blow, Replisome stall events have shaped the distribution of replication origins in the genomes of yeasts. Nucleic Acids Res. **41**(21), 9705–9718 (2013). doi:10.1093/nar/gkt728
15. S. Jun, J. Herrick, A. Bensimon, J. Bechhoefer, Persistence length of chromatin determines origin spacing in Xenopus early-embryo DNA replication: quantitative comparisons between theory and experiment. Cell Cycle **3**(2), 211–217 (2004). doi:10.4161/cc.3.2.655
16. A.G. Evertts, H.A. Coller, Back to the origin: reconsidering replication, transcription, epigenetics, and cell cycle control. Genes Cancer **3**(11–12), 678–696 (2012). doi:10.1177/1947601912474891
17. D. Remus, F. Beuron, G. Tolun, J.D. Griffith, E.P. Morris, J.F.X. Diffley, Concerted loading of Mcm2-7 double hexamers around DNA during DNA replication origin licensing. Cell **139**(4), 719–730 (2009). doi:10.1016/j.cell.2009.10.015
18. C. Evrin, P. Clarke, J. Zech, R. Lurz, J. Sun, S. Uhle, H. Li, B. Stillman, C. Speck, A double-hexameric MCM2-7 complex is loaded onto origin DNA during licensing of eukaryotic DNA replication. Proc. Natl. Acad. Sci. U.S.A. **106**(48), 20240–20245 (2009). doi:10.1073/pnas.0911500106
19. A. Gambus, G.A. Khoudoli, R.C. Jones, J.J. Blow, MCM2-7 form double hexamers at licensed origins in Xenopus egg extract. J. Biol. Chem. **286**(13), 11855–11864 (2011). doi:10.1074/jbc.M110.199521
20. A. Bielinsky, S. Gerbi, Where it all starts: eukaryotic origins of DNA replication. J. Cell Sci. **114**(4), 643–651 (2001)
21. M.L. Bochman, A. Schwacha, The Mcm2-7 complex has in vitro helicase activity. Mol. Cell **31**(2), 287–293 (2008). doi:10.1016/j.molcel.2008.05.020
22. M.L. Bochman, A. Schwacha, The Mcm complex: unwinding the mechanism of a replicative helicase. Microbiol. Mol. Biol. Rev. **73**(4), 652–683 (2009). doi:10.1128/MMBR.00019-09
23. T.J. Takara, S.P. Bell, Putting two heads together to unwind DNA. Cell **139**(4), 652–654 (2009). doi:10.1016/j.cell.2009.10.037
24. C.S. Newlon, J.F. Theis, The structure and function of yeast ARS elements. Curr. Opin. Genet. Dev. **3**(5), 752–758 (1993). doi:10.1016/S0959-437X(05)80094-2
25. K. Shirahige, T. Iwasaki, M.B. Rashid, N. Ogasawara, H. Yoshikawa, Location and characterization of autonomously replicating sequences from chromosome VI of Saccharomyces cerevisiae. Mol. Cell. Biol. **13**(8), 5043–5056 (1993). doi:10.1128/MCB.13.8.5043
26. S.P. Bell, A. Dutta, DNA replication in eukaryotic cells. Annu. Rev. Biochem. **71**, 333–374 (2002). doi:10.1146/annurev.biochem.71.110601.135425
27. C. Cvetic, J.C. Walter, Eukaryotic origins of DNA replication: could you please be more specific? Semin. Cell Dev. Biol. **16**(3), 343–353 (2005). doi:10.1016/j.semcdb.2005.02.009
28. M. Méchali, Eukaryotic DNA replication origins: many choices for appropriate answers. Nat. Rev. Mol. Cell Biol. **11**(10), 728–738 (2010). doi:10.1038/nrm2976
29. E. Besnard, A. Babled, L. Lapasset, O. Milhavet, H. Parrinello, C. Dantec, J.-M. Marin, J.-M. Lemaitre, Unraveling cell type-specific and reprogrammable human replication origin signatures associated with G-quadruplex consensus motifs. Nat. Struct. Mol. Biol. **19**(8), 837–844 (2012). doi:10.1038/nsmb.2339
30. C.-L. Chen et al., Replication-associated mutational asymmetry in the human genome. Mol. Biol. Evol. **28**(8), 2327–2337 (2011). doi:10.1093/molbev/msr056
31. J.J. Blow, A. Dutta, Preventing re-replication of chromosomal DNA. Nat. Rev. Mol. Cell Biol. **6**(6), 476–486 (2005). doi:10.1038/nrm1663
32. T. Kondo et al., Rapid degradation of Cdt1 upon UV-induced DNA damage is mediated by SCF-Skp2 complex. J. Biol. Chem. **279**(26), 27315–27319 (2004). doi:10.1074/jbc.M314023200
33. T. Senga, U. Sivaprasad, W. Zhu, J.H. Park, E.E. Arias, J.C. Walter, A. Dutta, PCNA is a cofactor for Cdt1 degradation by CUL4/DDB1-mediated N-terminal ubiquitination. J. Biol. Chem. **281**(10), 6246–6252 (2006). doi:10.1074/jbc.M512705200
34. J. Hu, Y. Xiong, An evolutionarily conserved function of proliferating cell nuclear antigen for Cdt1 degradation by the Cul4-Ddb1 ubiquitin ligase in response to DNA damage. J. Biol. Chem. **281**(7), 3753–3756 (2006). doi:10.1074/jbc.C500464200

35. M.L. DePamphilis, J.J. Blow, S. Ghosh, T. Saha, K. Noguchi, A. Vassilev, Regulating the licensing of DNA replication origins in metazoa. Curr. Opin. Cell Biol. **18**(3), 231–239 (2006). doi:10.1016/j.ceb.2006.04.001
36. T.K. GS Brush, DNA replication mechanisms. DNA Replication Eukaryot. Cells. **71**, 333–374 (1996)
37. A. Zembutsu, S. Waga, De novo assembly of genuine replication forks on an immobilized circular plasmid in Xenopus egg extracts. Nucleic Acids Res. **34**(13), e91 (2006). doi:10.1093/nar/gkl512
38. A. Gambus, R.C. Jones, A. Sanchez-Diaz, M. Kanemaki, F. van Deursen, R.D. Edmondson, K. Labib, GINS maintains association of Cdc45 with MCM in replisome progression complexes at eukaryotic DNA replication forks. Nat. Cell Biol. **8**(4), 358–366 (2006). doi:10.1038/ncb1382
39. M. Ruiz. DNA replication, http://en.wikipedia.org/wiki/File:DNA_replication_en.svg. Accessed 28 October 2013
40. J. Herrick, P. Stanislawski, O. Hyrien, A. Bensimon, Replication fork density increases during DNA synthesis in X. laevis egg extracts. J. Mol. Biol. **300**(5), 1133–1142 (2000)
41. H.J. Kriegstein, D.S. Hogness, Mechanism of DNA replication in Drosophila chromosomes: structure of replication forks and evidence for bidirectionality. Proc. Natl. Acad. Sci. U.S.A. **71**, 135–139 (1974). doi:10.1073/pnas.71.1.135
42. M.K. Raghuraman et al., Replication dynamics of the yeast genome. Sci. **294**(5540), 115–121 (2001). doi:10.1126/science.294.5540.115
43. M.D. Sekedat, D. Fenyö, R.S. Rogers, A.J. Tackett, J.D. Aitchison, B.T. Chait, GINS motion reveals replication fork progression is remarkably uniform throughout the yeast genome. Mol. Syst. Biol. **6**, 353 (2010). doi:10.1038/msb.2010.8
44. C. A. Müller et al. The dynamics of genome replication using deep sequencing. Nucleic Acids Res. (2013), gkt878. doi:10.1093/nar/gkt878
45. A.M. Woodward, T. Göhler, M.G. Luciani, M. Oehlmann, X. Ge, A. Gartner, D.A. Jackson, J.J. Blow, Excess Mcm2-7 license dormant origins of replication that can be used under conditions of replicative stress. J. Cell Biol. **173**(5), 673–683 (2006). doi:10.1083/jcb.200602108
46. D. McIntosh, J.J. Blow. Dormant origins, the licensing checkpoint, and the response to replicative stresses. Cold Spring Harb. Perspect. Biol. **4**(10) (2012). doi:10.1101/cshperspect.a012955
47. H.M. Mahbubani, T. Paull, J.K. Elder, J.J. Blow, DNA replication initiates at multiple sites on plasmid DNA in Xenopus egg extracts. Nucleic Acids Res. **20**(7), 1457–1462 (1992)
48. H.M. Mahbubani, Cell cycle regulation of the replication licensing system: involvement of a cdk-dependent inhibitor. J. Cell Biol. **136**(1), 125–135 (1997). doi:10.1083/jcb.136.1.125
49. N. Rhind, DNA replication timing: random thoughts about origin firing. Nat. Cell Biol. **8**(12), 1313–1316 (2006). doi:10.1038/ncb1206-1313
50. J. Bechhoefer, N. Rhind, Replication timing and its emergence from stochastic processes. Trends Genet. **28**(8), 374–381 (2012). doi:10.1016/j.tig.2012.03.011
51. J. Herrick, S. Jun, J. Bechhoefer, A. Bensimon, Kinetic model of DNA replication in eukaryotic organisms. J. Mol. Biol. **320**(4), 741–750 (2002)
52. S. Jun, J. Bechhoefer, Nucleation and growth in one dimension. II. application to DNA replication kinetics. Phys. Rev. E **71**(1), 011909 (2005). doi:10.1103/PhysRevE.71.011909
53. M. Fanfoni, M. Tomellini, The Johnson-Mehl- Avrami-Kohnogorov model: A brief review. Nuovo Cim. D **20**(7-8), 1171–1182 (1998). doi:10.1007/BF03185527
54. S. Jun, H. Zhang, J. Bechhoefer, Nucleation and growth in one dimension. I. The generalized Kolmogorov-Johnson-Mehl-Avrami model. Phys. Rev. E **71**(1), 011908 (2005). doi:10.1103/PhysRevE.71.011908
55. A. Goldar, M.-C. Marsolier-Kergoat, O. Hyrien, Universal temporal profile of replication origin activation in eukaryotes. PLoS One **4**(6), e5899 (2009). doi:10.1371/journal.pone.0005899
56. H. Zhang, J. Bechhoefer, Reconstructing DNA replication kinetics from small DNA fragments. Phys. Rev. E. Stat. Nonlin. Soft Matter Phys. **73**(5 Pt 1), 051903 (2006)
57. A. Goldar et al., A dynamic stochastic model for DNA replication initiation in early embryos. PLoS One **3**(8), e2919 (2008). doi:10.1371/journal.pone.0002919

58. M.G. Gauthier, P. Norio, J. Bechhoefer, Modeling inhomogeneous DNA replication kinetics. PLoS One **7**(3), e32053 (2012). doi:10.1371/journal.pone.0032053
59. M. Oehlmann, A.J. Score, J.J. Blow, The role of Cdc6 in ensuring complete genome licensing and S phase checkpoint activation. J. Cell Biol. **165**(2), 181–190 (2004). doi:10.1083/jcb.200311044
60. S.C.-H. Yang, N. Rhind, J. Bechhoefer, Modeling genome-wide replication kinetics reveals a mechanism for regulation of replication timing. Mol. Syst. Biol. **6**, 404 (2010). doi:10.1038/msb.2010.61
61. T.W. Spiesser, E. Klipp, M. Barberis, A model for the spatiotemporal organization of DNA replication in Saccharomyces cerevisiae. Mol. Genet. Genomics **282**(1), 25–35 (2009). doi:10.1007/s00438-009-0443-9
62. M. Barberis, T.W. Spiesser, E. Klipp, Replication origins and timing of temporal replication in budding yeast: how to solve the conundrum? Curr. Genomics **11**(3), 199–211 (2010). doi:10.2174/138920210791110942
63. A.P.S. de Moura, R. Retkute, M. Hawkins, C.A. Nieduszynski, Mathematical modelling of whole chromosome replication. Nucleic Acids Res. **38**(17), 5623–5633 (2010). doi:10.1093/nar/gkq343
64. R. Retkute, C. Nieduszynski, A. de Moura, Dynamics of DNA replication in yeast. Phys. Rev. Lett. **107**(6), 068103 (2011). doi:10.1103/PhysRevLett.107.068103
65. R. Retkute, C.A. Nieduszynski, A. de Moura, Mathematical modeling of genome replication. Phys. Rev. E **86**(3), 031916 (2012). doi:10.1103/PhysRevE.86.031916
66. A. Brümmer, C. Salazar, V. Zinzalla, L. Alberghina, T. Höfer, Mathematical modelling of DNA replication reveals a trade-off between coherence of origin activation and robustness against rereplication. PLoS Comput. Biol. **6**(5), e1000783 (2010). doi:10.1371/journal.pcbi.1000783
67. K. Koutroumpas, J. Lygeros, Modeling and analysis of DNA replication. Automatica **47**(6), 1156–1164 (2011). doi:10.1016/j.automatica.2011.02.007
68. N. A. Campbell, J. B. Reece, and L. G. Mitchell. Biology. Benjamin/Cummins, 1999.
69. B.I. Vaidyanathan Shantha, M. Kenward, G. Arya, Hierarchies in Eukaryotic Genome Organization: Insights from Polymer Theory and Simulations. BMC Biophys. **4**(1), 8 (2011). doi:10.1186/2046-1682-4-8
70. Z. Duan et al., A three-dimensional model of the yeast genome. Nature **465**(7296), 363–367 (2010). doi:10.1038/nature08973
71. P.R. Cook, The nucleoskeleton and the topology of replication. Cell **66**(4), 627–635 (1991)
72. I.I. Cisse et al., Real-time dynamics of RNA polymerase II clustering in live human cells. Sci. **341**(6146), 664–667 (2013). doi:10.1126/science.1239053
73. N. Saner et al., Stochastic association of neighboring replicons creates replication factories in budding yeast. J. Cell Biol. **202**(7), 1001–1012 (2013). doi:10.1083/jcb.201306143
74. A. Falaschi, Eukaryotic DNA replication: a model for a fixed double replisome. Trends Genet. **16**(2), 88–92 (2000). doi:10.1016/S0168-9525(99)01917-4
75. E. Kitamura, J.J. Blow, T.U. Tanaka, Live-cell imaging reveals replication of individual replicons in eukaryotic replication factories. Cell **125**(7), 1297–1308 (2006). doi:10.1016/j.cell.2006.04.041
76. A. Ligasová, I. Raska, K. Koberna, Organization of human replicon: singles or zipping couples? J. Struct. Biol. **165**(3), 204–213 (2009). doi:10.1016/j.jsb.2008.11.004
77. R. Berezney, D.D. Dubey, J.A. Huberman, Heterogeneity of eukaryotic replicons, replicon clusters, and replication foci. Chromosoma **108**(8), 471–484 (2000)
78. P.J. Gillespie, J.J. Blow, Clusters, factories and domains: The complex structure of S phase comes into focus. Cell cycle **9**(16), 3218–3226 (2010). doi:10.4161/cc.9.16.12644
79. T. Natsume, T.U. Tanaka, Spatial regulation and organization of DNA replication within the nucleus. Chromosome Res. **18**(1), 7–17 (2010). doi:10.1007/s10577-009-9088-0
80. D.S. Dimitrova, D.M. Gilbert, Temporally coordinated assembly and disassembly of replication factories in the absence of DNA synthesis. Nat. Cell Biol. **2**(10), 686–694 (2000). doi:10.1038/35036309

81. X.Q. Ge, J.J. Blow, Chk1 inhibits replication factory activation but allows dormant origin firing in existing factories. J. Cell Biol. **191**(7), 1285–1297 (2010). doi:10.1083/jcb.201007074
82. A.M. Thomson, P.J. Gillespie, J.J. Blow, Replication factory activation can be decoupled from the replication timing program by modulating cdk levels. J. Cell Biol. **188**(2), 209–221 (2010). doi:10.1083/jcb.200911037
83. D. Marenduzzo, C. Micheletti, P.R. Cook, Entropy-driven genome organization. Biophys. J. **90**(10), 3712–3721 (2006). doi:10.1529/biophysj.105.077685
84. D. Marenduzzo, K. Finan, P.R. Cook, The depletion attraction: an underappreciated force driving cellular organization. J. Cell Biol. **175**(5), 681–686 (2006). doi:10.1083/jcb.200609066
85. D. Marenduzzo, I. Faro-Trindade, P.R. Cook, What are the molecular ties that maintain genomic loops? Trends Genet. **23**(3), 126–133 (2007). doi:10.1016/j.tig.2007.01.007

Chapter 2
Optimal Origin Placement for Minimal Replication Time

Eukaryotic genomes vary in their size and are much larger than their bacterial counterpart, e.g. that of *Saccharomyces cerevisiae* is $\sim 10^7$ bp long, those of *Xenopus laevis* or humans are $\sim 10^9$ bp in length, whereas *Escherichia coli* is $\sim 10^6$ bp. Bacteria also only have one single origin locus of replication from which they start replication, with each fork propagating at ~4 kbp/min [1, 2]; this allows for replication completion in under 40 min. Eukaryotic replication forks however exhibit a much slower characteristic speed, and experimental data shows that the speed of synthesis is ~1.5 kbp/(min·fork) [3, 4] in *Saccharomyces cerevisiae* and at ~0.6 kbp/(min·fork) in early *Xenopus laevis* frog embryos [5]. Let us then consider the time required for *Saccharomyces cerevisiae* DNA replication here if there were only one single origin of replication: it would take *Saccharomyces cerevisiae* almost three days to complete its genome replication.[1] In a laboratory environment yeast completes replication of its entire genome in less than about 30 min [6, 7], more than 100 times faster than what we calculated—it is clearly not the case that there is only one of replication.

The time until replication completion is accelerated by partitioning the chromosome into smaller replication domains; each of these requires an origin of replication that has formed at an origin locus. Origin loci therefore need to be placed in a manner such that replication time is minimal, i.e. replication completes by the end of S-phase. An initial guess is to space origin loci at regular intervals across a chromosome (Fig. 2.1a), if we assume origins always become licensed and activate at the same time. Such a scenario is the optimal case to result in quickest replication as compared to having the same number of origins sparsely spaced but instead groups (Fig. 2.1). Within a group only one origin is able to become active which then means that replication forks must travel farther prolonging the overall replication process (Fig. 2.1b). Therefore grouping seems to be a waste of origin resources. However we do show in this chapter that grouping is necessary to achieve minimum replication time. This is if there is uncertainty for a locus to become licensed. To compensate for not activated origins, replication forks need to travel farther than in the ideal

[1] The replication time of the yeast genome for the case of replication starting from one single origin of replication is $1.2 \cdot 10^7$ bp/($2 \cdot 1.5 \cdot 10^3$ bp/min) = 2.9 days.

J. Karschau, *Mathematical Modelling of Chromosome Replication and Replicative Stress*, Springer Theses, DOI 10.1007/978-3-319-08861-7_2

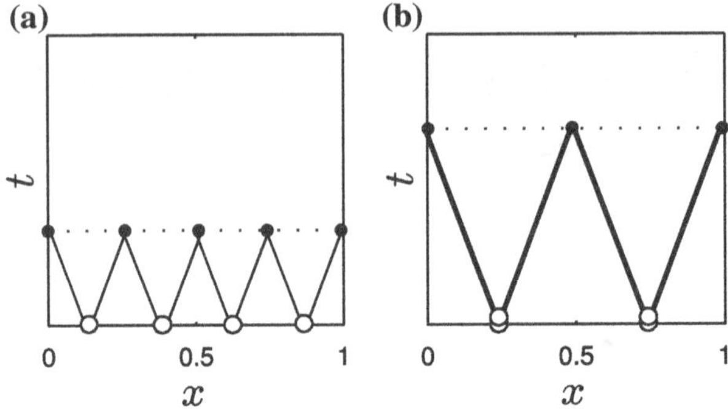

Fig. 2.1 Space–time diagram of four origins of replication (*hollow circles*). Schematic representation of origin loci distributed along the x-coordinate of a unit-sized chromosome. They have all been licensed and activate at the same time $t = 0\,\text{min}$. The replication fork movement (*black line*) along the x coordinate at a given point in time is shown, and forks terminate when they coalesce or arrive at an end of the chromosome (*black filled circles*). **a** The resulting replication time is minimal if all four origins are regularly spaced. **b** If origins are grouped (shown on top of each other) only one origin of a group is able to activate. The forks must travel a longer distance at the same speeds as in (**a**); the replication time is hence longer

scenario (Fig. 2.1a). It becomes a balancing act of either spreading out origins but risking failure and longer fork travelling times, or grouping origins to compensate for the likelihood of failure and initially have longer gaps between groups. Using mathematical modelling we show that there exist certain regimes between grouped and separated origin loci positions depending on the likelihood of activation.

We relate our modelling to budding yeast *Saccharomyces cerevisiae*, which has origin loci at specific genomic positions on a chromosome—some origins in groups and some separated. For the *Saccharomyces cerevisiae* origin distribution we investigate through our model what the optimal origin distribution must be, and find that grouping of origin loci is present within *Saccharomyces cerevisiae* origin distribution to minimise replication time. This is done through an evolutionary model which searches for loci positions to give minimum replication time, and our simulations results of optimal origin positions compare well to the experimental origin distribution. We also extend our model of specific genomic positions to apply it to the case of a circular chromosome. Finally, we also introduce uncertainty in origin activation time. An origin might never have the chance to activate if it has a high chance of activating later than other origins so that it always becomes replicated by forks that originated elsewhere. We show that in such a scenario origin grouping is also a means to minimise replication time. We use the example of *Xenopus laevis* where origins appear to take random positions. In experiments, groups of origins however appear to be regularly spaced [8] which we show gives indeed minimum replication time in our model.

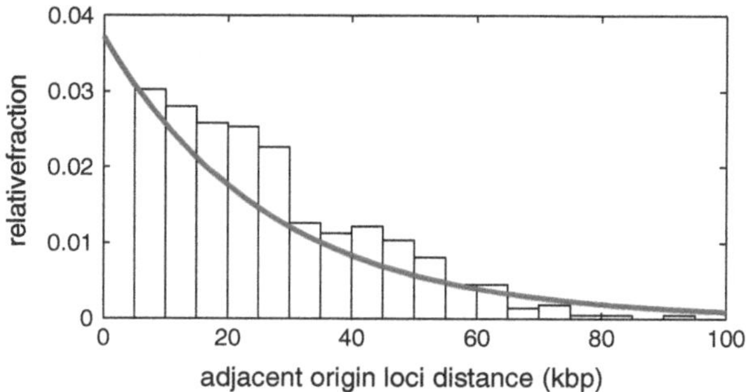

Fig. 2.2 Histogram of *Saccharomyces cerevisiae* inter-origin distances. The separation from one origin to its nearest neighbour is determined and then binned at intervals of 5 kbp (*black bars*). The origin position data was kindly provided by Hawkins et al. [9]. The mean of this data is 26 kbp, which is used to plot an exponential distribution with the same mean value (*blue solid line*)

2.1 Properties of Origins of Replication in *Saccharomyces cerevisiae*

If the origin loci in *Saccharomyces cerevisiae* would take their position within the genome randomly, then their nearest neighbour distances should be exponentially distributed. A histogram of inter-origin loci distances *Saccharomyces cerevisiae* however shows that this is not case. We show this in Fig. 2.2 where we plot a histogram of a recent study by Hawkins et al. [9]. The mean distance of the experimental data is 26 kbp which does not fit an exponential distribution with the same mean value. Also the inspection of a map for loci on the *Saccharomyces cerevisiae* genome reveals that there are groups of two or three very closely spaced origin loci which are prominent in most chromosomes [10]. We show such a map of *Saccharomyces cerevisiae* origin loci in Fig. 2.3 from the origin location data that was used in the study by Hawkins et al. [9]. Furthermore a similar map of origin loci of the fission yeast *Schizosaccharomyces pombe* gives a similar predominant grouping behaviour of origin loci (Fig. 2.4). It is to note that *Schizosaccharomyces pombe* has fewer but longer chromosomes than *Saccharomyces cerevisiae* which still require a large cohort of possible origin sites that have to be spaced with minimal gaps between to allow replication within the time allowed by the cell cycle. The data was taken from the oriDB database [10], and origin loci are shown for those classified as 'confirmed' or as 'likely'.

Previous theoretical works on *Saccharomyces cerevisiae* have used the experimentally determined loci as given parameters, without attempting to understand why the origins are located where they are [11–14]. Here, we will first show an analysis of *Saccharomyces cerevisiae* origin data addressing this, and then use mathematical modelling to explain the origin loci distribution for a specific chromosome.

As discussed in Sect. 1.4, DNA replication is divided into two distinct phases; the licensing phase and the synthesis phase (S-phase). Origins in budding yeast carry a

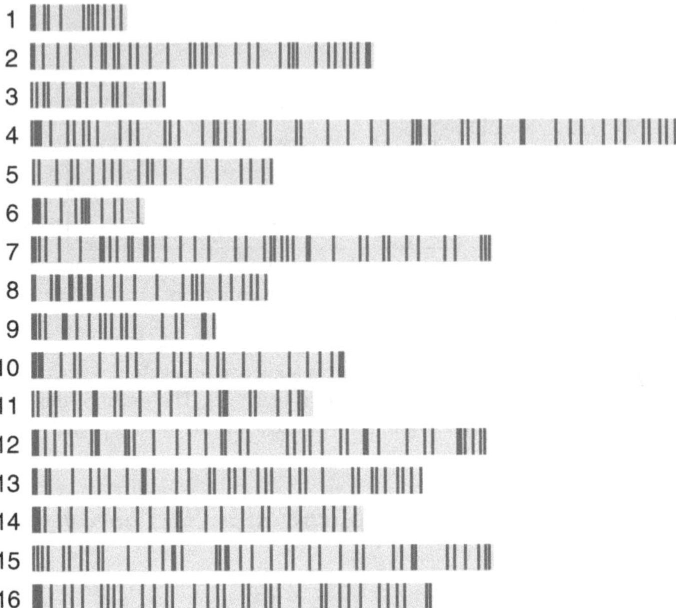

Fig. 2.3 Map of *Saccharomyces cerevisiae* origin positions. The location of origins (*red bars*) is shown along each individual chromosome as numbered (*blue horizontal line*). For reference, the length of the smallest chromosome, chromosome 1, is 230 kbp. The origin position data was kindly provided by Hawkins et al. [9]

Fig. 2.4 Map of *Schizosaccharomyces pombe* origin positions. The location of origins (*red bars*) is shown along each individual chromosome as numbered (*blue horizontal line*). For reference, the length of the smallest chromosome, chromosome 3, is 2450 kbp. The origin position data was taken from the oriDB data base [10], and only those classified as either 'confirmed' or 'likely' have been considered here

certain sequence motif which allows ORC to specifically bind to a target location during licensing. This means that *Saccharomyces cerevisiae* proteins take fixed origin positions along chromosomes, and we term these positions *origin loci* to distinguish them later from licensed positions to which we refer to as *origins*. Although origin loci are at specific sites on the *Saccharomyces cerevisiae* genome this does not mean that every origin locus is going to become an active origin during each and every round of the cell cycle; i.e. not all origin loci become licensed every time. This is because there are stochastic factors involved that hinder ORC from finding its DNA binding motif; also ever once licensed an origin might not become activated during S-phase.

For the analysis, we assign to every origin locus certain (simplifying) properties. The first one is what we term *competence*, and it describes the likelihood of an origin locus to actually become licensed which will give it the ability to become activated. It is a value between zero and one and for example, a 50 % competent origin becomes on average licensed in every other round of the cell cycle, a 25 % competent one is licensed in every fourth—the larger the value, the higher the likelihood of licensing. The second property defines the time when a licensed origin activates; it is the origin activation time distribution assuming that the origin is not passively replicated. We characterise this probability density to activate in S-phase by a distribution, which in case of a Gaussian distribution has mean time of activation μ and standard deviation σ. Previous analysis of the origin activation time distribution suggests a bell-shape-like function [15], and thus a Gaussian distribution is a good first approximation. In a previous mathematical model of DNA replication which incorporates these origin properties Hawkins et al. [9] determined parameters of the entire origin population in budding yeast using a model developed by Retkute et al. [16]. They fitted their model to experimental replication timing curves of *Saccharomyces cerevisiae* to determine the competence, mean and spread of an origin activation time distribution. For their study, Hawkins et al. and Retkute et al. chose a Hill-type function to represent their origin activation time distribution which depends on two parameters t_{12} and t_w which are similar to mean and standard deviation of a Gaussian distribution. Their choice of a variant function manifests in the possibility of having origin activation prior to the begin of S-phase, which is biologically unphysical. A Hill-type function however gives origin activation times well defined between zero and later times although any other choice of function can display replication time data equally well (*personal communication with Renata Retkute*). Hawkins et al. study uncovers valuable information on the spatial distribution of origins along chromosomes, and the parameters of origin loci.

We here analyse their data which we will discuss for the remainder of this section. Of particular interest is whether specific genomic regions for origin loci are random or whether their spacing depends on the competence value of their neighbours. We calculate the sum of the competence values for adjacent origin pairs, and look at a plot of this against their genomic separation. Figure 2.5 shows that this separates groups with a low value from those with a high value. We expect that most points would be roughly near the diagonal, and the two off-diagonal corners to be empty.

Plotting the distribution of origin data shows a somewhat linear trend between the competence of neighbouring loci pairs and their separation (Fig. 2.6a). We emphasise on the left-hand tail of the distribution which shows that low competent origins *per se* are closely located for a certain parameter regime up to about 2/3. Highly competent pairs tend to be further separated from their nearest neighbour whereas low competent pairs have a tendency to be very close to each other; although there are also close nearby pairs for the case of highly competent origins. This tendency is also reflected in the correlation coefficient of 0.331 (p-value $\sim 10^{-13}$) for this data. As we show

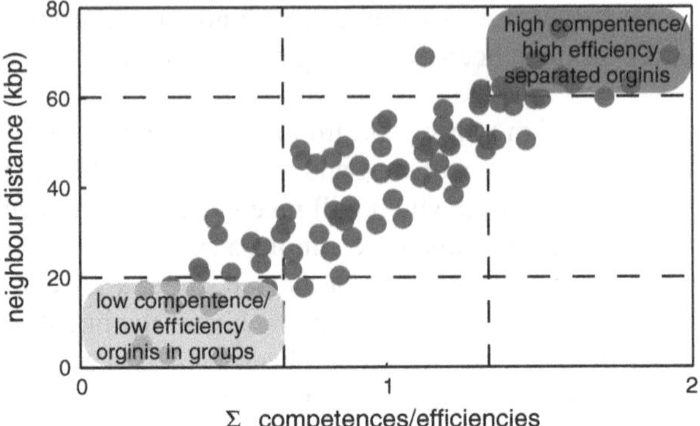

Fig. 2.5 Scheme for plotting origin neighbour distances. We plot the distance of adjacent origins of certain group size versus the sum of this competence or efficiency value of such a group. We expect that group with low competent/efficiency values have low distance to their neighbours and will be found in the *bottom left corner* (*green region*). As for highly competent/efficient origins, we expect these to be far away from their nearest neighbour and will be shown in the *top right hand corner* (*red region*)

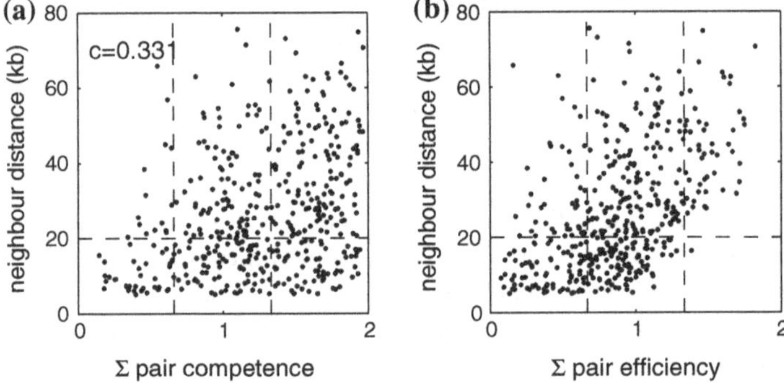

Fig. 2.6 Competence, efficiency and pair-wise neighbour distance in *Saccharomyces cerevisiae*. **a** Pairwise origin nearest-neighbour distance is plotted against their pairwise sum ($\sum$) of competences are. Highly competent pairs are found on the *right-hand side* of the *vertical line* at 4/3, and low competent ones at the *left-hand side* of the *vertical line* at 2/3. **b** Pairwise origin nearest-neighbour distances plotted here against the sum of their efficiency, i.e. the probability to become activated per round of the cell cycle

in Fig. 2.6b, a stronger trend for separation of highly competent origins holds for our analysis of efficiency—the probability of an origin being competent and also becoming activated in a particular round of the cell cycle. We emphasise that for the case of efficiency that there are no close and highly efficient origin pairs (bottom right corner) Fig. 2.6b.

This trend also persists if one considers sets of three nearest neighbouring origins. In Fig. 2.7a, b we compare the sum of competences with the maximal or minimal distance between direct origin neighbours out of a group of three adjacent origins.

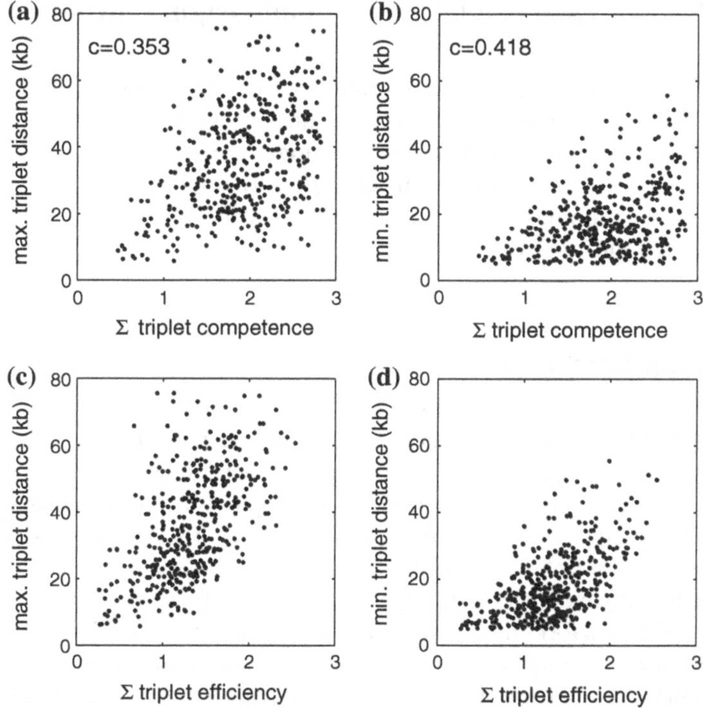

Fig. 2.7 Sets of three adjacent origins (*triplets*) are taken and either their maximum (**a, c**) or minimum (**b, d**) distance from one another within their triplet are plotted against either the $(\sum)$ sum of their competences (**a, b**) or the sum of their efficiencies (**c, d**)

There is a striking difference in maximal, or minimal separation when considering low competent and highly competent groups of three, consistent with data for a group of two. The linear correlation between origin separation and their ability to eventually activate is even clearer when we also consider efficiency (Fig. 2.7c, d). Figure 2.7c also shows that as the efficiency of a group of three origins increases at least one origin becomes further and further separated from the other two origins. This also applies to the minimum distance of a group (Fig. 2.7d). The data gives reason to speculate that origin positions have thus been chosen preferably to compensate for origins that have little likelihood to activate by others in their surroundings.

So this data in Figs. 2.6 and 2.7 show that the proximity of origin loci correlates with their competence. These properties are therefore not independent. The remaining question is however under what conditions do origins group and whether the positions of origin loci have been favourably selected to minimise the average replication time.

2.2 A Mathematical Model for Optimal Origin Positions

The data showed that the separation of origin loci correlates with origin competence and efficiency of their neighbour(s). Yet it is unclear whether those position found in experiments are actually optimal loci positions—i.e. those giving the minimum replication time for an average of a cell population. To re-phrase the question, we can ask whether evolution has driven origin loci to their positions on the chromosome where they are found today.

2.2.1 A Simplified Two Origin Model

In a first attempt to establish a many origin model we consider the case of having only two origin loci that are positioned on a stretch of DNA. We also simplify further that origins only have a probability to activate (or fail). In other words, we only consider competence p_i for the ith origin locus. The DNA is modelled as a one-dimensional line of unit length, and we denote competences of two loci p_1 and p_2. We initially make the assumption that origins activate at a well-defined time, $t = 0$. All replication forks travel at the same unit speed across the DNA. Specifically, we consider the geometry depicted in Fig. 2.8a where d_1 (d_2) is the distance from the left (right) end of the chromosome to the left (right) most locus. If both loci fail to be licensed we postulate that replication will eventually take place anyway, with a replication time T_0—for example, we can imagine that this stretch of DNA will be replicated by forks originating from origins outside of the region we are considering. It will be clear shortly that our results do not depend on T_0; this is just a mathematical device to prevent us dealing with infinite replication times.

If only one of the loci fails to become licensed, the replication time depends on the time it takes for the fork to reach the furthest end of the segment, so $T_{d_1} = 1 - d_1$ for locus 1 and $T_{d_2} = 1 - d_2$ for locus 2. If both loci have been licensed the replication time $T_{d_1,d_2} = \max\{d_1, d_2, (1 - d_1 - d_2)/2\}$ is defined by the longest time for a fork to reach the end of the segment or for two forks to collide. Figure 2.8b illustrates that the replication time of an asymmetric placement of loci is never less than a corresponding symmetric configuration (that is, with $d_1 = d_2$). Therefore we consider only symmetrical locus placements, and use $d_1 = d_2 = d$ with $0 \leq d \leq 1/2$. The average replication time is then given by

$$T_{\text{rep}}(d) = (1 - p_1)(1 - p_2)T_0 + (p_1 + p_2 - 2p_1p_2)(1 - d) + p_1p_2 \max\{d, (1 - 2d)/2\}. \quad (2.1)$$

This is a piecewise-linear function with discontinuity in its first derivative at $d = 1/4$, and with domain [0 1/2]. Hence, T_{rep} can only have a minimum at $d = 0$, $d = 1/2$, or at $1/4$. Placing loci at the end of a segment ($d = 0$) is obviously not a minimum of T_{rep}. Placing both loci in the middle ($d = 1/2$) we assume that

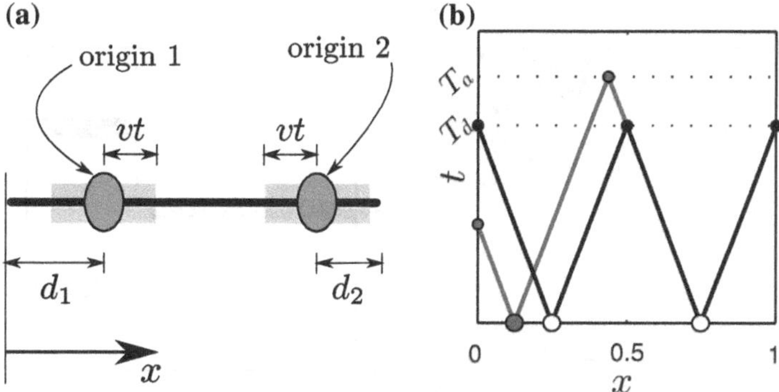

Fig. 2.8 Two origin model of DNA replication. **a** Coordinate system for origin loci with d_1, d_2 being the distance from the *left-* or *right-end* of the chromosome, respectively. x is the position coordinate along the chromosome. Replication forks travel at a speed v away from the origins. The *grey regions* show the replicated DNA at time t. **b** Space–time diagram of replication fork movement for the case of both origins starting replication at the same time $t = 0$ min. Forks move from each origin position and replication is completed once a fork reached the end of the chromosome or the last pair of forks coalesced. A symmetric placement of origins gives minimal replication time whereas an asymmetric one requires more time, i.e. $T_d < T_a$

both can activate at the same time, however the replication time is then 1/2 for the last term in Eq. (2.1) as well as for the second term when only one activates. The replication times for $d = 1/4$ and $1/2$ are

$$T_{\text{rep}}(d = 1/2) = (1 - p_1)(1 - p_2)T_0 + (p_1 + p_2 - p_1 p_2)/2$$

and

$$T_{\text{rep}}(d = 1/4) = (1 - p_1)(1 - p_2)T_0 + (3p_1 + 3p_2 - 5p_1 p_2)/4.$$

We conclude that the two loci group together ($d = 1/2$) to achieve minimum replication time if $T_{\text{rep}}(d = 1/2) < T_{\text{rep}}(d = 1/4)$, which leads to the condition

$$p_2 < \frac{p_1}{3p_1 - 1}. \tag{2.2}$$

Notice here that T_0 drops out. The inequality Eq. (2.2) defines two regions on the p_1–p_2 plane, corresponding to grouped or isolated loci being optimum. This is shown in Fig. 2.9a, where this analytical result is confirmed by stochastic simulations. These simulations are done employing a minimisation algorithm (using genetic algorithms [17]) which searches for the minimal replication time. The principal ingredients to the algorithms are as follows. First, origin loci are selected. Each origin locus is checked whether it will activate given its competence value, i.e. checking a random number against this probability. Finally the replication time is calculated, and this procedure repeats for several times to establish the average replication time. The positions of the origin loci are then changed, and the average replication time is

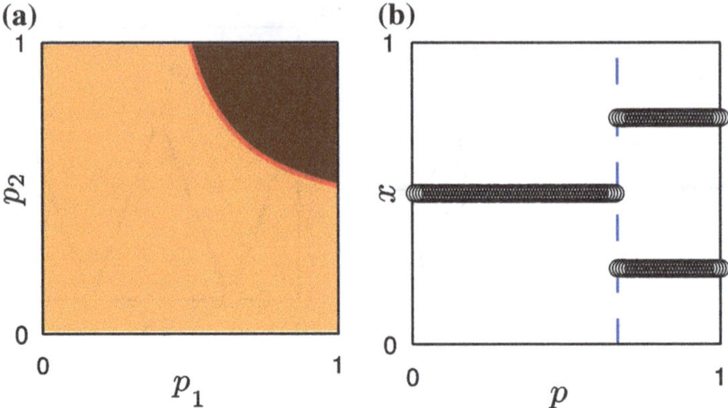

Fig. 2.9 Optimal locations in a two origin loci model. **a** Simulation results, showing optimal loci to achieve minimal $T_{\rm rep}$ for 2 loci with different competences, are shown for p_1–p_2 combinations on a lattice grid. Colour indicates $d_1, d_2 = 1/2$ (*beige*) or $d_1, d_2 = 1/4$ (*brown*). The two regimes are separated by a coexistence line matched by the condition Eq. (2.2) in *red*. **b** Optimal position of 2 identical loci with respect to their competence p to minimize the replication time $T_{\rm rep}$ (*circles*) and $p = 2/3$ (*dashed line*)

calculated for this new configuration. It is then compared to other randomly selected loci positions to whether or not it results in minimum replication time. In Fig. 2.9a, the region above the curve corresponds to competences for which $T_{\rm rep}$ is minimized by loci being apart ($d = 1/4$) and below the curve for organising these in a group ($d = 1/2$). In general, if one of the loci has low competence grouping gives the minimum replication time. In fact, it can be shown that if one of the loci has a competence lower than 50 %, grouping is the optimal situation regardless of the competence of the other—even if the other is close to 100 % competent. This becomes clear with if one imagines that once a replication fork from an origin has to cover a distance more than 1/2, such a grouped configuration becomes favourable. Figure 2.10 shows how the individual replication time ($T_{\rm rep}$) terms change depending on how many origins become activated.

For the case of equal competences, $p_1 = p_2 = p$, the grouped configuration is optimal if $p < 2/3$. We ran a numerical optimization algorithm again to find the loci corresponding to the least replication time for a range of p; these results are shown in Fig. 2.9b. The same transition also takes place for non-identical values of p_1 and p_2—whenever one crosses from the dark to the beige region of Fig. 2.9a.

The above results may seem at first quite counter-intuitive; one might expect that the configuration with the least replication time would correspond to isolated loci ($d = 1/4$). However, if the origins have a significant chance of failing to activate, this configuration would mean that often one side of the chromosome would have to wait for a fork which originated at the origin on the other site to replicate it, therefore increasing $T_{\rm rep}$. So in the case of low competences, it becomes advantageous to have

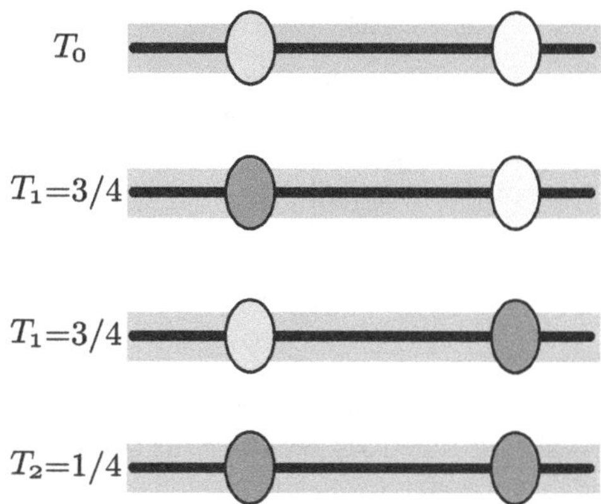

Fig. 2.10 The time it takes to replicate a given piece of DNA T_{rep} depends on the number of origins that activate (*orange filled ovals*) or not activating. This contributes to the different terms as for instance in Eq. (2.1)

both loci centered, which is near any point in the chromosome. This explains the condition for grouping if $p < 2/3$.

2.2.2 *Many Origin Loci*

In reality eukaryotic chromosomes have more than two loci [18], so next we investigate the case of a chromosome on which there are many loci and examine the conditions under which it becomes favourable to have isolated origin loci compared to groups. In this analysis we will assume for simplicity that the loci all have identical competence.

We consider a group of loci as one single locus with an effective competence p_{eff}. For a group consisting of m loci p_{eff} is the competence that at least one locus will be licensed there, and is given by

$$p_{\mathrm{eff}} = 1 - (1 - p)^m. \tag{2.3}$$

We assume that one large group of n identical loci breaks up into two groups of equal size, each consisting of $n/2$ loci. A locus organized with others in a group of size $m = n/2$ rather than with n loci will give minimum T_{rep}, as long as the locus' competence is larger than its critical probability p_c, given by $p_{\mathrm{eff}} = 2/3$, which yields

$$p_c = 1 - 1/\sqrt[n]{9}. \tag{2.4}$$

Figure 2.11 confirms our analytical result showing the value of p_c for increasing group sizes in our simulations. These results clearly show that large groups of many highly competent loci are unfavorable, but that groups tend to form for

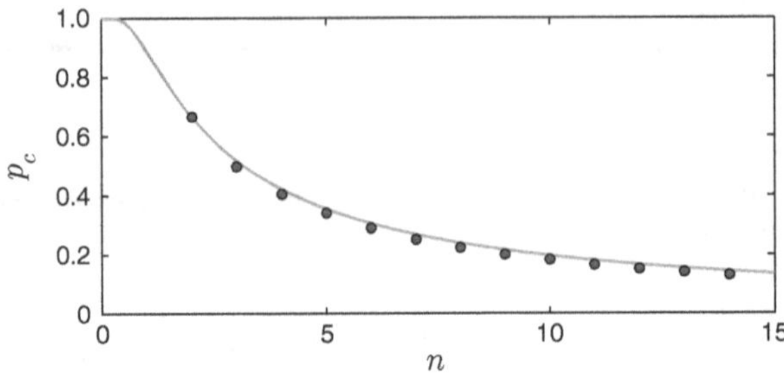

Fig. 2.11 Many origins with variable competence. **a** Probability at which groups separate p_c versus loci/group n. Shown are simulations (*circles*) and analytical prediction for $p_c = 1 - 1/\sqrt[n]{9}$ (*line*)

low-competence loci. Our formula is also a good approximation to predict the probability at which a transition occurs for an odd number of origins in a group.

So we would expect for example a group of four origins, to break up at $p_c \approx 0.42$. Our simulations do show this to be the case (Fig. 2.12a). However the groups of four origins does not break up symmetrically into two groups of two origins, but rather into three groups. As p_{eff} increases through p, we first see two origins move out to positions $x = 1/4$ and $x = 3/4$ leaving two at $x = 1/2$. Only at a slightly larger p do we get two clusters of two. This is due to the fact that we assumed the simple case of two origins can be directly applied to the more complicated case of more origins. Figure 2.12b shows this as well where we plot the replication time for the individual configurations. This also illustrates that at first only two loci break out of the four origin group which is the crossover of the black with the blue line in Fig. 2.12b; before the blue line crosses with the red one.

2.2.3 Evolutionary Pressure Drives Yeast Origin Loci to Optimal Positions

Our hypothesis from this modelling is that selective pressure has influenced the position of origin loci through the minimization of the replication time. The theoretical result—low competence loci group, high competence loci are spread out—is also in line with our data analysis presented in Sect. 2.1. The competence data used for the analysis there however resulted in silico by model fitting to experimental data. So it required a proxy that could be potentially biased, and as a further example we now use a *Saccharomyces cerevisiae* chromosome for which origin positions and competence values are experimentally known. We then apply a search algorithm for it to find the optimal loci positions to achieve minimal replication time. This will show that in silico optimisation matches a known set of locations.

We show in Fig. 2.14 locus competence and location data for *Saccharomyces cerevisiae* chromosome VI, which has been studied extensively [12, 19]. Competences

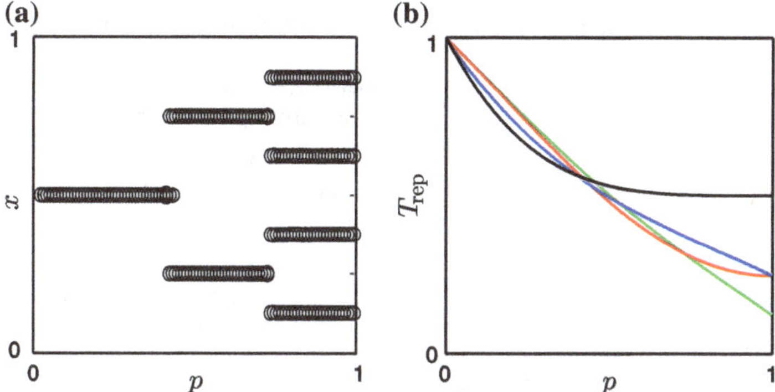

Fig. 2.12 Four origins with variable competence. **a** Simulation results for positions x of four identical origin loci with probability p. As p increases spreading loci along the chromosome of unit length results in minimal replication time. **b** The average replication time T_{rep} of arranging four origin loci positions with the same probability [corresponding to configuration shown in (**a**)]. The different colours of the curves correspond to: all 4 loci clustered at the middle position (*black*); 2 loci at $x = 1/2$, and 2 loci at either $x = 1/4$ or $x = 3/4$ (*blue*); groups of 2 individual loci at either $x = 1/4$ or $x = 3/4$ (*red*); individual loci $x = 0.2, 0.4, 0.6, 0.8$ (*green*)

cannot be measured for all loci (in white), because either they are too close to the end of the chromosome or to an adjacent locus. We performed a search for the optimal position for the loci in the region with known competences using a genetic algorithm [17]. The algorithm mimicks an evolutionary process by first selecting sets of random origin locations for a parent generation of 50 individuals. The parent generation is then tested for its individual set location to give minimum replication time. The most optimal of the minimal sets are selected for the next round of iteration. They then become reshuffled amongst each other to yield a new collection of origin loci positions on this chromosome. The sets of locations are in tournament. A pair of randomly selected individuals is set to tournament, meaning the one with lower replication time succeeds. Ten new sets of location are drawn randomly and replace the ten worst (maximal replication time) location sets out of the tournament. The remaining sets produce children. They result from crossing over 85 % of the parents which are selected randomly, i.e. 15 % of the best part of a population remains unchanged to the next generation. The selection of new locations from parents results from crossover of the two parental sets of locations, i.e. either picking location 1 from parent 1 or parent 2 and so forth. They produce two children sets so that each child inherits a particular location from a particular parent to 50 %; termed crossover. Note that the number of origins always stays fixed. We then determine the replication time for the individual position sets just as before. The genetic algorithm was run with a population of 100 chromosomes of the parent generation and optimised over 2,000 iterations meaning the genomes evolve over 2,000 generations. The procedure repeats for 18,000 times with different seeds of the random number generator. Figure 2.13 summarises the algorithm detailed above. The details of parameters here lead to a local minimum set of origin location in a reasonable amount of computation time.

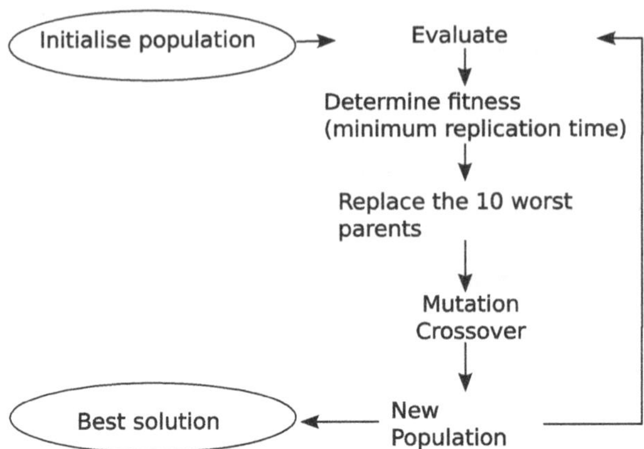

Fig. 2.13 Genetic algorithm. Summary of the steps of the genetic algorithm to determine the set of origin location to give minimum replication time

Although an appropriate choice of biological evolutionary-like parameters can be used to mimic evolution to occur over millions of years however this requires a substantial amount of extra computation time as most of the runs end in a local minimum similar to the one we find below (Figs. 2.14 and 2.15).

We remark that in our example of chromosome VI is an identifiability problem as all strong loci have $p \sim 90\,\%$, and we therefore constrained the ordering during the optimisation. Although in this result we do not consider inter-origin variations in the origin activation time, the predicted locus distribution from these simulations bears a good resemblance to the actual spacing with a score of $F = 0.11$[2]; in particular we recover the group in the middle, in which an origin locus with 58 % competence is placed next to one with 88 % competence. Even multiple repeats of the optimisation algorithm produce minimum replication time solutions which have on average $F = 0.12$ (Fig. 2.15). This indicates that evolution has generated a near optimal solution for the proper placement of origin loci over many generations. Our study here shows a possible means to minimise replication time by choosing optimal origin loci positions. Mutations such as the translocation of genetic sequences occur frequently in unicellular, eukaryotic organisms such as yeast [20]. The rearrangement of genetic sequences—origin loci in our model—over many generations is therefore also a legitimate device in an evolutionary context to achieve minimal replication timing.

[2] $F = \frac{1}{9}\sum_{i=1}^{n=9} d_i^o / d_i^r$ is a measure of the difference between the gap distribution of the optimised and random cases. A gap is defined as the separation between the ith experimental locus position p_i^e and that of the optimization p_i^o: $d_i^o = |p_i^e - p_i^o|$. d_i^r is akin; the average separation that arises from placing a locus uniformly randomly and p_i^e. $F = 0$ means that the optimization fits the experimental loci positions perfectly; $F \sim 1$ indicates no difference to that of a random placement.

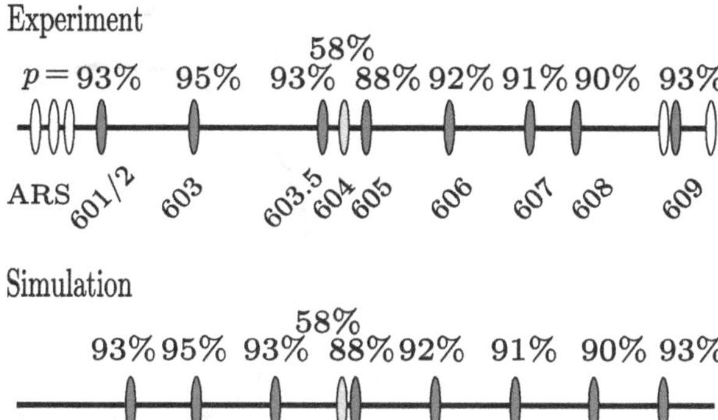

Fig. 2.14 Distribution of origin loci on yeast chromosome VI with known (*grey*) and unknown competences [12, 19]. The distribution results from our simulation in search for minimum T_{rep} (only *grey* origins considered). The group in the middle of the chromosome with a low and highly competent locus was recovered

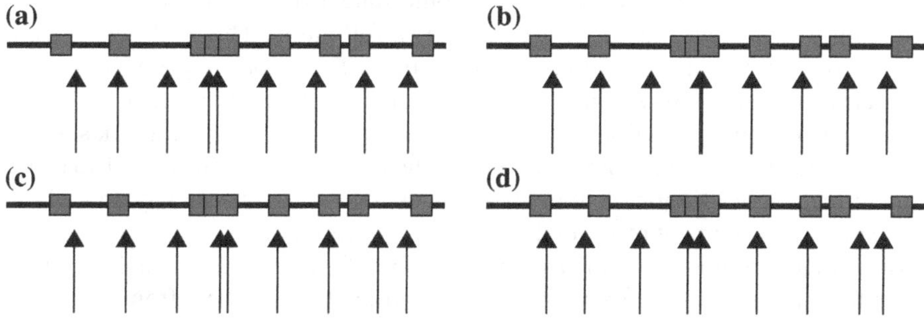

Fig. 2.15 Optimisation results for finding the minimum T_{rep} by varying the origin loci positions given their competences. The *blue boxes* are the experimental origin loci positions, the *arrows* show the positions found in simulations of individual runs. **a** Origin loci distribution that has the overall minimum replication time corresponds to Fig. 2.14. **b–d** Some distributions that give minimum replication time close to the overall minimum solution

2.2.4 Loci Competence and Circular Chromosomes

Most prokaryotes, for example the bacterium *Escherichia coli*, carry their genomic information on a single, circular chromosome. They have no compartmentalisation, meaning DNA is contained within the cytoplasm and not within a nucleus. Therefore there is no separation of licensing and origin activation as is in eukaryotes, and prokaryotes can start replication as soon as their origin locus becomes replicated. So here we can have re-replication since there is no separation of licensing from synthesis. This way they can produce concurrent copies of their DNA during exponential, unlimited growth conditions.

Their organisation of DNA replication on circular chromosome also has the advantage of only one replication fork being able to replicate its entire genome. For instance,

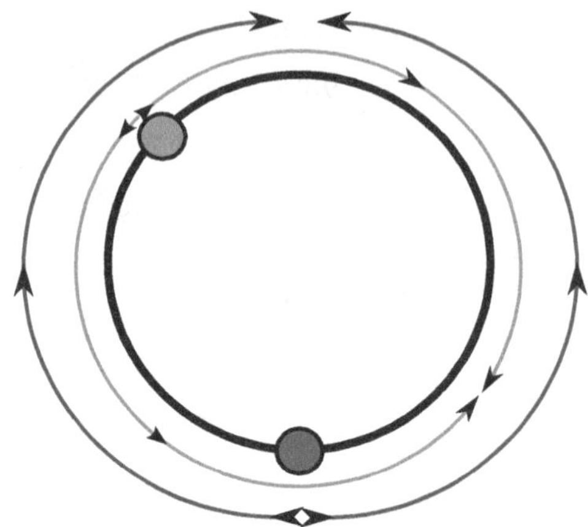

Fig. 2.16 One origin model of circular chromosome. The replication time for one origin (*blue or red*) is independent of its location due to the symmetry of a *circle*. Replication forks will always meet after travelling half circumference

the fork can start from any position on a chromosome, from which it takes the same time until to complete synthesis; it completes a full circle. This is different from the previous case of having a linear chromosome. There fork movement is more constrained because a fork cannot go around and one requires at least two forks travelling from either direction of an origin to complete DNA or have a fork starting from an edge of the chromosome. This edge effect was shown in Sect. 2.2.1 to result in preferred origin locations; only two locations that are symmetrically around the centre of a DNA segment result in the minimal replication time.

A circular chromosome also has advantage over failing origins or stalling replication forks to be easily recovered by a fork travelling towards them from elsewhere on the circle as illustrated in Fig. 2.16. So we note that all positions on a circle with a circumference we set to unit length result in the same replication time of $T_{\mathrm{rep1}} = 1/2$ (2 forks, each replicating half of the circle); and therefore any position serves equally well to act as an origin locus. In principle, we will always observe the same T_{rep1} for a population of cells no matter where each individual cell starts its replicating from. The remaining question is whether there also exist similar origin placement conditions as we observed previously—grouped or separated; and if, so how many origins are required along with their competence value to achieve minimal replication time. We consider growth to be limiting, so that there are at maximum two copies of a chromosome and not multiple ones as during exponential growth, and again ask the question which loci positions give minimum replication time.

2.2.4.1 Two Origins

The case of two origins, shown in Fig. 2.17, results in a shorter replication time of $T_{\mathrm{rep2}} = 1/4$, if both origins origins are maximally apart as is the case for a symmetric placement in Fig. 2.17a. An asymmetric placement however results in a replication time less optimal, depending on the maximum distance between the two origins it

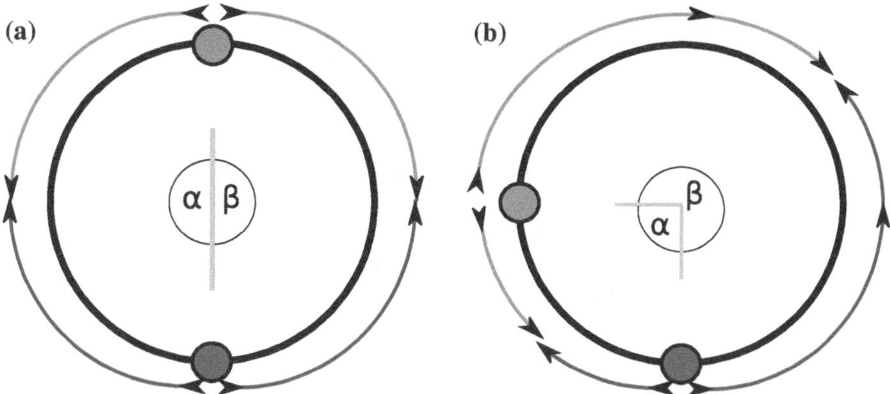

Fig. 2.17 Two-origin loci model with the angle α and β between them indicated by the *grey bar*. **a** The minimum replication time of $T_{\text{rep2}} = 1/4$ is achieved by placing the origin loci furthest apart from each other with distances clockwise and anticlockwise to the other origin being equal. **b** An asymmetric placement results in a longer replication time, because it takes longer for two forks to coalesce

will be $1/4 \leq T_{\text{rep2}} \leq 1/2$ (Fig. 2.17b). The other extreme is placing both origins on top of each other, for which we recover the same result as in the one-origin case. There exists only one optimal configuration, which is placing origins furthest apart which we show analytically. We define the angle between adjacent origins α and β. We note that the time of the replicated piece of the chromosome by two forks is defined by $T = \alpha/(2 \cdot 360)°$, which then gives the mean replication time

$$T_{\text{rep2}} = (1 - p_1)(1 - p_2)T_0 + p_1(1 - p_2)\frac{1}{2} + p_2(1 - p_1)\frac{1}{2} + p_1 p_2 \max\left\{\frac{\alpha}{2 \cdot 360°}, \frac{\beta}{2 \cdot 360°}\right\}. \tag{2.5}$$

The first term accounts for neither of the origins activating, the second and third terms account for only either origin to activate and the last term if both do. The angles are constrained by one full round around the circle $360° = \alpha + \beta$ which gives $\beta = 360° - \alpha$. We can only find the minimum of Eq. (2.5) at either $\alpha = 0°$, $\alpha = 360°$ or the discontinuity of the maximum function $\alpha = 360° - \alpha$ which is for $\alpha = 180°$. $\alpha = 0°$ and $\alpha = 360°$ mean that both origins would sit on top of each other; $\max\{\alpha, \beta\} = 360°$. This only leaves the configuration shown in Fig. 2.17a with both origins maximally apart to give minimum replication time.

We now write Eq. (2.5) in terms of different competence values p_1 and p_2 and include our knowledge that the minimum replication time can only be found for either $\alpha = 180°$ or $\alpha = 0°$, i.e. if both origins activate $T = 1/4$ or $T = 1/2$, respectively (cf. Fig. 2.17). We set $T_0 = 1$. The average replication time of both cases is then given by

$$T^{b}_{\text{rep2}}(p_1, p_2) = \frac{1}{4}p_1 p_2 - \frac{1}{2}p_1 - \frac{1}{2}p_2 + 1, \text{ and} \quad (2.6)$$

$$T^{b}_{\text{rep2}}(p_1, p_2) = \frac{1}{2}p_1 p_2 - \frac{1}{2}p_1 - \frac{1}{2}p_2 + 1. \quad (2.7)$$

The minimum is found using the configuration for $\alpha = 180°$ [Eq. (2.6)], because $T^{a}_{\text{rep2}}(p_1, p_2) < T^{b}_{\text{rep2}}(p_1, p_2)$ for $p_1, p_2 \in (0, 1]$. So even for origins with different competence it is always best to be farmost apart from each other. This result differs from our analysis of a linear chromosomes in Sect. 2.2.1. We showed that there exists a sharp transition from finding origins together or apart depending on the parameter p_1 and p_2 for a linear chromosome.

2.2.4.2 Three Origin Loci Break Circular Symmetry: And Group Together

We now examine an odd number of origin loci and continue our analysis in terms of the time a fork travels. We take the example of three origins and place them as depicted in Fig. 2.18. The case which results in minimum $T_{\text{rep3}} = 1/6$ is again placing all origins maximally apart from each other (Fig. 2.18a). Maximum replication time is achieved by placing all three origin loci on top of each other, which is obviously not the preferred configuration to achieve an optimal replication time. This leaves two possible scenarios to arrange the origins. We place two of them maximally apart and the third one on top of any of the two (Fig. 2.18b), or the third origin is placed somewhere in the remaining halves (Fig. 2.18c). We note that: if all origin loci are always competent to activate ($p = 100\,\%$) then the resulting $T_{\text{rep2}} = 1/2$ which is independent of the arrangement of the third origin locus. In a more general approach, we write an expression for the average replication time

$$T_{\text{rep3}}(p) = (1-p)^3 T_0 + 3p(1-p)^2 T_1 + 3p^2(1-p)T_2 + p^3 T_3, \quad (2.8)$$

with which we show analytically that placing origin loci maximally apart is the only optimal configuration. The four different terms in Eq. (2.8) account for the possible number of origins activating during a round of the cell cylcle. T_0 is the time resulting of all origins failing, but we note that it can be chosen arbitrarily as it will not influence our analysis. We choose $T_0 = 1$, as this is the longest time it takes for one single fork to complete replication. T_1 accounts for the time, if only one of the three origins activates is always independent of the placement of the failing origins. We know from the case of one origin locus that $T_1 = T_{\text{rep1}} = 1/2$. T_2 and T_3 both depend on the chosen configuration for the origin loci, and are defined by when the last coalescence event happens, so by the maximum distance a fork must travel.

The average replication times T^{a}_{rep3}, T^{b}_{rep3} and T^{c}_{rep3} for a circle of circumference $c = 1$ and origin loci at the positions shown in Fig. 2.18a–c are given by

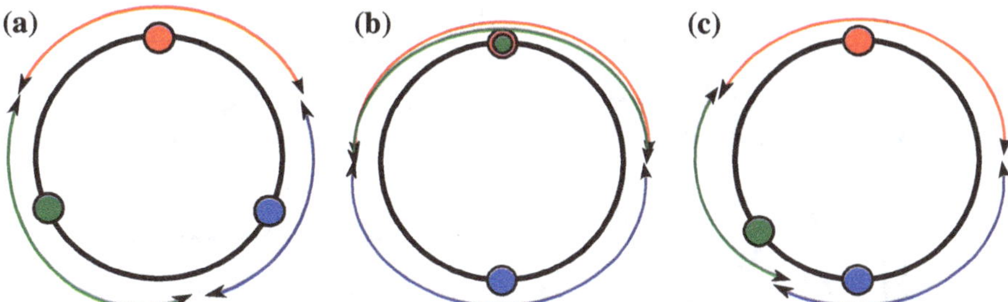

Fig. 2.18 Three origin loci on a circular chromosome. Three origin loci model with origins in either *green, blue* or *red*, and their corresponding forks shown as *lines*; origin loci 1, 2 and 3 respectively. Forks coalesce at the positions where two *arrowheads* meets. There exist three possible configurations to achieve minimum replication time. **a** All origins are spaced maximally apart. **b** Two origins are at either side along the diameter of the *circle* and the third origin at the same location of one of the two other. **c** The third origin can be placed in either half of the chromosome. However it does not contribute to the minimum replication time since it will always take longer to replicate the *right-hand side* of the *circle*

$$T^a_{\text{rep3}} = -1/3p^3 + p^2 - \frac{3}{2} + 1, \tag{2.9}$$

$$T^b_{\text{rep3}} = -1/4p^3 + p^2 - \frac{3}{2} + 1, \tag{2.10}$$

$$T^c_{\text{rep3}} = -1/4p^3 + p^2 - \frac{3}{2} + 1. \tag{2.11}$$

We note that $T^a_{\text{rep3}} < T^b_{\text{rep3}} = T^c_{\text{rep3}}$ as well as $T^b_{\text{rep3}} = T^c_{\text{rep3}}$ is for all origin sites with the same p; a group of two origin loci can either be situated at the top half or the bottom of the circle [configurations (2) and (3) in Fig. 2.19a]. We conclude that for all identical origin loci T^a_{rep} is the only optimal configuration, i.e. three origin loci are best placed maximally apart from each other. The cases for T^b_{rep3} and T^c_{rep3} both result in the same average replication time; the open boundary allows replication forks to travel around the circle. Those cases however are relevant for origin loci that differ in their competence as we show below.

We fix two loci with competence equal to 1, say $p_3 = p_2 = 1$ (red and blue loci respectively). Using a general expression for the average replication time [Eq. (2.8) for individual p_i values] one can show that the positioning of the third origin locus with variable competence has no contribution to the average replication. This is for as long as its competence value is below 0.5. We give the analytic expression of the average replication time for the configuration shown in Fig. 2.18a, c ($p_2 = p_3 = 1$), which we call $T^{a^*}_{\text{rep3}}$ and $T^{c^*}_{\text{rep3}}$ respectively:

$$T^{a^*}_{\text{rep3}} = 1/3 - 1/6p_1, \tag{2.12}$$

$$T^{c^*}_{\text{rep3}} = 1/4. \tag{2.13}$$

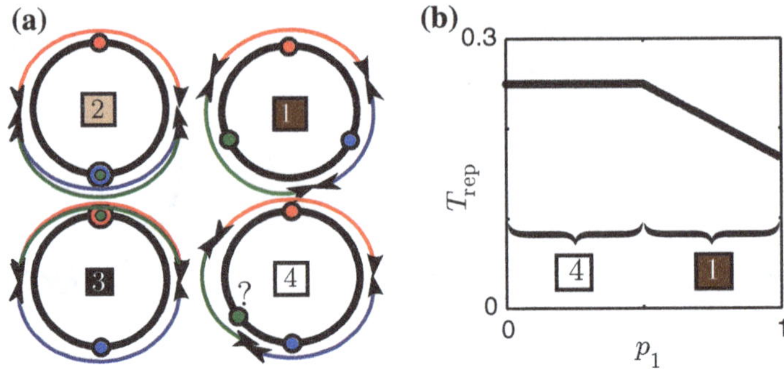

Fig. 2.19 Distribution of three loci on a circular chromosome. Origin 1, 2 and 3 have colours *green, blue* and *red*, respectively. **a** Three loci can be distributed in four different ways on a circular chromosome. In configuration (*1*) all origins are equally spread out, in configurations (*2*) and (*3*) one locus pairs with another one, and in configuration (*4*) the third locus can positioned anywhere. **b** Average replication time T_{rep} of a 3 origin system with two loci of competence 100 % and one origin having varying competence p_1. T_{rep} is independent of p_1 for $p_1 < 0.5$ [configuration (*4*) in (**a**)] and for values $p_1 > 0.5$ it contributes [configuration (*1*) in (**a**)]

We see that Eq. (2.13) is independent of p_1, the green origin, which is confirmed through stochastic simulations shown in Fig. 2.19a. There are only two possible configurations for this setting which are depicted as configuration (1) and (4) in Fig. 2.19b. Origin loci are either best placed far apart from each other, or only two origins contribute to the replication time. Minimum average replication time is achieved for the condition $T^{a^*}_{\text{rep3}} < T^{c^*}_{\text{rep3}}$ for $p_1 > 0.5$. Therefore a less competent origin will not influence the average replication time if combined with two highly competent origins.

Now we vary the competence of two origins, say the red origin that has $p_3 = 1$ here. We will see that there are four different configurations for this case. These are shown in Fig. 2.19a. Again using the general expression Eq. (2.8), we find that the other two green and blue origins cluster together; the red origin, origin 3, stays isolated as in Fig. 2.19a configuration (2). This is if the following condition is justified

$$p_1 < \frac{p_2}{3p_2 - 1}, \tag{2.14}$$

which corresponds to the beige region in Fig. 2.20a. The relative position of origin 1 and 2 (green and blue loci) to origin 3 (red locus of Fig. 2.19) is plotted in this figure; beige indicates locus 1 and 2 group together [configuration (2) in Fig. 2.19a], black they are 1/2 apart from each other [configuration (3) in Fig. 2.19a], brown all loci are maximally apart from each other [configuration (1) in Fig. 2.19a].

We now lower p_3 as in for example Fig. 2.20b–d where $p_3 = 0.75,\ 0.50,\ 0.25$, respectively. This makes the above mentioned four regions more visible; each corresponds to an optimal configuration. If two origin loci have same competence, the location of the weaker third origin locus can be chosen freely as it will not affect

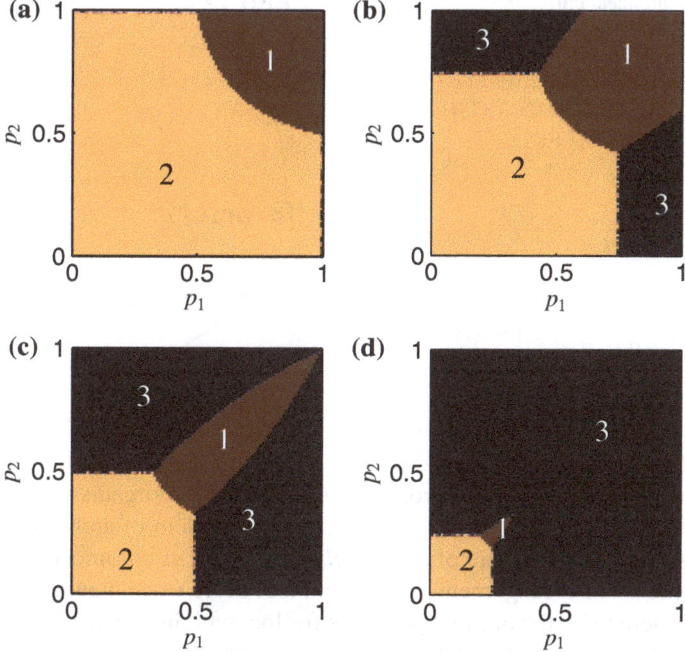

Fig. 2.20 The configurations giving minimal replication are shown for the case of three origin loci. The competence of locus 3 is fixed to either the value of $p_3 = 1.00$ in (**a**), $p_3 = 0.75$ in (**b**), $p_3 = 0.50$ in (**c**), or $p_3 = 0.25$ (**d**). Competences p_1 and p_2 of loci 1 and 2 are varied. The colour code and numbering correspond to the configurations as shown in Fig. 2.19a. The *brown* (*1*) colour indicates complete separation of all loci. *Beige* (*2*) and *black* (*3*) colours correspond to grouping of two loci, i.e. configurations (*2*) and (*3*) of Fig. 2.19a. There is a fourth regime along $p_1 = p_2 = 1.00$ in (**a**), $p_1 = p_2 = 0.75$ in (**b**), $p_1 = p_2 = 0.50$ in (**c**), and $p_1 = p_2 = 0.25$ in (**d**) where the position of the fourth locus positions can be chosen arbitrarily. As the competence p_3 decreases the number of possible configurations of (*1*), where we find maximal separation, decrease; as do those for configuration (*2*)

the result of the average replication time, [cf. Fig. 2.19a configuration (4)]. This is the case for the randomly coloured shades as one crosses from the beige to the black region at $p_2 = p_3 = 0.50$; the configurations change from (2)→(4)→(3) (Fig. 2.19a) in Fig. 2.20b. As p_3 decreases even further the region of configuration (1) shrinks even further. Once p_3 drops below 0.50, i.e. going from Fig. 2.20c, d, the regime of configuration (3) increases. This is in agreement with Fig. 2.19b where we showed that grouping or not requires a minimum value to contribute to the average replication time.

This analysis shows that origin loci grouping is also a means of minimising replication time for a circular chromosome. If all origins are sufficiently competent they will be furthest apart from each other. A transition from where it becomes best to group two origins if they are weaker compared to a third. Then the individual loci and the group of two take a configuration similar to a two origin model; they are

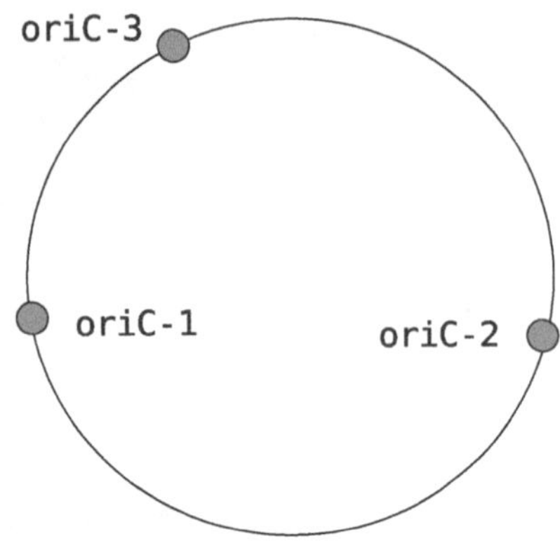

Fig. 2.21 An archaeal chromosome with 3 origin loci. Schematic representation of the arrangement of the origin loci (oriC-1, oriC-2, oriC-3) of the archaea *Sulfolobus solfataricus*

$1/2$ apart from each other. There are only a few examples in nature where there are three origins on a circular chromosome. Most of the organisms with circular chromosomes and multiple origins are part of the kingdom of archaea [21, 22]. In Fig. 2.21, we show an example of a *Sulfolobus solfataricus* chromosome with three origin loci [23]. The arrangement of its origin loci bears resemblance with what we have shown here to be the optimal positions for loci with high competence (see also Figs. 2.19a and 2.18), and there are also several further examples as for instance in *Haloferax volcanii* [24] or *Sulfolobus islandicus* [25] with similar loci arrangements.

2.3 Optimal Origin Loci and Stochasticity in Origin Activation Time

The above discussions focused on the case of pre-defined loci in yeast and archaea, and ignored additional noise such as the variation in origin activation time. Stochastic origin activation is also well accepted by biologists and we now examine the case of stochastic activation time for *Xenopus laevis* embryos as a model organism. We remind that unlike loci in *Saccharomyces cerevisiae*, any DNA locus in a *Xenopus laevis* embryo is capable of binding with pMcm to become an origin. Surprisingly, biologists find roughly equally-spaced groups of 5–10 pMcms separated by approximately 10 kbp [26–28]. However do these give minimal replication time for biological relevant parameters with such an activation time distribution?

We first turn to the case where origin loci have been licensed, and there is a delay during their activation given by some activation time distribution. For simplicity we assume that the pMcms at an origin can activate with uniform probability at any time within a window which has a lower boundary at $t_0 = 0$ min and an upper at t_b, which is at maximum the length of an S-phase (20 min). The probability for an origin to activate at some time t is distributed according to

$$f_T(t) = \begin{cases} 1/t_b & 0 \le t \le t_b \\ 0, & \text{otherwise} \end{cases} \tag{2.15}$$

This distribution has mean $\mu = t_b/2$ and standard deviation $\sigma = t_b/\sqrt{12}$ and represents, for example the grey area in Fig. 2.22a. As an origin activates later than its neighbour the overall replication is delayed as well. In this scenario replication completes when all forks have either coalesced or reached the end of the DNA segment. If an origin does not activate by the time its locus is replicated from a replication fork which originated elsewhere, it then cannot become activated anymore. The replicating fork then has to continue synthesis until it reaches the end of the chromosome; which prolongs overall replication time.

We will use the same approach as for a linear chromosome in Sect. 2.1 now incorporating the uniform activation time distribution. In this case, an "origin" is defined as a locus where at least one pMcm has bound to it, and so it corresponds to 100 % competent locus in the notation we have used so far. In addition, pMcms are assumed to be all identical with the same activation probability distribution (standard deviation $\sigma = t_b/\sqrt{12}$). We apply this probability distribution to the two-origin model depicted in Fig. 2.22a, and we also use the genetic search algorithm [17] to find the positions resulting in minimum replication time as σ increases. The expectation is that we will again see a transition of the optimal configuration from isolated pMcms to groups as σ increases; this is akin to varying competence in our previous scenario. If for most cases an origin activates too late it becomes replicated and cannot activate anymore. The active replication fork then has to travel a much farther to complete replication at a much later time as if all origins had activated. We test this prediction using the two-origin model with one pMcm bound to one origin; we find numerically the optimal (minimum average replication time) positions for the origins as a function of σ which are shown in Fig. 2.22b. These results show that origin grouping is also preserved in the two-origin model with stochastic variation in origin activation time. Grouping is important for swift replication under conditions of low competence and large noise which we will explain in the remainder of this chapter. We again use a segment of unit length and forks progress at unit speed of $v = 1$ kbp/min. We observe a sharp transition at $\sigma \approx 0.25$ min, above which it is best to place both origins in the middle of the segment, as observed in the case with varying competence. This is consistent with Fig. 2.22c which shows the average replication time. A minor difference between this case and the previous one in Sect. 2.1 is that for $\sigma < 0.25$, the optimal location of the origins is not constant. Origins move by a small amount further towards the edges of the chromosome. Using a Gaussian activation time distribution, as suggested by for example Goldar et al. [15] or Herrick et al. [29], also gives the transition from separated to grouped origin for a similar σ-value of around 0.25 if we fix the mean at zero (cf. also Fig. 2.23b). A uniform distribution is thus a good approximation and further has the advantage that replication can only occur after a set time $t = 0$. A Gaussian distribution however has the complication that by its definition an activation prior to the begin of S-phase is possible. The transition for the uniform distribution we use here is also

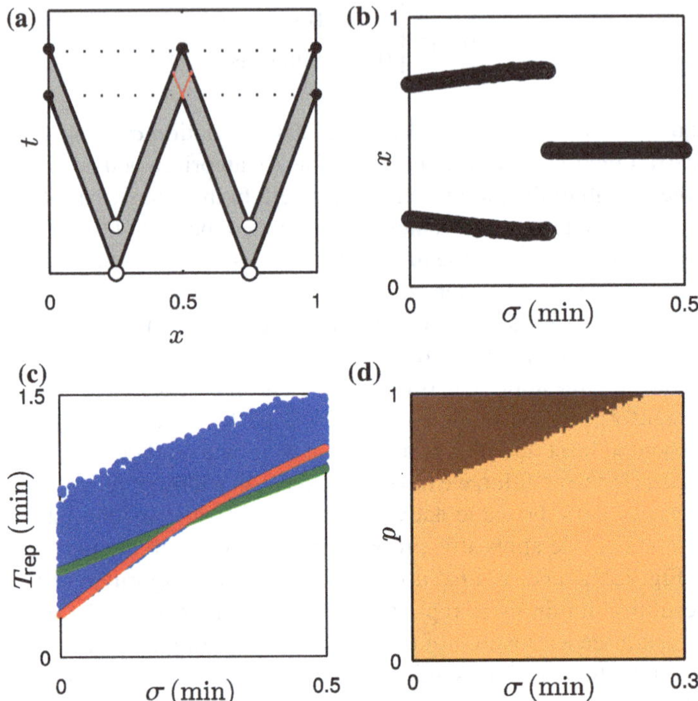

Fig. 2.22 **a** Schematic representation of space–time diagram for a two-origin system. Origins (*hollow circles*) can activate randomly within a time window (*grey area*). This will change the replication completion time (*dotted lines*). Forks arrive later at an edge (*filled circle*), and also forks from an early origin have to travel further until they coalesce with those of a late origin (*red dotted line*). **b** Origin position x so that the average replication T_{rep} for 2 pMcms is minimal on a segment of unit length, when the standard deviation σ for their activation time increases. **c** T_{rep} curves for two-origin systems of (**b**) at fixed positions (*green* $x = 1/2$; *red*: $x = 1/4$ and $x = 3/4$); or both at random sites (*blue*). **d** Phase diagram of the two-origin model to minimize replication time with changing competence and increasing the σ. Colour indicates origin position relative to chromosome ends $d_1, d_2 = 1/2$ (*beige*) or $d_1, d_2 = 1/4$ (*brown*)

reflected in Fig. 2.22c where the fixed positions at $x = 1/4$ and $x = 3/4$ (red solid line) result in a slightly higher replication time than compared to a random sampling of all possible configurations (blue area). Intuitively speaking, the origins group if the fork travelling towards the middle position needs to travel beyond the position of the other, i.e. it travels a distance longer than 0.5 and then has to continue until it reaches the end (see also 2.22a). Figure 2.22d shows that the transition between the group and ungrouped regimes also holds if we vary competence as well as varying σ of the uniform activation time distribution.

We also remark that our result is independent from the particulars of origin activation time distribution. Figure 2.23 depicts examples for the case of two origins and using either a distribution where an origin can activate with probability 1/2 at

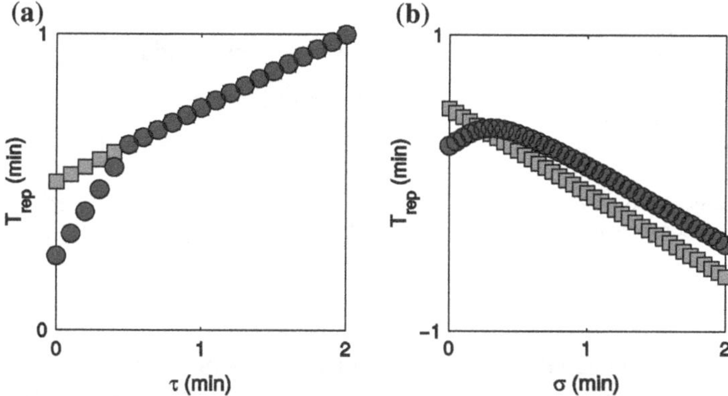

Fig. 2.23 Spread of replication times using different activation time distributions and varying the time between activations. Two origins are placed on a line of unit length either at positions $x = 1/4$ and $x = 3/4$ (*blue circles*), or both at position $x = 1/2$ (*red squares*). In (**a**) an origin can either activate at time $t = 0$ min or later with equal probability, thus τ denotes the difference between those times. In (**b**) the origin activation time is given by a Gaussian activation time distribution with zero mean. We increase its standard deviation σ. This allows for activation at times earlier than zero, hence the decreasing (and 'negative') average replication times

t=0 min or with equal probability at some later time. The difference between these times is shown as τ in Fig. 2.23a. It is clear that once the difference in origin activation time is larger than 1/2 the configuration of having origins positioned at 1/4 and 3/4 does not display any advantage compared to the case of having both origins at the middle position. Similarly as the standard deviation σ of a Gaussian activation time distribution passes over a threshold value the grouped configuration gives minimum replication time (Fig. 2.23b). We note here that once the Gaussian activation time distribution becomes very wide we achieve minimum replication times as the mean is fixed at zero, however left hand tail of the distribution stretches towards negative value allowing (at least one of the) origins to start at some 'negative' time.

We now apply this model for more origins and pMcms, using realistic parameters so that we can relate the results to what is experimentally known about pMcm distribution of *Xenopus laevis*. We model a stretch of DNA of size 100 kbp and $v = 1$ kbp/min [3]. To determine whether the minimum-replication-time configuration requires pMcm grouping, we distributed 64 pMcms in total, i.e. that there is on average $1/1.5$ pMcm/kbp as found in nature [26]. The pMcms are then placed in $64/n$ groups of $n \in \{1, 2, 4, 8, 16, 32, 64\}$ origins, so that the origins are uniformly distributed through the 100 kbp chromosome, or completely random. As the group size decreases the spacing between origins becomes closer as for instance shown in Fig. 2.24. Other authors have identified σ to be 6–10 min and $\mu \sim 15$ min (Gaussian-like) in *X. laevis* [29, 30] as well as in *S. cerevisiae* [3, 4, 12, 14]. As works by Herrick et al. and Goldar et al. [29, 30] have identified the activation distribution at a fixed mean in *Xenopus laevis*, using a uniform distribution and varying σ is a good approximation for our analysis here. Our results (Fig. 2.25a) indicate

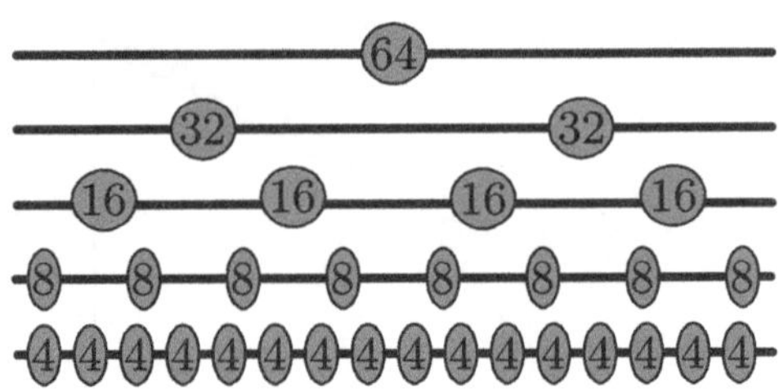

Fig. 2.24 Cartoon illustration of distributing a total of 64 pMcms at origins in groups of varying sizes to simulate the pMcm distribution in *Xenopus laevis*. As the groups of pMcms at an origin decrease the separation between individual origins decreases as well

that grouping with an equal spacing of up to 12.5 kbp achieves precise and fast DNA synthesis before the end of S-phase (20 min) for σ within these limits. We also find that 8 groups of 8 pMcms gives the advantage of a 1.1 min quicker T_{rep} than using random loci; even when the number of pMcms at these 8 groups varies, a quicker T_{rep} is achieved (data not shown). Grouping pMcms also protects the overall replication process against fluctuations from one round of the cell cycle to another; a similar problem is discussed in [31]. This is because one initiation event at an origin is sufficient to activate replication forks and result in a shorter mean time for an activation event at an origin, as we show below.

The probability of the ith pMcm activating by the time t^* given our uniform activation time distribution is

$$P(X_i = t^*) = \frac{t^*}{t_b}, \tag{2.16}$$

and the probability that a pMcm activates later than t^* is

$$\begin{aligned} P(X_i > t^*) &= \int_{t^*}^{t_b} \frac{t'}{t_b} \mathrm{d}t' \\ &= \frac{t_b - t^*}{t_b}, \end{aligned} \tag{2.17}$$

We consider there to be a group of n identical pMcms at an origin. The probability of at least one of those activating by t^* then follows as

$$\begin{aligned} P(\min(X_i) = t^*) &= \sum_{i=1}^{n} \left\{ P(X_i = t^*) \prod_{j=1, j \neq i}^{n} P(X_j > t^*) \right\}, \\ &= nP(X_i = t^*)P(X_j > t^*)^{n-1}, \qquad (2.18) \\ &= n\frac{1}{t_b}\left(\frac{t_b - t^*}{t_b}\right)^{n-1} \qquad (2.19) \end{aligned}$$

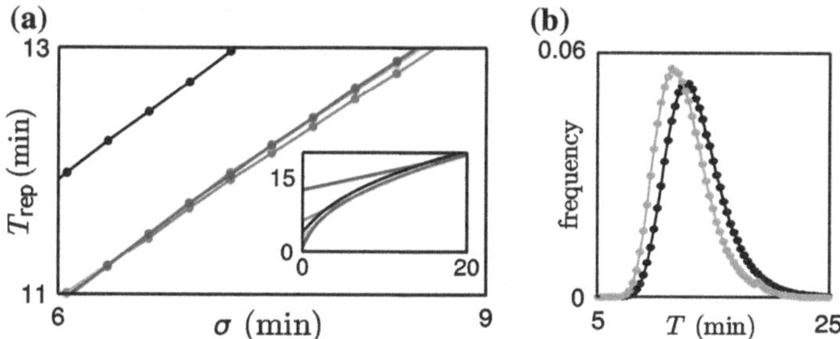

Fig. 2.25 Replication timing in *Xenopus laevis*. **a** Inset: T_{rep} as a function of σ for realistic parameters as given in the text. Origins are distributed in 4 equally-spaced groups of 16 pMcms (*blue*); 8 groups of 8 pMcms (*green*); 16 groups of 4 pMcms (*red*); 32 groups of 2 pMcms (*cyan*); 64 single pMcms (*magenta*); 64 pMcms placed randomly (*black*). Main: zoom around realistic $\sigma \sim 8$ min. For $6 < \sigma < 20$ min minimal T_{rep} is achieved for groups of 8 pMcms. **b** Distribution of replication times T for a 100 kbp chromosome under the condition that $\sigma = 8$ min. Shown is the distribution of 64 pMcms in 8 equally-spaced groups of 8 pMcms (*green*) and placed randomly (*black*)

According to this origin activation time distribution the mean activation time is $t_b/(n+1)$. This shows that activation is earlier for a certain group of pMcm compared to an individual that has mean activation time $t_b/2$. So as the average activation increases through t_b it becomes a balancing act to be able to activate before a replication fork has moved across from another origin elsewhere. The origin must also not be too sparsely placed to leave small enough gaps between groups to replicate on time. Grouping is therefore a useful tactic to achieve this by lowering the overall activation time of a group of pMcm.

In a natural environment, one might expect that there would not be strict equal spacing of groups as we show it here. We now relax our previous assumption by taking evenly-spaced groups and perturb the location of each group by a small random amount drawn from a Gaussian distribution. The introduction of such variation allows us to compare our simulation with available experimental data of replicated genomic regions, which were captured as centre-centre distances at around 5 min after the onset of replication (for instance in Blow et al. [27]). Figure 2.26 shows that our result is in agreement with the current understanding of the biological community, i.e. groups of 5–10 pMcms about every 10 kbp. This may be achieved by a regulation of pMcm—loading proteins, whose affinity to bind decreases around existing origins [32, 33]. Although a random placement represents the data similarly well, T_{rep} remains smaller in this case where the origin groups are not equally-spaced as seen before (cf. Fig. 2.25b).

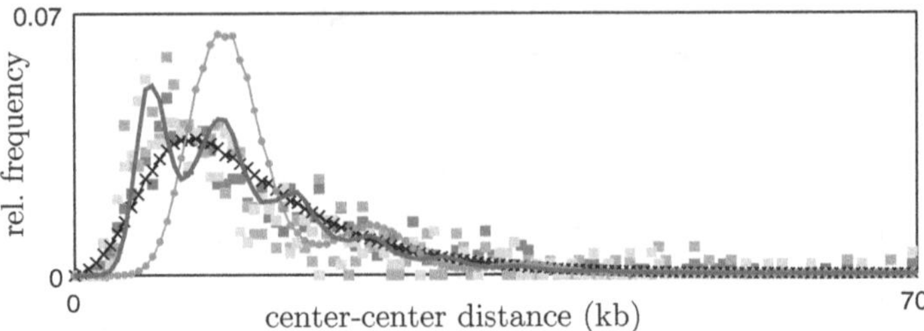

Fig. 2.26 Centre–centre distribution from three experiments [27] (*squares*) and from simulations 5 min after replication started. The simulation is positioning groups of 4 pMcms every 6.3 kbp (*solid line*), groups of 8 pMcms every 12.5 kbp (*circles*), or all randomly (*crosses*). A small random amount was added to the group location of fixed distances which was picked from a Gaussian distribution with $\sigma \sim 16\,\%$ of group distances. The pMcm/length ratio was fixed with a total of 64 origins distributed per 100 kbp of DNA (cf. Fig. 2.25a)

2.4 Summary

Grouping is a means by which replication time is minimised and it strongly depends on the parameters of an origin. Some of the previous models of DNA replication neglected this fundamental question of where origins should be placed to minimise replication time.

We have shown that random fluctuations in the formation of origins, and the subsequent activation of proteins lead to variations in the replication time. We analysed these stochastic properties of DNA and derive the positions of origins corresponding to the minimum replication time. This was done calculating the relation between the competence of the origin to activate and the replication time; low-competence replication origins tend to group in order to minimise replication, and so do origins with long delay in their activation time. This delay is independent of the shape of the activation time distribution of the origins. Moreover we intuitively showed that origin grouping occurs to compensate for the origin failure. It thus only depends on whether or not an origin had become activated before it becomes passively replicated by a replication fork that originated elsewhere.

We have related this to experimental data in a number of species. All of those organisms show that origin grouping on linear as well as circular chromosomes is a means for minimising replication time. We finally showed arguments to prove our hypothesis that evolution has driven origins to the locations where they are found today. For this we used *Saccharomyces cerevisiae* as an example, however we propose that our results also applies to other yeast species such as *Schizosaccharomyces pombe*.

References

1. R. Reyes-Lamothe, C. Possoz, O. Danilova, D.J. Sherratt, Independent positioning and action of Escherichia coli replisomes in live cells. Cell **133**(1), 90–102 (2008). doi:10.1016/j.cell.2008.01.044
2. T.M. Pham, K.W. Tan, Y. Sakumura, K. Okumura, H. Maki, M.T. Akiyama, A single-molecule approach to DNA replication in Escherichia coli cells demonstrated that DNA polymerase III is a major determinant of fork speed. Mol. Microbiol. (2013). doi:10.1111/mmi.12386
3. M.K. Raghuraman et al., Replication dynamics of the yeast genome. Science **294**(5540), 115–21 (2001). doi:10.1126/science.294.5540.115
4. M.D. Sekedat, D. Fenyö, R.S. Rogers, A.J. Tackett, J.D. Aitchison, B.T. Chait, GINS motion reveals replication fork progression is remarkably uniform throughout the yeast genome. Mol. Syst. Biol. **6**, 353 (2010). doi:10.1038/msb.2010.8
5. H.M. Mahbubani, T. Paull, J.K. Elder, J.J. Blow, DNA replication initiates at multiple sites on plasmid DNA in Xenopus egg extracts. Nucleic Acids Res. **20**(7), 1457–1462 (1992)
6. A. Lengronne, P. Pasero, A. Bensimon, E. Schwob, Monitoring S phase progression globally and locally using BrdU incorporation in TK+ yeast strains. Nucleic Acids Res. **29**(7), 1433–1442 (2001)
7. C.A. Müller et al., The dynamics of genome replication using deep sequencing. Nucleic Acids Res. **42**(1), e3 (2013). doi:10.1093/nar/gkt878
8. J.J. Blow, Control of chromosomal DNA replication in the early Xenopus embryo. EMBO J **20**(13), 3293–3297 (2001). doi:10.1093/emboj/20.13.3293
9. M. Hawkins, R. Retkute, C.A. Müller, N. Saner, T.U. Tanaka, A.P. de Moura, C.A. Nieduszynski, High-Resolution Replication Profiles Define the Stochastic Nature of Genome Replication Initiation and Termination. Cell Rep. **5**(4), 1132–1141 (2013). doi:10.1016/j.celrep.2013.10.014
10. C.A. Nieduszynski et al., OriDB: a DNA replication origin database. Nucl. Acids Res. **35**, 40–46 (2007). doi:10.1093/nar/gkl758
11. T.W. Spiesser, E. Klipp, M. Barberis., A model for the spatiotemporal organization of DNA replication in Saccharomyces cerevisiae. Mol. Genet. Genomics **282**(1), 25–35 (2009). doi:10.1007/s00438-009-0443-9
12. A.P.S. de Moura, R. Retkute, M. Hawkins, C.A. Nieduszynski, Mathematical modelling of whole chromosome replication. Nucleic Acids Res. **38**(17), 5623–5633 (2010). doi:10.1093/nar/gkq343
13. S.C.-H. Yang, N. Rhind, J. Bechhoefer, Modeling genome-wide replication kinetics reveals a mechanism for regulation of replication timing. Mol. Syst. Biol. **6**, 404 (2010). doi:10.1038/msb.2010.61
14. A. Brümmer, C. Salazar, V. Zinzalla, L. Alberghina, T. Höfer, Mathematical modelling of DNA replication reveals a trade-off between coherence of origin activation and robustness against rereplication. PLoS Comput. Biol. **6**(5), e1000783 (2010). doi:10.1371/journal.pcbi.1000783
15. A. Goldar, M.-C. Marsolier-Kergoat, O. Hyrien, Universal temporal profile of replication origin activation in eukaryotes. PLoS One **4**(6), e5899 (2009). doi:10.1371/journal.pone.0005899
16. R. Retkute, C.A. Nieduszynski, A. de Moura, Mathematical modeling of genome replication. Phys. Rev. E **86**(3), 031916 (2012). doi:10.1103/PhysRevE.86.031916
17. D. Levine, Users guide to the PGAPack parallel genetic algorithm library. (1996), http://ftp.mcs.anl.gov/pub/pgapack/, doi: 10.2172/366458
18. O. Hyrien, A. Goldar, Mathematical modelling of eukaryotic DNA replication. Chromosome Res. **18**(1), 147–161 (2010). doi:10.1007/s10577-009-9092-4
19. K. Shirahige, T. Iwasaki, M.B. Rashid, N. Ogasawara, H. Yoshikawa, Location and characterization of autonomously replicating sequences from chromosome VI of Saccharomyces cerevisiae. Mol. Cell. Biol. **13**(8), 5043–5056 (1993). doi:10.1128/aANMCB.13.8.5043
20. B. Alberts, D. Bray, J. Lewis, M. Raff, K. Roberts, J.D. Watson, *Molecular Biology of the Cell* (Garland Publishing, New York, 1994)

21. L.M. Kelman, Z. Kelman, Multiple origins of replication in archaea. Trends Microbiol. **12**(9), 399–401 (2004). doi:10.1016/j.tim.2004.07.001
22. O. Hyrien et al., From simple bacterial and archaeal replicons to replication N/U-domains. J. Mol. Biol. **425**(23), 4673–4689 (2013). doi:10.1016/j.jmb.2013.09.021
23. I.G. Duggin, N. Dubarry, S.D. Bell, Replication termination and chromosome dimer resolution in the archaeon Sulfolobus solfataricus. EMBO J. **30**(1), 145–153 (2011). doi:10.1038/emboj.2010.301
24. C. Norais, M. Hawkins, A.L. Hartman, J.A. Eisen, H. Myllykallio, T. Allers, Genetic and physical mapping of DNA replication origins in Haloferax volcanii. PLoS Genet. **3**(5), e77 (2007). doi:10.1371/journal.pgen.0030077
25. R.Y. Samson et al., Specificity and function of archaeal DNA replication initiator proteins. Cell Rep. **3**(2), 485–96 (2013). doi:10.1016/j.celrep.2013.01.002
26. H.M. Mahbubani, Cell Cycle Regulation of the Replication Licensing System: Involvement of a Cdk-dependent Inhibitor. J. Cell Biol. **136**(1), 125–135 (1997). doi:10.1083/jcb.136.1.125
27. J.J. Blow, P.J. Gillespie, D. Francis, D.A. Jackson, Replication origins in Xenopus egg extract Are 5–15 kilobases apart and are activated in clusters that fire at different times. J. Cell Biol. **152**(1), 15–25 (2001)
28. M.C. Edwards, A.V. Tutter, C. Cvetic, C.H. Gilbert, T.A. Prokhorova, J.C. Walter, MCM2-7 complexes bind chromatin in a distributed pattern surrounding the origin recognition complex in Xenopus egg extracts. J. Biol. Chem. **277**(36), 33049–33057 (2002). doi:10.1074/jbc.M204438200
29. J. Herrick, S. Jun, J. Bechhoefer, A. Bensimon, Kinetic Model of DNA Replication in Eukaryotic Organisms. J. Mol. Biol. **320**(4), 741–750 (2002). doi:10.1016/S0022-2836(02)00522-3
30. A. Goldar et al., A dynamic stochastic model for DNA replication initiation in early embryos. PLoS One **3**(8), e2919 (2008). doi:10.1371/journal.pone.0002919
31. S.C.-H. Yang, J. Bechhoefer, How Xenopus laevis embryos replicate reliably: investigating the random-completion problem. Phys. Rev. E: Stat. Nonlin. Soft Matter Phys. **78**(4), 41917 (2008)
32. A. Rowles, S. Tada, J.J. Blow, Changes in association of the Xenopus origin recognition complex with chromatin on licensing of replication origins. J. Cell Sci. **112**, 2011–2018 (1999)
33. M. Oehlmann, A.J. Score, J.J. Blow, The role of Cdc6 in ensuring complete genome licensing and S phase checkpoint activation. J. Cell Biol. **165**(2), 181–90 (2004). doi:10.1083/jcb.200311044

Chapter 3
Actively Replicating Domains Randomly Associate into Replication Factories

In the previous chapter DNA was treated as a stiff, one-dimensional line. However within a cellular environment DNA diffuses and organises into structures on different scales as for instance being wrapped around nucleosomes or forming chromatin. This brings otherwise far-away genomic regions into physical contact with each other. Yet it is unclear what leads to such an organisation of structures in three dimensions—especially during DNA replication. Recent advances using chromosome conformation capture data, e.g. HiC, 3C, 4C techniques, shed some light on the way chromosomal regions (domains) interact with each other for example during protein expression or genome duplication (see review and commentary [1, 2]). The technology captures the organisation of chromosomes in form of contact maps that can help to understand the organisation of chromosomes in a given cell subject to particular (growth) conditions. There is also an increasing body of work modelling chromosome interaction data using techniques from graph theory [3] or polymer theory [4, 5]. One disadvantage of these technologies is that they also captures random collisions of chromosomal region with another. The experimental result thus also contains information of unspecific interaction that occurred among genomic loci and the signal must be sufficiently from those regions that specifically come into contact. A further confounding factor is that the majority of experiments, that use the chromosome capture techniques, average over population measurements when establishing interaction and chromosome contact data. They therefore pursue a top–down approach by inferring single-cell operations from population studies. It is difficult to draw conclusions from these studies about mechanism occurring on a single-cell level.

We present here—on basis of single-cell experiments—the mechanism that causes replication forks (replisomes) in *Saccharomyces cerevisiae* to establish chromosomal interaction which affects further organisation into *replication factories*. We show that these factories stem from random interaction events of adjacent replication forks. Our theoretical model establishes from experimental grounds. Data is derived from a technique initially established by Kitamura et al. [6] for single *Saccharomyces cerevisiae* cells to visualise replication on DNA. Their data shows that during DNA synthesis genomic regions (domains) undergoing replication—so called *replicons*—

J. Karschau, *Mathematical Modelling of Chromosome Replication and Replicative Stress*, Springer Theses, DOI 10.1007/978-3-319-08861-7_3

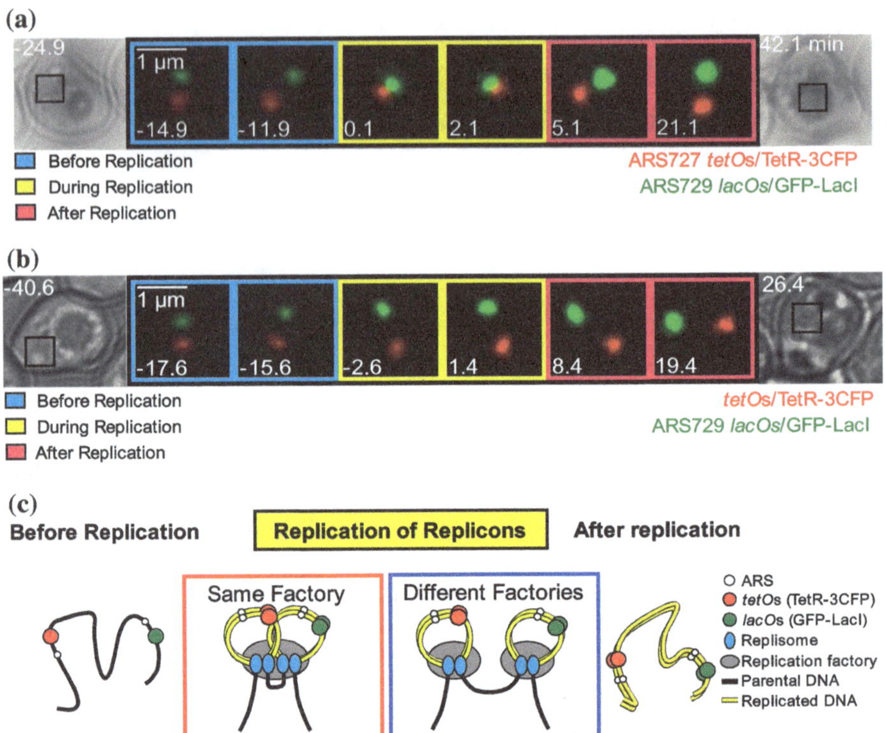

Fig. 3.1 Observations of two replicating dots. Two genomic loci have been labelled either in *green* or in *red*. If these loci undergo replication the observed intensity at these loci doubles. With this information one can establish whether or not both loci are seen in close contact (**a**), or whether they are localised far apart (**b**) during DNA replication. Panel (**c**) shows a graphical interpretation of close dot localisation, which can lead to replication in the same factory, or not as in (**a**) and (**b**). Details for the experimental are provided in Saner et al. [8]

become associated with each other. They label DNA near origin loci sites which allows them to observe when a replicon becomes replicated; the fluorescent intensity at a replicated region doubles. This is illustrated in Fig. 3.1. Moreover labelling two regions also shows that those sometimes become associated (Fig. 3.1a) forming *replication factories* of about 90 nm in diameter [7]. In some other cases, labelled regions do not associate when a region undergoes replication as for example in Fig. 3.1b. It is currently an open question how association occurs and an extension of the labelling technique by our experimental collaborators using multiple labelled sites produces new experimental data of replicon associations (see also Saner et al. [8]).

This data alone is incomplete and requires a physics approach for a holistic comprehension to whether or not association is a deterministic or stochastic process. We complement their data using a mathematical model to allow further insight. We test our model numerically first using a Metropolis-Monte-Carlo algorithm. This then

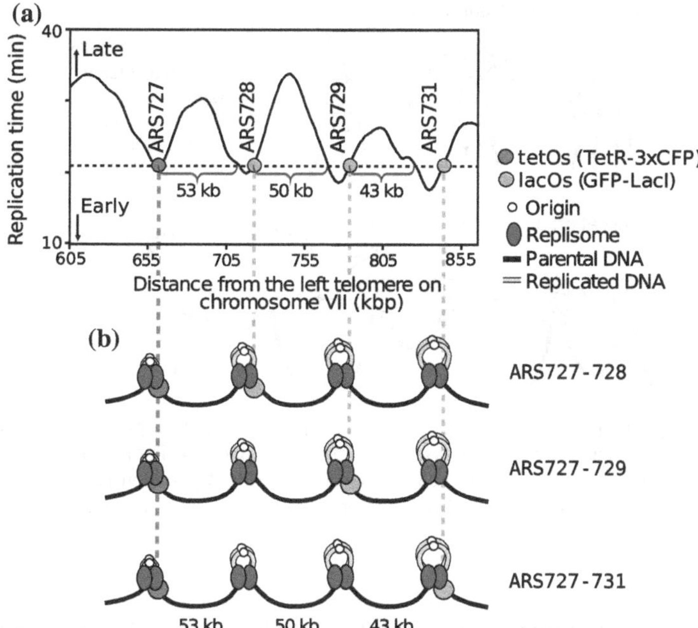

Fig. 3.2 Tagged replisome pair distances on chromosome VII. **a** Replication profile of the relevant genomic region on chromosome VII obtained from [9]. Origin loci (ARS727–731) are the values of the timing profile and tetO (*red*) or lacO (*green*) where integrated in three different strains as a combination of ARS727–728, ARS727–729, and ARS727–731. **b** Diagram of the length scale of sites which were labelled near replicating origins. Each of three different strain had ARS727 labelled as a reference (*red dot*) and in *green* in that strain either ARS728, ARS729, or ARS731 was labelled (*green dot*). Length scales between neighbouring points is given in kbp. The chromosomal distance d between relevant replisome pairs upon replication of fluorescent dots (i.e., tetO and lacO arrays) is estimated assuming that upon replication sister replisomes stay together. Thus, to obtain the chromosomal distance d between replisome pairs, only the integration sites of tetOs and lacOs **a** need to be considered, but not the length of these arrays, as shown by the distances

allows us to extend it from a four origin in vivo experiment to a whole-genome in silico one. Without further need for any parameter we relate back to observations of entire cells and the size distribution of their replication factories.

3.1 Summary of Experimental Procedure

To investigate the organisation of replication factories Saner et al. [8] analysed the behaviour of replicons using live-cell microscopy in *Saccharomyces cerevisiae*. They chose a region on chromosome VII with four adjacent replication origin loci (Fig. 3.2) and selected one locus on each replicon such that all four loci show the same average replication timing [9]. They integrated two DNA sequences into a chromosome.

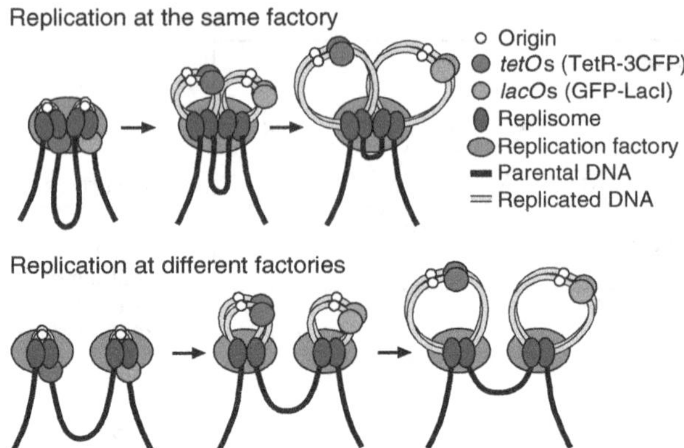

Fig. 3.3 Concept of replication factories. Models for replication of two replicons at the same factory and at different factories. If two replicons are processed for replication in the same factory, CFP and GFP fluorescent dots should come into close proximity during replication i.e. when the intensity of the dots increases. In contrast, if replicons are processed in different factories, they do not come closer during replication

Those sequences are normally repressed by the binding of a fluorescent protein. Those inserted genes are tetO and lacO arrays producing a separate strain for each of the three different red–green combinations of Fig. 3.2. These arrays bound TetR and LacI proteins, fused with cyan and green fluorescent proteins (CFP, GFP), respectively, and were thus visualised as small fluorescent dots. The fluorescent dots increased in intensity upon DNA replication as the number of arrays was doubled, thus defining their replication timing by microscopy [6].

To analyse how replicons are gathered into factories, only cells whose two marked loci replicated with similar timing, i.e. their difference in activation was <3 min, were taken into account. When both loci replicated and they were observed in close spatial proximity of less than 350 nm apart for more than 2 min, they were considered to be replicating in the same factory (Fig. 3.3). In contrast, if replicons are processed in different factories, the fluorescent dots do not come close during replication.

Using this protocol, it was found that the two marked loci in the first strain (ARS727–728: 53 kb apart) replicated in the same factory in 43 % of cells (10 out of 23) and in different factories in 57 % of cells (13 out of 23). This suggests that grouping of replicons within factories can vary from cell to cell. In contrast, in the other two strains ARS727–729 and ARS727–731, the two marked loci replicated in the same factory less frequently: 11 % (2/19) and 5 % (1/19), respectively. Thus, replicons that are close along a chromosome were often processed for replication in the same factory, but replicons that are farther apart replicated more frequently in different factories. The manner by which this occurs is not directly inferable from the data alone and requires additional modelling to explain the association of replisomes and the amount replisomes per factories. We therefore introduce a

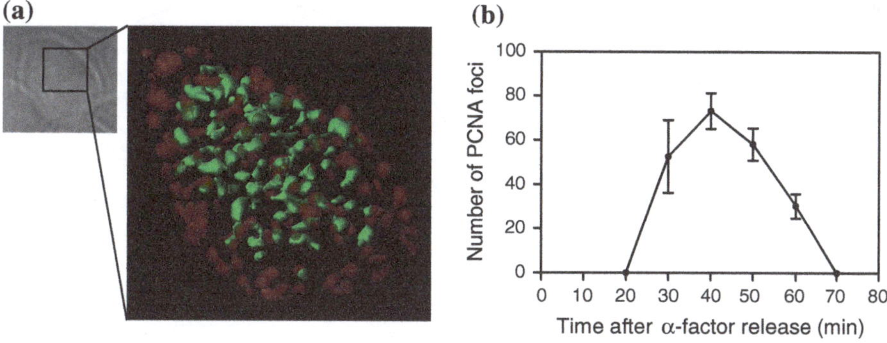

Fig. 3.4 Replication factories observed by super-resolution microscopy. Cells (T8375) with GFP-POL30 (PCNA), SPC42-mCherry (a component of spindle pole body, SPB), and NIC96-mCherry (a component of the nuclear pore complex, NPC) were released from α-factor treatment (defined as 0 min). **a** A bright-field image, a fluorescence image (GFP, *green*; mCherry, *red*), and the 3D rendering of a fluorescence image (GFP, *green*; mCherry, *red*) in a representative cell, which was fixed at 40 min. **b** The number of PCNA foci (mean ± SD) within the nucleus along the time course. For further experimental procedures refer to Saner et al. [8]

mathematical model that will help us to understand the meaning of the above mentioned association probabilities.

A further set of data from this study contains single-cell images of fluorescent PCNA; a unique replication fork component which shows where replication forks localise (cf. Sect. 1.5, page 10ff). Images as shown in Fig. 3.4a contain size distributions and the count of PCNA foci at a particular time point (Fig. 3.4b). We will use our mathematical model and apply it to genome-wide yeast replication simulation to establish the number of forks per factory in silico as well as determine this number independently in vivo.

3.2 The Diffusion Time Scale of Two Replicating Dots

In the above experiment for replicon grouping probabilities, two dots appear associated if they are in close proximity. This can occur via two routes (i) replication forks have reached the location of an adjacent dot or (ii) two dots meet randomly due to diffusion. In experiments, the diffusion coefficient of one dot was obtained and found to be $D_1 = 0.2\,\mu\text{m}^2/\text{min}$. The typical diffusion time scale for one dot to travel some distance L is calculated using [10]:

$$t_D = \frac{L^2}{2D}. \tag{3.1}$$

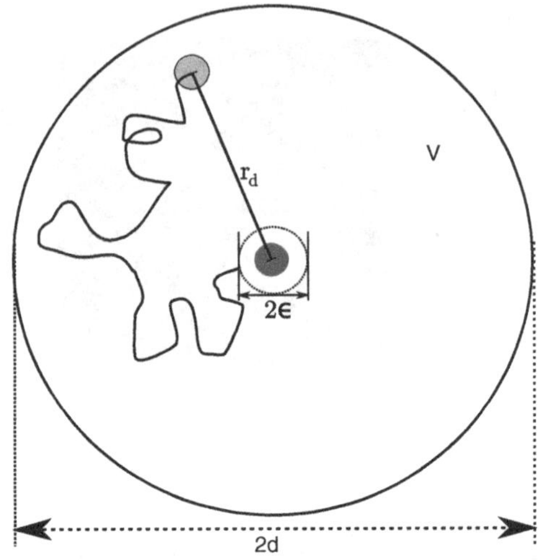

Fig. 3.5 Target finding time. To establish the target finding time we fix one replisome pair at the centre of spherical volume V which has radius r. The moving pair (*green*) performs diffusion with twice the diffusion coefficient of one particle until it hits the centre particle (*red*). This target region has a diameter of 2ϵ, i.e. twice of that of one particle. illustration

Since we have two particles diffusing, this is equivalent to one particle diffusing with $D = 2D_1$. Hence, we double the diffusion coefficient in the Eq. (3.1). The DNA is not as fully stretched as is shown in Fig. 3.2b for instance. We therefore apply a chromatin packaging ratio of 10 nm/kbp, based on a ratio of measured spatial distances over the chromosomal distances between two fluorescently labelled chromosomal loci. This matches a reported value [11]. For the maximum distance between the origins in the second strain with ARS727–729, $L = 1.3\,\mu\text{m}$ corresponding to chromosomal distance of 129 kbp between the fluorescent dots [12]. The diffusion time-scale for this length is ~2 min. In this strain it takes 4–6 min after replication initiation at ARS727 and ARS729 until tetO/lacO dots are replicated (i.e. until replication forks reach the middle of tetO/lacO arrays, which are 10–11 kb in length). Replication from one dot to another, i.e. replicating a distance of 50 kbp (cf. Fig. 3.2), takes about 15 min. So diffusion can in principle account for two dots to meet and to be seen associated under the microscope. However the diffusion time scale alone does not mean that the two dots will actually meet within this time.

We therefore establish a further property for a system of two diffusing dots which is the *mean target finding time*. This measure allows to estimate whether the dots not only have time to explore a certain distance, but also whether they actually meet with another, i.e. the time scale until one dot will encounter another. We derive the target finding time in analogy to Sneppen and Zocchi [10] by rephrasing our problem as depicted in Fig. 3.5. Instead of describing two sister replisome pairs diffusing in a spherical volume, it is equivalent to fix one sister replisome pair (red) at the center—it becomes the target—and the second pair (green) diffuses around this target (shown in Fig. 3.5). Hence, the diffusion constant of the second pair D is the sum of its own diffusion constant and that of the target, which we place at a fixed position. The spherical volume V, in which the mobile pair diffuses to find its target, has radius r_d. This radius $r_d = d$ is defined by the distance of the pairs to be at a distance d

maximally apart from each other (cf. Fig. 3.2). The radius of the spherical volume (dotted circle) that two sister replisome pairs occupy once the mobile pair meet the target, is twice the diameter of one and therefore 2ϵ.

We describe this process using the standard diffusion equation

$$\frac{\partial p(\vec{r},t)}{\partial t} = D\nabla^2 p(\vec{r},t), \tag{3.2}$$

with position probability density $p(\vec{r},t)$ for finding the mobile pair at a particular position $\vec{r}$ at a time t. We are interested in the equilibrium state, that is for once the systems has reached steady-state. We therefore set the left hand-side of Eq. (3.2) to zero as the system will be independent from time

$$0 = D\nabla^2 p(\vec{r},t). \tag{3.3}$$

We simplify the equation by assuming that $p(\vec{r},t)$ is independent from any particular direction (isotropic), and only depends on the radial distance r_d to the fixed pair. Using spherical coordinates we show that the probability distribution satisfies

$$\int_{r=0}^{d}\int_{\theta=0}^{\pi}\int_{\phi=0}^{2\pi} p(r,\theta,\phi)\, r^2 \,\sin\theta \,\mathrm{d}r\mathrm{d}\theta\, \mathrm{d}\phi = 1. \tag{3.4}$$

It then follows from the position probability density distribution $p(r,\theta,\phi) = \text{const}$ and

$$\int_{r=0}^{d}\int_{\theta=0}^{\pi}\int_{\phi=0}^{2\pi} r^2 \,\sin\theta \,\mathrm{d}r\mathrm{d}\theta\, \mathrm{d}\phi = V \tag{3.5}$$

that

$$p(r,\theta,\phi) = 1/V. \tag{3.6}$$

In order to solve the second-order differential equation, Eq. (3.3), we choose two boundary conditions:

1. When the mobile pair is away from the fixed one ($r_d > \epsilon$), there is a flux I towards the fixed origin
$$I = -4\pi Dr^2 \frac{dp(r_d)}{dr_d}, \tag{3.7}$$
2. When the mobile pair is far away from the fixed one, the probability of finding the particle is $p(\infty) = 1/V$.

We then obtain,

$$p(r_d) = \frac{I}{D4\pi r_d} + p(\infty) \tag{3.8}$$

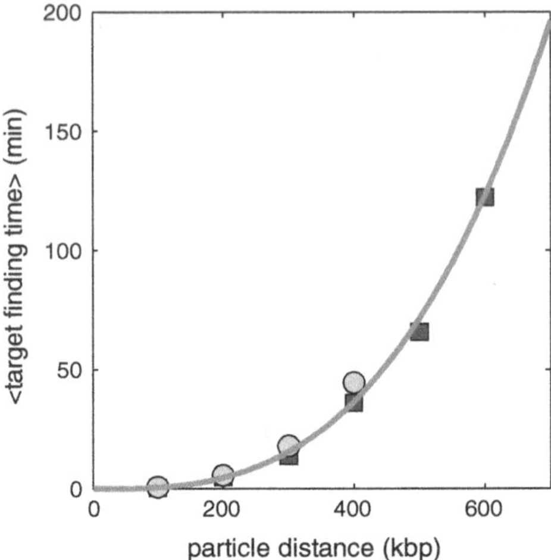

Fig. 3.6 Simulation of average target finding times. Two particles move freely in a given volume (*green squares*), or one dot moves with the sum of the diffusion constant of both particles for the average time it takes for both particle to be found associated if they diffuse in the given volume, i.e. given by the maximum separation allowed. The solid red line shows the analytical result for the average target finding time τ_{on} given by Eq. (3.9) for $D = 0.2\,\mu\text{m}^2/\text{min}$ and $\epsilon = 62.5$ as chosen in these simulations

as the solution for Eq. (3.3). The probability of finding the mobile origin at the target is $P(\epsilon) = 0$. We now solve Eq. (3.8) for the flux I which is the inverse of the time it takes for the mobile origin to find the target

$$\tau_{on} = \frac{1}{|I|} = \frac{V}{4\pi D\epsilon} = \frac{r_d^3}{3D\epsilon}. \tag{3.9}$$

We check our analytical result of Eq. (3.9) numerically by simulating the diffusion of both origins given some maximum separation distance. We also check this against the consideration of one being fixed at the origin and the other moving with a diffusion coefficient that is the sum of both. Figure 3.6 shows the results for this and it also confirms that our analytical derivation of τ_{on} appropriately describes the average target finding time. We remark that the simulation result here is for illustration purposes only as we have $D = 0.2\,\mu\text{m}^2/\text{min}$ and $\epsilon = 62.5$ chosen in these simulation; their actual values become refined in the discussion further below.

The above derivation assumed that replisomes find each other from initial maximally-extended DNA length, i.e. the distance is always as shown in Fig. 3.2. In an experimental setting this clearly not the case, cells are selected at random, and replisomes within each cell can take their initial position during replication anywhere within a volume that has a maximal diameter as the length of the DNA connecting them. We therefore calculate the mean radial distance $\langle r_{\text{act}}\rangle$ of those two. The probability density distribution to be anywhere in that spherical volume of fixed V

(thus $d = \text{const}$) is the same throughout (uniform). Hence the probability density $p(d_{\text{act}})$ of replisome pairs being at an actual distance d_{act} away, i.e. the moving replisome lies on a spherical segment $4\pi d_{\text{act}}^2$, is given by

$$p(d_{\text{act}}) = \frac{4\pi d_{\text{act}}^2}{V}, \tag{3.10}$$

which satisfies

$$\int_{d_{\text{act}}=0}^{d} p(d_{act})\, \mathrm{d}d_{\text{act}} = 1.$$

In a collection of individual cells we therefore find the average distance between replisomes as

$$\langle d_{act} \rangle = \int_0^d d_{\text{act}}\, p(d_{act})\, \mathrm{d}d_{\text{act}},$$

$$\langle d_{act} \rangle = \frac{3}{4} d. \tag{3.11}$$

This means that we rescale the known chromosomal distance d by 3/4 which yields for the average target finding time of a collection of cells

$$\tau_{\text{on}}^{\text{pop}} = \frac{1}{|I|} = \frac{(3/4d)^3}{3D\epsilon} = \frac{9d^3}{64D\epsilon}. \tag{3.12}$$

We now determine the duration for two sister replisome pairs to meet each other based on Eq. (3.12). This is the time required for the system to approach equilibrium. As a result of taking both replication and diffusion processes into account, the time needed for two sister replisome pairs to find each other is approximately in the the range of 1–5 min in strain ARS727–728 and ARS727–729, respectively. The time of diffusion suffices so that nearby replisomes can associate by the replication of the tetO/LacI arrays. It further allows us to draw an adiabatic assumption—the association probability relaxes to its local equilibrium on a time-scale which is smaller than replication time-scale. This is important to establish an equilibrium model of random associations of replisomes in the following section.

In a wider context, the organisation of DNA inside the cellular nucleus can influence diffusion. The data used to determine the diffusion in the experiment by Saner et al. [8] displays a mean squared displacement which shows saturation at longer times (Figs. 3.7, 3.8 and 3.9). This is characteristic for anomalous diffusion as for example occurs in crowded environments such as the cellular nucleus. The saturation is particularly visible in Figs. 3.8 and 3.9. Previous work, as for example the one by Heun et al. [13], also showed that when cells undergo replication diffusion

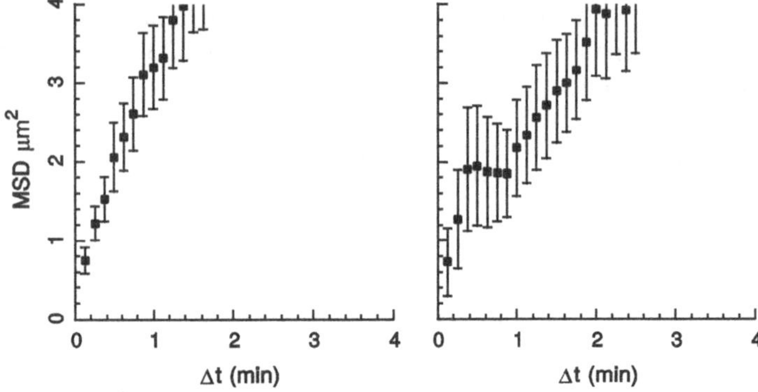

Fig. 3.7 Diffusion of a DNA locus. Mean squared displacement (MSD) of a tagged DNA locus is plotted as a function of the time interval of observation Δt. This was done for a stage of S-phase in the experiment by Saner et al. [8] observing the locus at 25–33 min after α-factor release. Shown here are examples for two cells

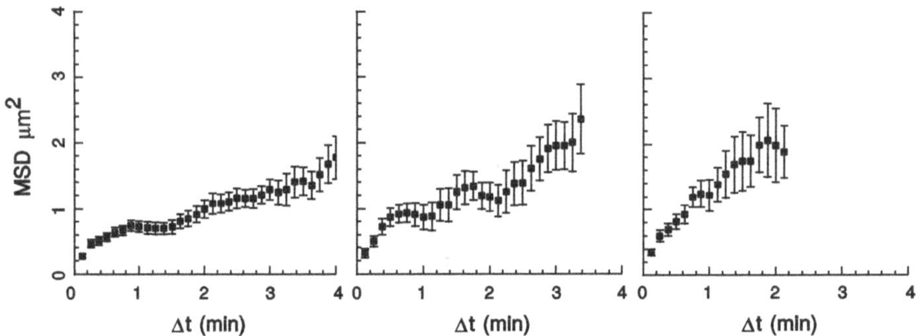

Fig. 3.8 Diffusion of a DNA locus. Mean squared displacement (MSD) of a tagged DNA locus is plotted as a function of the time interval of observation Δt. This was done for a stage of S-phase in the experiment by Saner et al. [8] observing the locus at 35–43 min after α-factor release. Shown here are examples for three cells

slows down, which authors claim to depend on the openness of the chromatin. Of relevance here for our estimate of the target finding is diffusion at short time scales ($\sim$2 min) which allows us to draw a rough estimate of the target finding time as we have done above. In particular the plots shown in Fig. 3.8 which correspond to the time point relevant of replication of the origin loci tagged in the experiment by Saner et al. [8]. However we remark a model also accounting for anomalous diffusion will give a more accurate approximation.

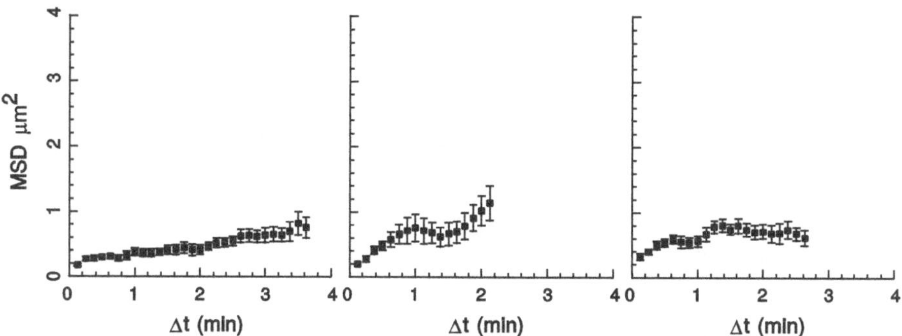

Fig. 3.9 Diffusion of a DNA locus. Mean squared displacement (MSD) of a tagged DNA locus is plotted as a function of the time interval of observation Δt. This was done for a stage of S-phase in the experiment by Saner et al. [8] observing the locus at 45–53 min after α-factor release. Shown here are examples for three cells

3.3 Binding Energy

Using the above assumption that we can treat the system to be in thermodynamic equilibrium allows us to use an analogy for the different strains. Each strain has two replisomes connected by DNA of varying length.

We therefore rephrase our problem as two particles tethered by a string of length d. This describes two sister replisome pairs that are apart from each other at a chromosomal distance d (Fig. 3.10). Each sister replisome pair is thereby a particle fixed to the end of the string. Each particle is considered to be a sphere with diameter ϵ. We assume the string has no stiffness, given that the persistence length of yeast chromatin is short (2.5 kbp [12]) relative to the distance between replication origins and between marked chromosome loci analysed here. The particles perform a random walk within a sphere of radius $d/2$ in three dimensions (illustrated in two dimensions, for simplicity, in Fig. 3.10). If both particles come close within interaction radius, i.e. the distance between their centres is ϵ or less, they associate. Note that we here place the centre of reference at the middle of the string (the centre of mass), compared to the derivation in the previous section were the coordinate system was fixed at a particle.

The two particle system can be in two conditions. First, when particles are separated; the energy of the system is then $E = 0$ (Fig. 3.10a, b). Second, when particles are in close proximity and become associated; the energy of the system is then $E = J$, where J is a binding energy (Fig. 3.10c). Therefore, J is negative, meaning that the particles' interaction is attractive.

Our aim is to estimate the probability of finding the system in any of these conditions—particles separated or particles associated—depending on the string length between them. The probability that the two particles meet and associate with each other when the system is in thermodynamic equilibrium is

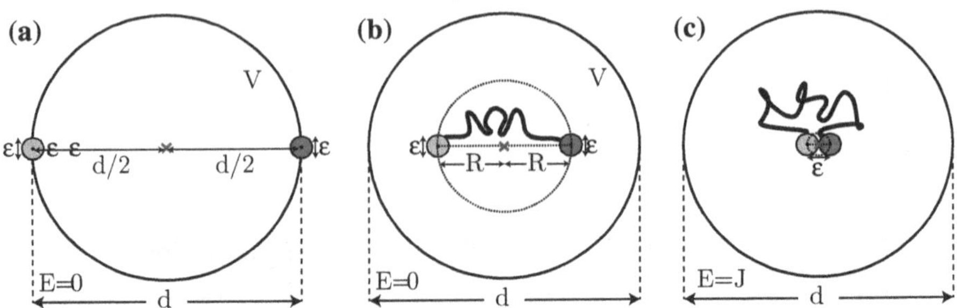

Fig. 3.10 Schematic diagram of the *particles on a string* model. Two particles are connected with a string of length d. The two particles and the string represent two pairs of sister replisomes and the chromosome region between them, respectively. **a, b** The particles move by a random walk and the energy remains $E = 0$ as long as they are separated (*left, central panels*). **c** If the two particles are associated with each other, i.e. the distance between the centres of the particles is, the energy is reduced ($E = J$, J is the binding energy with a negative value)

$$P_a = \frac{n_a B_a}{n_a B_a + n_s B_s}, \tag{3.13}$$

where n_a and n_s are the normalised numbers of states in which particles are associated and separated, respectively. B_a and B_s represent corresponding Boltzmann factors (weighing factors). Each Boltzmann factor $B = e^{-E/(k_B T)}$ depends on temperature, T, and energy, E, of the system. k_B is the Boltzmann constant.

The normalized number of states is derived as follows. As the reference frame is centered at the midpoint, states corresponding to the particles separated by a distance R lie on a spherical shell of radius $R/2$. Particles are considered to associate once the distance between their centres is less than ϵ, i.e., they are within a sphere of radius $\epsilon/2$ around the origin. The volume of this sphere is

$$V_a = \frac{4}{3}\pi \left(\frac{\epsilon}{2}\right)^3. \tag{3.14}$$

We normalise the number of states to the total volume

$$V = \frac{4}{3}\pi \left(\frac{d}{2}\right)^3. \tag{3.15}$$

The normalised number of states in which two particles associate is then given by

$$n_a = \frac{V_a}{V} = \left(\frac{\epsilon}{d}\right)^3. \tag{3.16}$$

The energy of the system at this association state is minimised, thus $E_a = J$, with the corresponding Boltzmann factor

$$B_a = e^{-J/(k_B T)}. \tag{3.17}$$

The normalised number states in which particles are not associated is

$$n_S = \frac{V - V_a}{V} \approx 1, \tag{3.18}$$

for a small interaction radius ($\epsilon << d$). The energy of the system when the particles are apart is $E_S = 0$, and the Boltzmann factor is $B_s = 1$.

Therefore the association probability from Eq. (3.13) is then

$$P_a = \frac{\left(\frac{\epsilon}{d}\right)^3 B_a}{1 + \left(\frac{\epsilon}{d}\right)^3 B_a} = \frac{1}{Ad^3 + 1}, \tag{3.19}$$

where $A = e^{J/(k_B T)}/(\epsilon^3)$ is a constant with constant temperature. Equation (3.19) describes the probability of two particles, separated by a distance $\leq d$, being associated in an equilibrium system.

3.4 Test of the Analytical Result Versus Computer Simulations

In the previous Sect. 3.3, we derived an analytical expression for the probability of observing two dots in a joined configuration. Our assumption is that we can treat the system to be at equilibrium and that the state of having both particles in a joined configuration minimises the energy of the system. In this section, we test our theory with help of computer simulations, and we use an algorithm known as Metropolis Monte Carlo simulations [14].

It allows for testing the different configurations of the system and the sampling of transitions from one state to another depending on the binding energy J, e.g. from associated to non-associated particle configurations. For the simulations here we simplify to problem by placing the particles on a cubic grid. For example a particle can be at position (0, 5, 0), i.e. particle positions are direct integer coordinates in our simulations. If both particles have the same coordinates that means they occupy the same grid point and we recognise them to be in an associated configurations and the energy of the system is E, or they are not associated and the energy of the system is 0 otherwise. Note that the interaction radius is thus of the order of a unit cell. When a new, random configuration for the particles is chosen the energy is calculated and whether or not the new configuration is accepted depends on the energy from the old to the new configuration. Specifically, the algorithm is outlined as follows:

1. Generate a random configuration Z_0 for both particles to be at some coordinates that satisfies the maximum separation constraint, i.e. their distance must be $\leq d$.
2. Determine the corresponding energy J_0 of the system, i.e. test whether particles are associated or not.

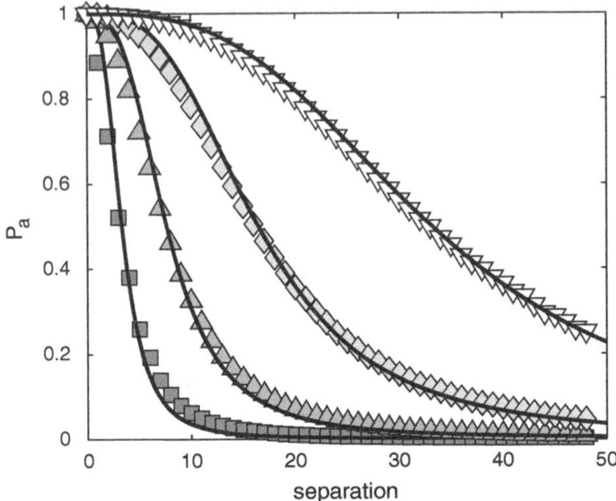

Fig. 3.11 Metropolis-Monte Carlo simulations. Fitting of the model for the association probability $P_a(d) = 1/(Ad^3 + 1)$ [Eq. (3.19)] of individual replisome pairs to simulation results. For simplicity we set $k_B T = 1$, so that $A = \exp(-J)$. Particles move on a three dimensional grid with grid points along a dimension indicated by the maximum separation. The association energy J increases for the different simulation results: $J = -4$ (*squares*), $J = -6$ (*upward triangles*), $J = -8$ (*diamonds*), $J = -10$ (*downward triangles*). The solid lines indicate the best fit of the simulation data with the association model Eq. (3.19); their values in ascending order are: −3.6, −6.1, −8.4, −10.5

3. Choose a new, random configuration for both particles again under the constraint that both particles can only have some maximum separation d.
4. Determine the energy J_1 for this new configuration.
5. Calculate the energy difference of both configuration $\Delta J = J_0 - J_1$ and the corresponding Boltzmann factor: $F_B = \exp\{\frac{\Delta J}{k_B T}\}$.
6. If $F_B > 1$, the new configuration is accepted.
7. If $F_B < 1$, the new configuration is a priori not immediately accepted.
8. Test a uniformly chosen random number $w \in [0, 1)$ against F_B:
   (a) If $w < F_B$ accept the new configuration.
   (b) If $w > F_B$ reject the new configuration, and keep the old one.
9. Chosen configuration becomes Z_0. Continue the simulation and return to step 3.

We simulate the process in accordance with the rules above as well as under the constraints of maximum separation and association energy. For simplicity we set $k_B T = 1$ so that F_B becomes $\exp(\Delta J)$. We simulate for a series of parameters ranging over $J = -4, -6, -8, -10$ and plot the result for the probability of particle association in Fig. 3.11. We find that if we fit our numerical results to the equation of particle association Eq. (3.19), we can recover the energies we had used in these simulations. Although the fit is does not match to 100 % with the assigned binding energies, we remark that we have simplified the problem from a spherical, continuous

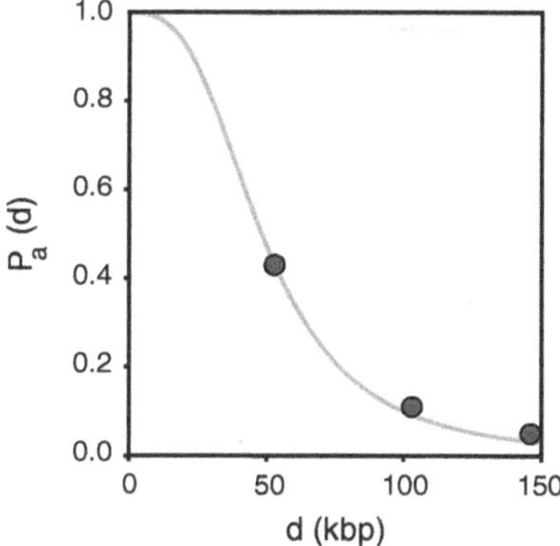

Fig. 3.12 Fitting of the model for the association probability $P_a(d) = 1/(Ad^3 + 1)$ [Eq. (3.19)] of individual replisome pairs with another. In experiments (*blue circles*) origin loci were tagged and their association frequency was determined depending on their chromosomal distances d from each other. The fitting for the single model parameter results in $A = 8.7 \cdot 10^6\,\text{kbp}^{-3}$

one to a cubic, discrete one. This leads to slight differences in our fit to Eq. (3.19) and the actual parameters used in our simulations. Overall our simulation confirms the trend that we expect for the probability of particle association given by Eq. (3.19), so that we can now use our formula for biological relevant experimental data for sister replisome pair associations, and the investigation of their dependence on maximum allowed separation (cf. Saner et al. [8]).

3.5 Fit to Experimental Data of Replisome Association

We fit Eq. (3.19) to the biological data of probability of replicons grouping in the three yeast strains in order to determine the single parameter A. The function $P_a(d)$ fits the data well (Fig. 3.12), with the best fitting for $A = 8.7 \cdot 10^{-6}\,\text{kbp}^{-3}$ ($R^2 = 0.99$, Fig. 3.12). The binding energy of two sister replisome pairs is $J = k_B T \ln(A^3) = -5.1\,k_B T = -12.5\,\text{kJ/mol}$, for the best-fitting A, $\epsilon = 90\,\text{nm}$ and $T = 298.2\,\text{K}$. Here we estimate the diameter of a single sister replisome pair from the minimum size of a replication factory of $\epsilon = 90\,\text{nm}$ [7]. We again apply the chromatin packaging ratio of 10 nm/kb to account for the actual distance between replicating dots [12]. The calculated binding energy of sister replisome pairs ($-12.5\,\text{kJ/mol}$) is in the range of a typical weak protein–protein interaction [15, 16]. It is also in agreement with the estimated energy for the association of DNA polymerases bound on two replication origins [17]. So there is a relatively strong force which keeps replisomes together in factories once they meet. The experimental data of Saner et al. [8] show that dots randomly co-localise and stay closely together for periods of about 2 min. Their data also shows that when loci undergo replication in the same factory their movement is more restrained than compared to those loci that do not co-localise

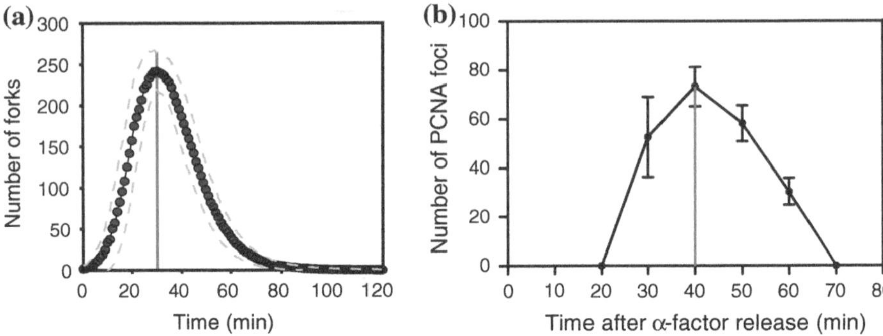

Fig. 3.13 **a, b** In silico and in vivo (respectively) distributions of the number of active replication forks. The experimental distribution **b** shows the number PCNA foci (*dots*) which is a unique component of a replication fork. This number is however incomplete and requires the in silico data so that it can be related to the number forks present in vivo. We chose to relate this number at the peak of S-phase (*red line*), when most replication forks are present in the cell

during replication [8]. Between intervals of co-localisations, the loci are seen to move rapidly before and after replication independent from their localisation during replication (see for instance Fig. S2 in Saner et al. [8] and also Kitamura et al. [6]). This then further suggests a strong interaction of replisomes as we calculate here.

3.6 Genome-Wide Replication Data and the Number of Forks Per Factory

Next we establish the size distribution of replication forks that correspond to microscope images of the distribution of PCNA foci (see Fig. 3.4 on page 53). In experiments, cells were observed at the peak of S-phase, i.e. when most forks are active corresponding to 40 min after α-factor release.

This data showed that the number of replication factories increased to a peak value of 73 $\pm$ 8 (mean $\pm$ standard deviation) in mid-S-phase (Fig. 3.13b). We next evaluated the number of replisome pairs present in each replication factory. Published replication profiles showing the replication timing of the whole genome [9, 18] are an average from a large number of cells and do not accurately represent replication in individual cells. To estimate the total number of forks, we used data, which Hawkins et al. kindly provided to us [19–21]. This fitting determined origin parameters such as competence, mean activation time, and standard deviation of activation timing for origins in *Saccharomyces cerevisiae* (unpublished data); excluding ribosomal DNA. We applied Hawkins et al.'s data to our dynamical model which simulates stochastic origin activation, according to these parameters, as well as fork progression at a speed of 1.5 kbp/min [18]. In simulations, origins are first selected to become licensed or not; which is done by testing a uniform random number against the competence value

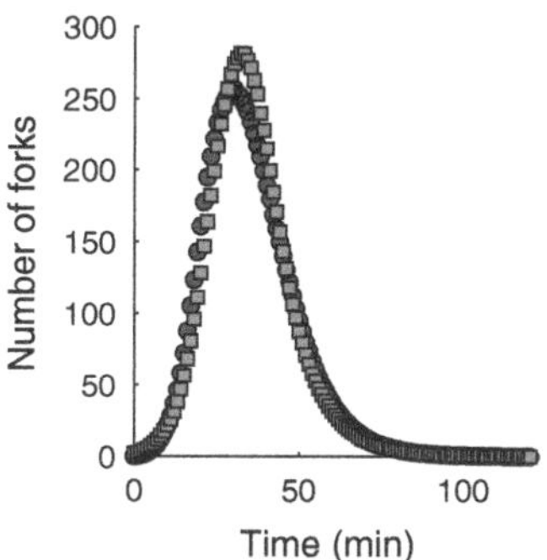

Fig. 3.14 The number of replication forks during S-phase using a Hill- (*blue circles*) or Gaussian-type (*green squares*) activation time distribution. We simulate the data without using a variability of ±4 min in onset of S-phase as we do in Fig. 3.13a. The data is in good qualitative agreement with Fig. 3.13b independent of the activation type used

of each origin. Second, origins are assigned their activation times which are drawn randomly from their activation time distribution with mean and standard deviation. Finally, a point in time during S-phase is selected and fork progression up to then is recorded, e.g. within an array representing a chromosome '0' marks a places with unreplicated DNA, '1' represents replicated DNA. The simulation runs per chromosome and the number of active forks results as the number of edges of regions with '1'. Repeating the simulations several times produces the statistics of fork numbers at a particular time which is plotted in Fig. 3.13a. This allows to correlate the size distribution of replication foci which had been measured earlier (Fig. 3.4a). Using our simulation, we estimated that 242 ± 24 (mean ± standard deviation) replication forks were present at the peak of DNA replication (Fig. 3.13). We also remark that using a Hill-type function for origin activation over time or some other type such as a Gaussian origin activation time function will not change our result. Either type shown in Fig. 3.14 is in good qualitative agreement with the experimental distribution in Fig. 3.13b.

Using published data [22, 23], we estimated that 60 replication forks were present, on average, in the ribosomal DNA region. This brings the estimate to 302 forks (242 + 60) to be found in the whole nucleus at the peak of DNA replication. In the cell imaging data these 302 replication forks are assigned to each of the replication factories, assuming that the integrated GFP-PCNA signal in each factory is proportional to the number of forks it contains (Fig. 3.16). We also show the distribution of the number of forks that are found in a particle cell at 25, 30, and 35 min in Fig. 3.15. It becomes apparent that at the peak of S-phase (30 min), the distribution is thinner in comparison to some earlier or later times. In this way, we are able to estimate the in vivo number of replisome pairs (at sister replication forks) present in each replication factory—in particular at the experimental relevant time at the peak of S-phase.

Next, we relate our simulated fork profiles, that contain information of fork position along the DNA at the peak of S-phase, to the in vivo replication factory dis-

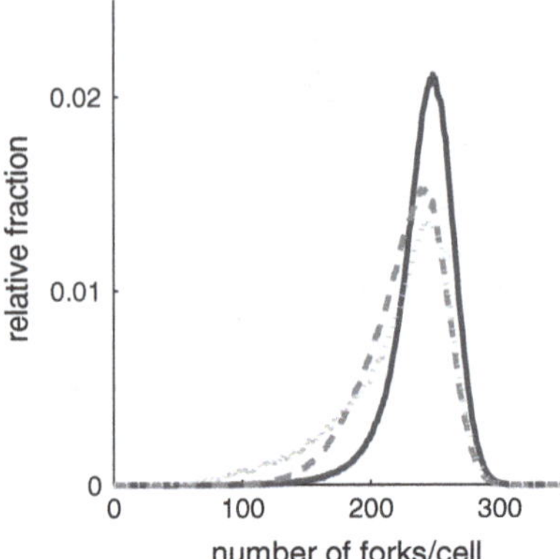

Fig. 3.15 In silico distributions of the number of active replication forks per cell at 25 min (*green dotted line*), 30 min (*blue solid line*), and 35 min (*red dashed line*). The data indicates that at the peak of S-phase, i.e. at 30 min, the distribution centres at around 242 forks per cell

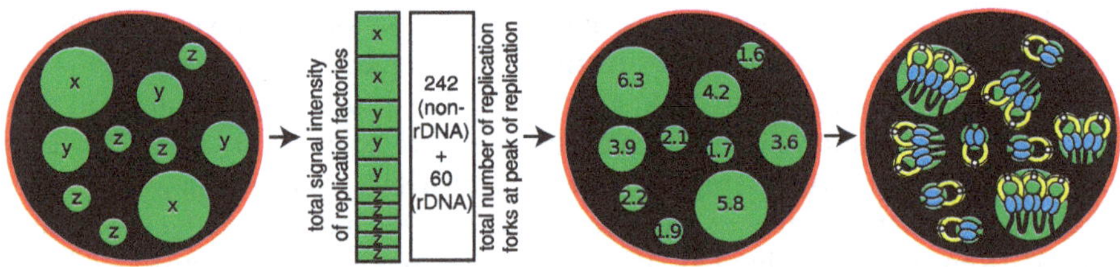

Fig. 3.16 Schematic diagrams explaining how the number of replisomes (at replication forks) was estimated at each factory. The intensity of each replication factory from the first sequence was correlated with simulation data for the number of replication forks present at the peak of S-phase (242 forks + 60 forks in ribosomal DNA regions) in the second sequence. This binned number of the third sequence was binned to even integers as sister replisomes associate [6]. This represents the number of replication forks per factory in the fourth sequence

tribution. We derived the dependence of grouping probability on fork distances in the previous section [Eq. (3.19)] which we now apply to our in silico fork distributions. This establishes an in silico distribution of sister replisome pairs per replication factory in the manner depicted in Fig. 3.17. Specifically, we ran the simulation in one million cells and took snapshots of replisome positions on chromosomes at the peak of replication after cells had entered S-phase with 4 min variation to allow for noise in cell synchronisation during experiments. Based on these snapshots, we determined whether adjacent sister replisome pairs were grouped in the same factory or not, depending on the chromosomal distance between them and corresponding probability of grouping [Fig. 3.12 and Eq. (3.19)].

Let us designate each sister replisome pair along a chromosome as A, B, C, D, …etc. in order from left to right. To determine whether A and B are grouped to the same factory, we drew a uniformly distributed random number from (0, 1], which is tested against the distance-dependent value $P_a(d)$ of those two pairs. If the random

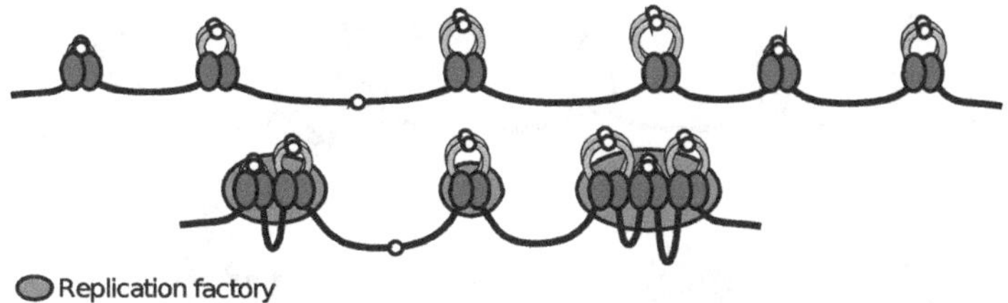

Fig. 3.17 Pairing of replication forks into replication factories. The top panel shows the genomic distances between active replicating units (replication forks in *blue*). Using Monte-Carlo simulations along with Eq. (3.19) one can then establish the number of active replication forks that associate within a replication factory

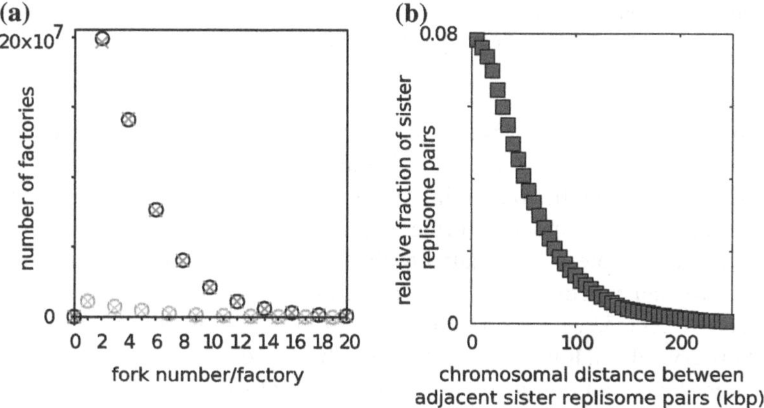

Fig. 3.18 In silico fork and fork distance distributions. **a** The computer algorithm used for pairing neighbouring replication forks into factories is directionally independent, i.e. it does not depend whether association starts from the left (*circles*) or the right (*crosses*) end of a chromosome. It produces the same fork per factory distribution. **b** Distribution of the distance (replicated DNA is not counted) between neighbouring sister replisome pairs along a chromosome, obtained from the simulation. Relative fractions of the pairs at the indicated distance (each 5 kbp window) are obtained from one million simulations, at the peak of DNA replication (at 30 min in Fig 3.13)

number was below $P_a(d)$, the pairs are assumed to be part of the same factory. Next, we examine the association of pairs B and C in the same way. If A and B are in the same factory and if B and C were in the same factory, then we conclude that A, B, and C are grouped together in the same factory; if not then C has the chance to form a factory with D etc. We performed this pairwise clustering of adjacent sister replisome pairs into factories in the rightward direction along each chromosome. Nonetheless, we also confirmed that clustering in the left direction gave a very similar result (Fig. 3.18).

In this study, we assume that sister replisomes are always associated with each other during replication of a relevant replicon. This assumption was based on Kitamura et al. [6] previous results that sister replisomes were associated in vivo

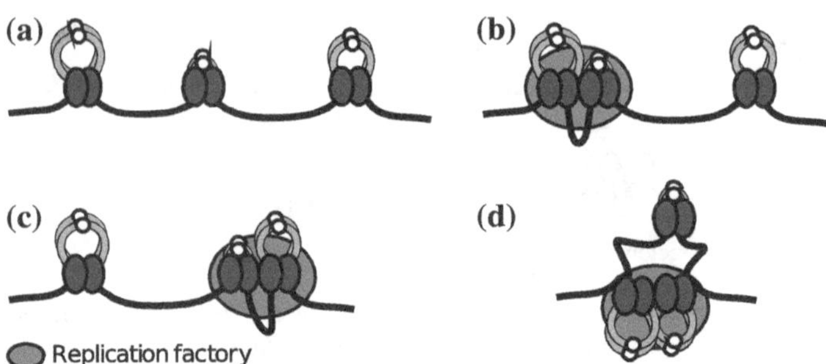

Fig. 3.19 Factory grouping for an example of three neighbouring replisome pairs. We consider three directly adjacent replisome pairs. They are initially isolated (**a**). Some other possible configurations are the immediate neighbours association (**b**) and (**c**), or the association of the farthest neighbours (**d**). We show in the main text that this configuration has a small likelihood

in most of the cells. We also assume that, when two replisome pairs encounter one another (head-on-head fork collision and coalescence), one sister replisome in each pair disappears, leaving the remaining two replisomes associated. This mechanism allows the new pair to undergo further replication. This assumption is consistent with a low energy state of associated replisome pairs; i.e., once two pairs become associated, we can expect that they stay associated for some time (see also diffusion time scales in Sect. 3.2, page 53). Nonetheless, in the above mathematical simulation, we observe also a low number of cases where one replisome is present without its sister, producing an odd number of forks per factory (Fig. 3.18a). This happens when one replisome has completed replication at the end of a chromosome (which is linear) while its sister is still engaged in replication. This led to generation of a small number of replication factories containing odd numbers of replisomes (Fig. 3.18a). However, for a direct comparison of the distribution of sister replisome pairs in factories obtained from in vivo and in silico data, we partitioned factories with odd numbers of forks (replisomes) proportionally to the nearby categories with even numbers of forks. For example factories with three forks were recategorised to those with two and four forks proportionally to their factory numbers.

In the above mathematical modeling, we assume that replisome pairs A and C only associate when both A/B and B/C associate. In other words, we consider association between immediate neighbours but not between others. It is actually difficult to consider direct association between A and C because we would need to consider all possible permutations: the presence and absence of A/C (Fig. 3.19d) association separately depending on whether A/B (Fig. 3.19b) and B/C (Fig. 3.19c) association is present or not. Doing this for genome-wide simulations is impractical. Nonetheless, our assumption—direct pairwise association only—is justified only when A/C (second neighbour) association is relatively low compared with A/B and B/C (direct neighbour) association. We test this in a simplified case of equal chromosomal distances d between A and B and between B and C. The ratio of the A/C association probability to the A/B and B/C association probability is $\eta = P_a(2d)/(2P_a(2d))$.

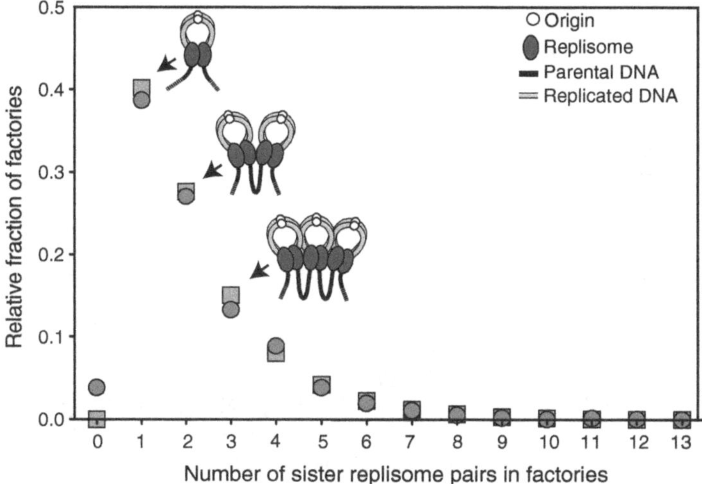

Fig. 3.20 Genome-wide association probabilities of forks per factories. Simulations are shown as *green squares* and in vivo observation are shown as *red circles*. There is an offset at the origin in the experimental data. This is an artifact of noise in the experimental technique. Depicted are also the number of sister replisome pairs (*ovals*), replicated (*yellow*) as well as unreplicated DNA (*black*) and the origin of replication (*small white circles*)

Considering the median chromosomal distances between two neighbouring replisome pairs (Fig. 3.18b) $d = 36\,\text{kbp}$ and $\text{A} = 8.7 \cdot 10^{-6}\,\text{kbp}^{-3}$ equates to $\eta = 0.17$. From first principles, $\eta = 0.17$ is not negligible however taken into account the accuracy of the experimental procedure we estimate this to be of similar magnitude, and also an association of A/B and B/C is about six times more likely than A/C. In the initial experimental setting of observing two dots it is for instance not possible to distinguish when A/C are seen associated whether this is in a configuration of A/C, A/B/C. So there is also an intrinsic error introduced in the measurement when reporting A/C association.

In this way, we are able to compare in vivo and in silico estimates of the number of replisome pairs in each replication factory as shown in Fig. 3.20. Simulations and microscopy observation are very similar. Thus, from the frequency that adjacent sister replisome pairs associate with one another we are able to accurately recapitulate the genome-wide distribution in replication factories by assuming stochastic assembly of replicons. Our result shows that it is mainly neighbouring replicons on a chromosome that are brought together in factories; the association of replicons is random. The result further suggests that factory organisation is intra-chromosomal (replicons on the same chromosome), albeit other factors constituting to inter-chromosomal factory formation for a minor part of the population of factories.

In Fig. 3.21, we also compare the experimentally obtained distribution with in silico experiments at some time before (25 min) and after (35 min) the peak of S-phase (30 min). The tail of the distribution for large factories still matches the experimental well, however diverges for the data point when two sister replisome pairs associate,

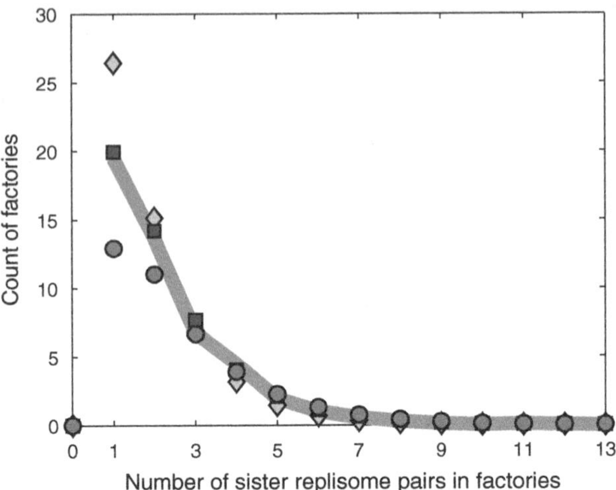

Fig. 3.21 Genome-wide association of sister replisome pairs per factories at different times in silico. Simulations are shown as an average of 10,000 in silico cells. This is done by taking snapshots at different times for each of the 10,000 individual simulations: t = 25 min (*green diamonds*), t = 30 min (*blue squares*), t = 35 min (*red circles*). The *grey line* shows the trend of the experimental from the count of two sister replisome pairs per cell (as seen in Fig. 3.20). For an actual comparison of the different settings we here show the actual count of factories rather than the relative fraction as is done in Fig. 3.20

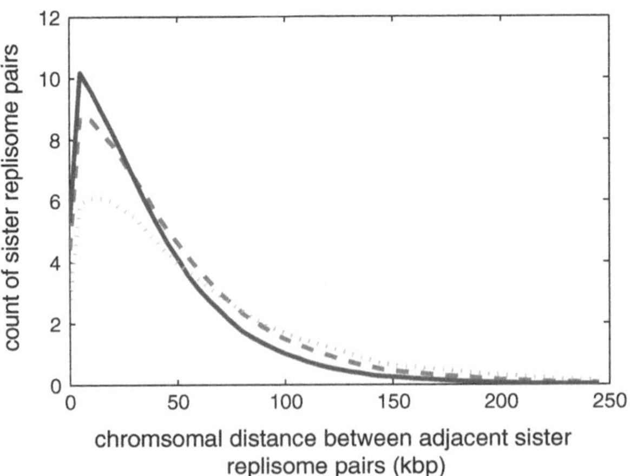

Fig. 3.22 In silico fork distribution of the distance (replicated DNA is not counted) between neighbouring sister replisome pairs along chromosomes. The count of the pairs at the indicated distance (each 5 kbp window) are obtained at t =25 min (*green dotted line*), t = 30 min (*blue solid line*) at the peak of DNA replication (cf. Fig 3.13), and at t =35 min (*red broken line*). This was done for 10,000 simulation runs for each time point

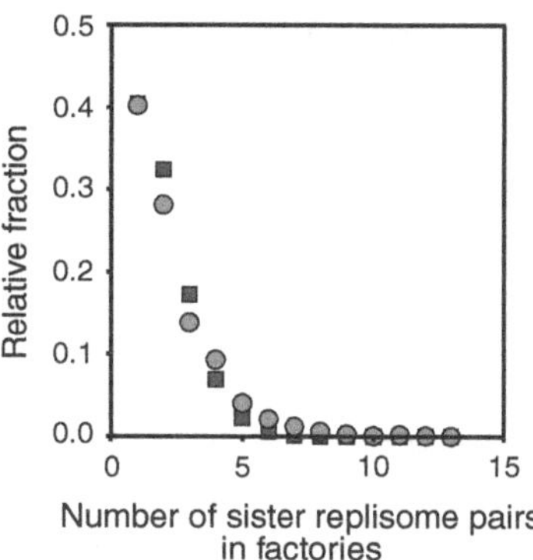

Fig. 3.23 The distribution of in vivo sister replisomes per replication factory (*red circles*) approximately fits a Poisson distribution with $\lambda = 1.60$ $R^2 = 0.98$ (*blue squares*)

i.e. one pair of those. Along with Fig. 3.15 as well as with Fig. 3.22 the data indicates that the immediate neighbour interactions lead to their increase or decrease over the course of replication. Its consequence is then felt mostly in the number of two sister replisome pairs because their formation is driven by forks are either being further or closer away from a neighbouring one. This is in agreement with recent data published by Cisse et al. [24] who showed that replication factories constantly become assembled and disassembled over time course of S-phase rather than displaying a completely fixed entity within the cellular nucleus. We propose that it is a natural consequence of fork coalescence events (decreasing the number of two sister replisome pairs), or for example the nucleation nearby some other fork which then leads to the formation of factories of size two. A further point of consideration is that in a factory containing many sister replisome the energy required to break it up into to single individual sister replisomes has to be rather large; although this has to be tested in a different kind of simulation that studies their dynamics over the entire course of S-phase at an individual cell level instead as we did here where we took an equilibrium assumption for our model. Constant assembly and disassembly also occurs for other structures, e.g. the growth of filamentous structures inside cells, the formation of centromeres, and thus is of particular interest to further understanding of physical mechanisms that lead and control cellular functions.

In summary, our result is in line with the current biological model [11, 25] and it is consistent with observed clustering of active replicons on DNA fibre [26] as well as a high rate of association of neighbouring DNA sequences observed in chromosome conformation capture assays [27]. We also supplement this random association hypothesis showing a fit of *zero-truncated* Poisson distribution, i.e. a Poisson distribution under the assumption that there is no observation for a count of $k = 0$ forks per factory. The probability distribution is then given by

$$P(Z = k|X > 0) = \frac{P(X = k)}{P(X > 0)} = \frac{\lambda^k e^{-\lambda}}{k!(1 - e^{-\lambda})}, \tag{3.20}$$

with $\lambda = 1.60$ as a result of a least-squares fit with the in vivo distribution and Eq. 3.20 (Fig. 3.23).

3.7 Summary

We have shown that replisomes associate randomly with each other using an adiabatic assumption for our model, and we verify our analytical results numerically using Metropolis-Monte-Carlo stimulations. A stochastic assembly mechanism may provide robustness to factory organisation. It is relatively easy to establish—all that is required is that some replisome components have an affinity for another replisome component. In a deterministic assembly scheme, failure to incorporate one component might cause failure of the entire factory network, whereas in a stochastic scheme, each individual interaction is independent of the status of the others. This has particular importance for example in human and animal cells responding to replication stress when a replication factory defines the boundary, inside of which dormant origins can initiate and complete replication for the region between two stalled replication forks [28, 29].

In addition to organising DNA replication, replication factories (foci) are likely to represent a fundamental feature of chromosome organisation [11, 30]. Using *Saccharomyces cerevisiae* as a model organism for our mathematical modelling, we find that individual replication factories creating replicons are highly variable from cell to cell. Their group size also depends on a particular of the cell size as distances from one replisome to another constantly changes and fork movement bringing replisome pairs closer into contact, hence promoting the formation of replication factories. Our results show adjacent replicons assemble stochastically and stay associated together to maintain replication factories in a stable manner. Their formation is also essential to then build up replication factories containing a larger number of sister replisome pairs. Our study elucidates the importance of not only organisation of DNA replication within the nucleus, but also to general mechanisms by which chromosomes organise sub-nuclear structures such as transcription factories and repair foci [31, 32]. Their further investigation is required, especially in light of new experimental data which shows that transcription factories are very dynamic structures which constantly assemble and disassemble inside a cluster with a typical life time of 5 s [24]; rather than sticking together for long times (>2 min) as is the case of replication factories here.

References

1. M. Tark-Dame, R. van Driel, D.W. Heermann, Chromatin folding-from biology to polymer models and back. J. Cell Sci. **124**(6), 839–845 (2011). doi:10.1242/jcs.077628
2. V. Dion, S.M. Gasser, Chromatin movement in the maintenance of genome stability. Cell **152**(6), 1355–1364 (2013). doi:10.1016/j.cell.2013.02.010
3. R.E. Boulos, A. Arneodo, P. Jensen, B. Audit, Revealing long-range interconnected hubs in human chromatin interaction data using graph theory. Phys. Rev. Lett. **111**(11), 118102 (2013). doi:10.1103/PhysRevLett.111.118102
4. M. Barbieri, M. Chotalia, J. Fraser, L.-M. Lavitas, J. Dostie, A. Pombo, M. Nicodemi, Complexity of chromatin folding is captured by the strings and binders switch model. Proc. Natl. Acad. Sci. U. S. A. **109**(40), 16173–16178 (2012). doi:10.1073/pnas.1204799109

5. S. Hahn, D. Kim, Physical origin of the contact frequency in chromosome conformation capture data. Biophys. J. **105**(8), 1786–1795 (2013). doi:10.1016/j.bpj.2013.08.043
6. E. Kitamura, J.J. Blow, T.U. Tanaka, Live-cell imaging reveals replication of individual replicons in eukaryotic replication factories. Cell **125**(7), 1297–1308 (2006). doi:10.1016/j.cell.2006.04.041
7. D. Baddeley et al., Measurement of replication structures at the nanometer scale using super-resolution light microscopy. Nucleic Acids Res. **38**(2), e8 (2010). doi:10.1093/nar/gkp901
8. N. Saner et al., Stochastic association of neighboring replicons creates replication factories in budding yeast. J. Cell Biol. **202**(7), 1001–1012 (2013). doi:10.1083/jcb.201306143
9. N. Yabuki, H. Terashima, K. Kitada, Mapping of early firing origins on a replication profile of budding yeast. Genes Cells **7**(8), 781–789 (2002)
10. K. Sneppen and G. Zocchi, Timescales for target location in a cell. Phys. Mol. Biol. 178–182 (2005)
11. R. Berezney, D. D. Dubey, and J. A. Huberman, Heterogeneity of eukaryotic replicons, replicon clusters, and replication foci. Chromosoma **108**(8), 471–484 (2000)
12. J. Dekker, K. Rippe, M. Dekker, N. Kleckner, Capturing chromosome conformation. Science **295**(5558), 1306–1311 (2002). doi:10.1126/science.1067799
13. P Heun, T Laroche, K Shimada, P Furrer, and S. M. Gasser, Chromosome dynamics in the yeast interphase nucleus. Science 294(5549), 2181–2186 (2001). doi:10.1126/science.1065366
14. D.P. Landau, K. Binder, *A Guide to Monte Carlo Simulations in Statistical Physics* (Cambridge University Press, Cambridge, 2005). doi:10.1017/CBO9780511614460
15. C.A. Baxter, C.W. Murray, D.E. Clark, D.R. Westhead, M.D. Eldridge, Flexible docking using Tabu search and an empirical estimate of binding affinity. Proteins **33**(3), 367–382 (1998). doi:9829696
16. K. Rippe, Dynamic organization of the cell nucleus. Curr. Opin. Genet. Dev. **17**(5), 373–380 (2007). doi:10.1016/j.gde.2007.08.007
17. D. Marenduzzo, C. Micheletti, P.R. Cook, Entropy-driven genome organization. Biophys. J. **90**(10), 3712–3721 (2006). doi:10.1529/biophysj.105.077685
18. M.K. Raghuraman et al., Replication dynamics of the yeast genome. Science **294**(5540), 115–121 (2001). doi:10.1126/science.294.5540.115
19. A.P.S. de Moura, R. Retkute, M. Hawkins, C.A. Nieduszynski, Mathematical modelling of whole chromosome replication. Nucleic Acids Res. **38**(17), 5623–5633 (2010). doi:10.1093/nar/gkq343
20. R. Retkute, C.A. Nieduszynski, A. de Moura, Mathematical modeling of genome replication. Phys. Rev. E **86**(3), 031916 (2012). doi:10.1103/PhysRevE.86.031916
21. M. Hawkins, R. Retkute, C.A. Müller, N. Saner, T.U. Tanaka, A.P. de Moura, C.A. Nieduszynski, High-resolution replication profiles define the stochastic nature of genome replication initiation and termination. Cell Rep. **5**(4), 1132–1141 (2013). doi:10.1016/j.celrep.2013.10.014
22. M.H. Linskens, J.A. Huberman, Organization of replication of ribosomal DNA in Saccharomyces cerevisiae. Mol. Cell. Biol. **8**(11), 4927–4935 (1988)
23. P. Pasero, A. Bensimon, E. Schwob, Single-molecule analysis reveals clustering and epigenetic regulation of replication origins at the yeast rDNA locus. Genes Dev. **16**(19), 2479–2484 (2002). doi:10.1101/gad.232902
24. I.I. Cisse et al., Real-time dynamics of RNA polymerase II clustering in live human cells. Science **341**(6146), 664–667 (2013). doi:10.1126/science.1239053
25. P.J. Gillespie and J.J. Blow, Clusters, factories and domains: The complex structure of S phase comes into focus. Cell Cycle **9**(16) (2010). doi:10.4161/cc.9.16.12644
26. S. Tuduri, H. Tourrière, P. Pasero, Defining replication origin efficiency using DNA fiber assays. Chromosome Res. **18**(1), 91–102 (2010). doi:10.1007/s10577-009-9098-y
27. Z. Duan et al., A three-dimensional model of the yeast genome. Nature **465**(7296), 363–367 (2010). doi:10.1038/nature08973
28. X.Q. Ge, J.J. Blow, Chk1 inhibits replication factory activation but allows dormant origin firing in existing factories. J. Cell Biol. **191**(7), 1285–1297 (2010). doi:10.1083/jcb.201007074

29. A. M. Thomson, P. J. Gillespie, and J. J. Blow, Replication factory activation can be decoupled from the replication timing program by modulating Cdk levels. J. Cell Biol. 188(2), pp. 209–221 (2010). doi:10.1083/jcb11037
30. D.A. Jackson, Replicon clusters are stable units of chromosome structure: evidence that nuclear organization contributes to the efficient activation and propagation of S phase in human cells. J. Cell Biol. **140**(6), 1285–1295 (1998). doi:10.1083/jcb.140.6.1285
31. M. Lisby and R. Rothstein, DNA damage checkpoint and repair centers. Curr. Opin. Cell Biol. 16(3), pp. 328–334 (2004). doi:10.1016/j.ceb.03.011
32. H. Sutherland, W.A. Bickmore, Transcription factories: gene expression in unions? Nat. Rev. Genet. **10**(7), 457–466 (2009). doi:10.1038/nrg2592

Chapter 4
Summary and Conclusions

Life is only possible because the genomic information in a cell's chromosomes is copied from one generation to the next, by means of DNA replication. Components of the complex biological machinery responsible for replication in eukaryotes act in concert to ensure that replication takes place rapidly and accurately, at the right time within the cell cycle, and crucially that every piece of the chromosome is replicated once and only once per round of the cell cycle. The two key elements of this process—establishing the starting points for replication (*origins*) and the activation of replication forks at those origins—are stochastic events which occur during two distinct phases of the cell cycle. From each origin, replication forks propagate from either side, synthesising DNA at an apparently fixed speed. Hence, the time required to replicate the DNA content of a cell is dictated by the distances between origins.

The work presented here examined theoretically, and in close collaboration with experimentalists, how replication can be brief and on time as is the case in nature, how robust timing is possible under fluctuating and noisy conditions, and how replication forks organise spatially within the cell.

In brief, we developed a timing–model of DNA replication which has identified optimal origin positions induced depending on failure probabilities and evolutionary pressure. The emergence of such optimal positions is still to be investigated, however previous experimental results in *Xenopus laevis* suggest that this could be achieved as an effect of limitting space on DNA due to pMcm binding. We also introduced a general theory for active forks in this work which shows that their random assembly leads to higher–order structures or *replication factories*, and for the first time theory accurately predicts factory size distributions from genome–wide yeast data in silico which agree with quantitative in vivo experiments.

In detail, the work here described those aspects as follows.

1. The balancing act to spread out origins in a certain manner to compensate for variations in activation timing and lack of proteins stochastically binding to sequences. We showed both analytically and through numerical simulations (similar to a 1D nucleation and growth process) that there exists two regimes for origins, either positioned together in groups spaced far away from the next, or

J. Karschau, *Mathematical Modelling of Chromosome Replication and Replicative Stress*, Springer Theses, DOI 10.1007/978-3-319-08861-7_4

as equally–scattered single origins depending on the uncertainty when activation occurs. We applied the model to known origin locations in yeast and showed that grouping is a means of organisation driven by evolutionary pressure. The model is able to reproduce origin distributions of Xenopus which are thought to be random, and showed contrarily that grouping must occur in order to swiftly complete replication. The model also holds when considering a circular DNA topology as for instance archaeal genomes have, as well as if applied to the whole replication profiling data of yeast.

2. The second topic aimed at the organisation of replication forks within the cellular nucleus. For simplicity, cartoons often depict DNA replication on a straight one–dimensional line. In fact we deal with a polymer that is packed and modified on different levels yielding higher order structures of organisation. A project in experimental collaboration focussed on the aspect of spatial organisation of active replication forks during the time–course of replication. These forks are observed to organise in clusters of *replication factories* which we investigated by describing the process with a particles on a string model. We calculated analytically the probability for forks to meet using Boltzmann–statistics. The model was then used to describe properties of measured experimental distributions such as fork numbers per cluster during the DNA synthesis phase. Analysis was extended to the whole yeast–genome which yielded a near–perfect match with the data suggesting that actively replicating units of DNA randomly associate with each other to form *replication factories*.

Particular emphasis on the stochastic processes that work here at different scales allowed us to describe key aspects of replication. The models developed here allow for further extensions to describe DNA replication at various scales of organisation; e.g. at the DNA sequence level, an investigation of origin positioning under perturbing conditions, i.e. epigenetic factors that forbid binding to a chromosomal region, and the effect on replication completion times. At larger scales, formation of these origins is linked to fluctuating levels of proteins, e.g. during embryogenesis or under starvation conditions. More importantly at tissue–level, a treatment of noise in these processes combined with a modelling of replication fork movement could then provide a comprehensive model for tissue homeostasis.

Ultimately, we expect the outcome of such studies to also provide understanding of stochasticity in protein synthesis and usage of cellular resources. The theoretical investigation and new modelling tools can be integrated with experiments. In the long–term view, extensions to the work presented here has potential to address challenges in cancer therapy. For example, a model could be used alongside data to predict critical shifts in the replication pattern that trigger cancer or how to achieve optimal cellular growth conditions. This must be tested using a holistic model incorporating the physical process involved in replication licensing, origin activation. Such a model is then testable against experimental replication timing profiles and yields insight into organisation of DNA replication at a single cell level.

Zeitfracht Medien GmbH
Ferdinand-Jühlke-Straße 7
99095 Erfurt, Deutschland
produktsicherheit@kolibri360.de